Supplement 1965 to

A BIBLIOGRAPHY OF
HIGHER EDUCATION IN CANADA

Supplément 1965 de

BIBLIOGRAPHIE DE
L'ENSEIGNEMENT SUPÉRIEUR
AU CANADA

T0334998

Studies in Higher Education in Canada

NUMBER 3

Etudes dans l'Enseignement Supérieur au Canada

NUMÉRO 3

Supplement 1965 to

A BIBLIOGRAPHY
OF HIGHER EDUCATION
IN CANADA

Supplément 1965 de

BIBLIOGRAPHIE
DE L'ENSEIGNEMENT
SUPERIEUR
AU CANADA

Robin S. Harris

UNIVERSITY OF TORONTO PRESS

LES PRESSES DE L'UNIVERSITÉ LAVAL

© UNIVERSITY OF TORONTO PRESS 1965
REPRINTED 2017
ISBN 978-1-4875-9140-3 (paper)

Foreword

READERS OF *A Bibliography of Higher Education in Canada* may recall a statement there that a supplement was being planned. Largely because of the intelligent zeal and industry of Principal Harris the plan has become a reality in this volume which now brings the total number of items recorded to between seven and eight thousand as of the end of 1963. The organization of the original volume has been maintained with slight modification, some new sections having been added, about which Principal Harris comments in the Introduction. Among them are two worthy of note: first, one devoted to institutions which although post-secondary, do not grant degrees; second, one entitled fiction which includes plays and novels set wholly or partly in actual or fictitious Canadian universities.

The Committee on Higher Education is again indebted to the Carnegie Foundation of New York for assistance in making possible the publication of this volume. It also wishes to express its gratitude to Principal Harris and to those who have unselfishly collaborated with him.

FRANK STILING
Chairman of the Committee
on Higher Education

Contents

Introduction

[1960]

TO CONSULT the primary sources for the study of higher education in Canada it is normally necessary to go to particular libraries or to particular institutions. Most of the relevant documents published by governments, notably legislative acts, the transcripts of parliamentary debates, and ministerial reports, can most conveniently be consulted in legislative libraries, while the universities themselves are in most instances the only location for complete files of Calendars, Year Books, Examination Papers, and the Annual Reports of Presidents, Deans, and Boards of Governors. The universities are certainly the only location for unpublished material such as Faculty Minutes and Committee Reports which in special circumstances are available to the qualified scholar.

The present volume, which is properly entitled "A Bibliography of Higher Education in Canada," includes no basic documents among its nearly 4,000 entries. There is little point in listing such documents relevant to the history of Dalhousie University since the scholar must go to Halifax to consult them; the Dalhousie Librarian is surely justified in refusing to send on interlibrary loan the only known copy of, let us say, the Dalhousie *Calendar* for 1867. The scholar who does go to Halifax will have no difficulty in obtaining a complete list of the official documents relevant to his investigation.

"A Bibliography of Higher Education in Canada" is, rather, a list of secondary sources—the books, pamphlets, theses, and dissertations, and the articles in journals and magazines—which supplement the basic documents by supplying context and commentary. Since all such works are available at all major libraries in Canada, either immediately or through interlibrary loan, there is considerable point in listing them. All the items listed in the present volume under "Dalhousie University" can be obtained in Victoria, B.C. Only two sections of the bibliography contain items which are likely to pose problems of location, those entitled "Canadian Culture" and "Canadian Universities." The National Library at Ottawa will normally provide the answer in the first case, the institution concerned in the second.

The compilers have not attempted to indicate where particular works can be obtained. They have restricted themselves to providing the information necessary to identify the work: for books and pamphlets, *author, title, place* and *year of publication,* and (except for publications prior to 1920) *publisher;* for theses and dissertations, *author, title, institution* and *year of submission;* for articles, *author, title* and *journal* (with *volume* and *year*). Pagination has been provided for books, pamphlets, and articles as an indication of relative length—one's interest in examining a given work may depend on whether it is 20 or 400 pages in length. Pagination has not been given for multi-volume works or for theses and dissertations; the treatment can be assumed to be lengthy.

The Bibliography has two Parts. Part I provides the context for the study of higher education in Canada. Our universities do not exist in a vacuum; they are conditioned by (and in turn condition) the economic, political, religious, and social life of the country itself. It is impossible to study any aspect of Canadian higher education without taking into full account the basic forces which motivate Canadian life. Hence a section called "Canadian Culture," listing histories of Canada and its provinces, histories of its religious and social institutions, histories of its art, its economy, its racial groups, its relation with other countries. But it is also impossible to study higher education in Canada without reference to other levels of Canadian education. Our universities are what they are partly because our elementary and secondary schools are what they are. Hence a section called "Canadian Education," listing works concerned with educational developments and problems at all levels.

Part II lists works which bear directly on higher education in Canada. Section I, "History and Organization," contains a subsection devoted to works which concern the Canadian universities considered as a group and subsections for each of twenty-nine institutions—the classical colleges have been treated as a single institution. Section II, "Curriculum and Teaching," contains subsections for each academic subject and professional field and for the following general areas: Adult Education, Enseignement secondaire classique, Faculty of Arts, Graduate Studies and Research, Humanities, Sciences, Social Sciences. Sections III and IV contain no subsections. Under "The Professor" are listed works which bear on the status of the Canadian university teacher, his academic freedom, his salary, his professional qualifications. Under "The Student" are listed works which concern the student's status—the availability of scholarships and bursaries, the special problems of the foreign student, the adequacy of matriculation requirements.

An entry which is appropriate to more than one subsection has been listed under each. For example, "Twenty-five Years of Chemistry at Laval" is listed under "Université Laval" and "Chemistry."

As a general rule, the compilers have excluded newspaper articles, journal articles of less than five pages, and articles in alumni and student publications. The principal exceptions are articles in *Relations*, whose pages are long and whose print is fine, addresses in the *Proceedings of the National Conference of Canadian Universities*, where the fact that a subject was discussed at all is of special significance, and newspaper or alumni articles which present the only known treatment of a topic.

The entries are arranged in chronological order in all sections in order to present the progressive development of each topic. In certain subsections, for example "Classics" and "Université de Montréal," the dates of the entries are themselves of interest, the sequence revealing periods of active debate and silence. No distinction has been drawn between English- and French-language publications—Chemistry and Chimie are one subject. The decision to provide separate subsections for "Faculty of Arts" and "Faculté des Arts" is not a departure from this principle; the inclusion of instruction at the secondary school level in the curricula of the classical colleges causes the problems of the Faculté des Arts to differ markedly from those of the Faculty of Arts.

The relative proportion of English and French entries in a section is often significant. "Orientation professionnelle" is a recognized field of study in the French-speaking universities, but "Vocational Guidance" is not a subject of study in the English-speaking universities. Nursing has long been a recognized profession in English-speaking Canada; in Quebec, university training for *l'infirmière* is a recent development—the French language contains no word which corresponds to *nursing*. "Religion," "Journalism," "Law," and "The Professor" are other sections which reflect interesting variations in the frequency of English- and French-language entries.

"A Bibliography of Higher Education in Canada" is in part based on the fourteen earlier bibliographies listed at the end of this introduction. The majority of entries, however, have been obtained through a search of the files of over 150 Canadian journals. These journals are also listed at the end of the introduction, together with an indication of the years searched and the abbreviation adopted for each journal in the bibliography. A number of entries involve journals published outside Canada. The country of origin has been indicated in parenthesis unless it is obvious from the title; thus *Am. Econ. Rev.* but *Jour. Pol. Econ.* (U.S.).

The compilers have not drawn upon two important sources of information about higher education in Canada, the recently published *Encyclopedia Canadiana* and the obituary notices in the *Proceedings of the Royal Society of Canada.* The latter provide full biographical details of many persons intimately connected with the development of our universities as well as an assessment of their contribution to that development. *Encyclopedia Canadiana* contains articles on all institutions, all academic disciplines, all professions, and on such topics as *adult education, classical colleges, libraries,* and *Student Christian Movement.*

Over 100 university presidents, professors, and librarians have co-operated in the preparation of this bibliography. An authority in the field has vetted the draft of each subsection; a physicist has examined the tentative list for "Physics," a McGill librarian the subsection for McGill, a Dean of Pharmacy the subsection for Pharmacy. The degree to which each subsection is an adequate list of the literature in the field is in large measure the result of the many additional entries proposed by these correspondents.

The compilers are aware that the present list, like all bibliographies, will contain errors and that it is incomplete. Since the terminal date of entries was set at December 31, 1958, the bibliography is already out of date. Supplements will be published from time to time. Readers are urged to report errors and to suggest additions in letters addressed to the compilers in care of the University of Toronto Press.

The compilers wish to acknowledge formally the assistance of Miss Annabel Connell and Mlle Annette Faucher in the preparation of the draft and final manuscripts, the co-operation of their colleagues on Dean Stiling's Committee, and the editorial guidance of Miss Francess Halpenny of the University of Toronto Press. Miss Connell prepared the index.

R. S. H.
A. T.

Introduction

[1960]

PARMI les sources primaires auxquelles doit puiser l'histoire de l'enseignement supérieur au Canada, il y a d'abord les documents officiels publiés par les universités elles-mêmes ou par les gouvernements. Les lois concernant les universités, les comptes rendus des débats parlementaires que les lois ont provoqués et, d'une façon générale, tous les actes législatifs ou administratifs dont les universités ont pu être l'objet de la part d'organismes gouvernementaux, sont conservés dans les bibliothèques ou les dépôts d'archives du Parlement et des législatures. On peut aussi trouver dans toutes les universités les documents administratifs qui concernent chacune d'elles en particulier : annuaires, rapports annuels du recteur ou du président, procès-verbaux du conseil universitaire ou des conseils de facultés, etc.

L'ouvrage que nous présentons aujourd'hui ne contient aucune référence à cette sorte de documents auxquels, dans bien des cas, le chercheur ne peut avoir accès qu'à l'endroit même où ils sont conservés. Ainsi, par exemple, le bibliothécaire de l'Université Dalhousie est parfaitement justifié de ne pas se départir, même pour très peu de temps, de l'unique exemplaire connu de l'annuaire 1867 de son université. Par conséquent, le chercheur désireux de se renseigner sur l'histoire de cette institution devra nécessairement se rendre à Halifax même et, dans ce cas, les indications bibliographiques que nous pourrions lui fournir sur les documents officiels relatifs à l'Université Dalhousie ne lui seraient d'aucune utilité puisqu'il trouvera sur place toutes ces indications.

Voilà pourquoi la « Bibliographie de l'enseignement supérieur au Canada » constitue plutôt un index de sources secondaires : livres, brochures, thèses de maîtrise ou de doctorat, articles de revues, susceptibles de compléter les documents de base et de les situer dans le contexte plus général de l'évolution de la culture canadienne et du mouvement des idées en matière d'enseignement universitaire. Un tel index trouve sa justification dans le fait que tous ces documents sont facilement accessibles au chercheur dans la plupart des grandes bibliothèques, qui les possèdent déjà en dépôt ou qui peuvent se les procurer grâce un système de prêt entre bibliothèques. Tous les items classés dans le présent ouvrage sous la rubrique « Université

Dalhousie » sont disponibles à Victoria, C.B. Deux chapitres seulement de la bibliographie, ceux qui portent sur le « Contexte socio-culturel canadien » et sur les institutions particulières, poseront peut-être des problèmes de localisation des ouvrages. La Bibliothèque nationale à Ottawa ou le bibliothécaire de l'institution concernée devraient pouvoir repondre sans difficulté aux demandes de renseignements à ce sujet.

Les compilateurs n'ont pas indiqué l'endroit où l'on peut se procurer les divers ouvrages qui apparaissent dans la bibliographie. Ils se sont contentés de fournir les indications nécessaires à l'identification du document : pour les livres et les brochures, ils fournissent le nom de l'auteur, le titre de l'ouvrage, l'endroit et la date de publication, le nom de l'éditeur (sauf pour les écrits publiés avant 1920); dans le cas des thèses de maîtrise ou de doctorat, seuls le nom de l'auteur, le titre, l'université où elles ont été soumises et la date de leur parution sont mentionnés; enfin, pour les articles de revues, on fournit le nom de l'auteur, le titre de l'article et le nom du périodique où il a paru, accompagnés du numéro de volume et de la date. Dans le cas des livres, des brochures et des articles de revues, l'on a ajouté le nombre de pages à titre d'indication grossière de la longueur de l'écrit : la décision de consulter par la suite un ouvrage donné peut en effet dépendre de sa dimension. Le nombre de pages n'a cependant pas été indiqué pour les ouvrages en plusieurs tomes ou les thèses; on peut, en effet, supposer que, dans tous ces ouvrages, la question étudiée comporte des développements considérables.

La bibliographie se divise en deux parties. La première partie, elle-même subdivisée en deux chapitres, se rapporte au contexte socio-culturel canadien. Nos universités n'existent pas dans le vide; elles subissent l'influence du milieu dont elles font partie et elles-mêmes, à leur tour, agissent sur ce milieu. Quel que soit l'aspect considéré, toute étude sur l'enseignement supérieur au Canada doit tenir compte des multiples forces qui animent et orientent la vie canadienne. C'est pourquoi l'on a consacré un chapitre de la bibliographie à la « Culture canadienne »; ce chapitre contient des références se rapportant à l'histoire du Canada et de ses provinces, à l'histoire des institutions religieuses, politiques et sociales, à l'évolution des groupes ethniques au Canada et aux relations de notre pays avec l'étranger.

Pour des raisons analogues, le deuxième chapitre de la bibliographie groupe des ouvrages traitant de l'évolution de l'enseignement et de ses problèmes à tous les niveaux. Nos universités, sous plusieurs rapports, dépendent intimement des systèmes scolaires dont elles font partie intégrante; dans une large mesure les traits qui les caractérisent proviennent de ce que nos écoles élémentaires et secondaires sont elles-mêmes d'un certain type.

La deuxième partie qui porte sur l'enseignement supérieur proprement dit, contient un premier chapitre sur « l'histoire et les cadres institutionnels » des universités canadiennes. La première section de ce chapitre rassemble les textes traitant des universités canadiennes en général, la seconde consacre une sous-section à chacune des 28 universités du Canada et aux collèges classiques qui ont été considérés, en l'occurrence, comme une seule institution.

Le chapitre intitulé « Programmes d'études et enseignement » comporte au delà de 40 sections portant sur les divers domaines de l'enseignement professionnel et une section pour chacune des sept catégories suivantes de disciplines générales : « Faculty of Arts », « Enseignement secondaire classique », « Humanités », « Sciences sociales », « Sciences », « Recherches », « Education des adultes ».

Les deux derniers chapitres de cette partie sont beaucoup plus courts que les précédents et ne comportent pas de section particulière. Ils contiennent des références à des ouvrages qui ne traitent ni d'une institution en particulier ni d'une discipline d'enseignement, mais plutôt du statut du professeur et de l'étudiant universitaires. Dans le chapitre consacré au « professeur », on a classé des sujets tels que la liberté académique, les salaires, la formation du professeur universitaire. Dans le chapitre intitulé « les étudiants » apparaissent tous les écrits où l'on discute des questions comme celles des bourses d'étude, de l'adaptation de l'étudiant étranger, etc.

Il est arrivé à plusieurs reprises qu'un même ouvrage ou un même article traite de plusieurs sujets à la fois; dans ce cas, l'ouvrage a été classé autant de fois que nécessaire aux endroits appropriés. Par exemple, l'article intitulé « Historique de la Faculté des Arts à l'Université Laval » apparaît à la fois sous la rubrique « Université Laval » et sous la rubrique « Faculté des Arts ».

Règle générale, les compilateurs n'ont pas relevé les articles de journaux ni les articles de revue de moins de cinq pages, ni les textes publiés par les associations d'anciens ou d'étudiants. On a toutefois fait exception à ces règles dans le cas des articles de la revue *Relations*, dont le format dépasse celui des revues ordinaires, dans le cas également des comptes rendus des réunions de la Conférence nationale des Universités canadiennes, le fait qu'un sujet y soit discuté ayant une signification particulière, et, enfin, dans le cas des articles de journaux qui semblaient être le seul écrit connu sur le sujet.

A l'intérieur de chaque rubrique, l'on a respecté l'ordre

chronologique de façon à montrer les variations dans le temps de l'intérêt manifesté pour chaque thème. Il n'est pas rare, en effet, que les dates de publication des textes énumérés soient particulièrement intéressantes en elles-mêmes et permettent de constater jusqu'à quel point un sujet a pu donner lieu à des débats animés, à certaines époques, et n'a suscité aucun intérêt à d'autres époques. L'on n'a pas séparé les unes des autres, pour en constituer deux listes distinctes, les références de langue française et les références de langue anglaise; l'enseignement supérieur n'a pas à se préoccuper des frontières linguistiques : Chemistry et Chimie constituent un seul sujet; aussi toutes les références à ce thème ont-elles été groupées sous la même rubrique, quelle que soit la langue dans laquelle elles ont été écrites. Une seule exception à cette règle : deux sections séparées ont été attribuées à la « Faculté des Arts » et à la « Faculty of Arts »; la raison qui justifie cette exception est la suivante : l'enseignement secondaire classique régi par la « Faculté des Arts », dans les universités de la Province de Québec, est à la fois de niveau « secondaire » et « collégial »; en outre, il se donne dans les collèges classiques c.-à-d. dans une institution indépendante, au point de vue administratif, de l'université elle-même; ces deux faits ont évidemment pour conséquence que la notion de « Faculté des Arts » dans les universités de langue française et celle de « Faculty of Arts » dans les universités de langue anglaise sont tout à fait différentes, et que les problèmes relatifs à l'organisation de l'enseignement, aux programmes d'étude, etc., dans les deux cas, ne sont absolument pas comparables : il valait donc mieux, malgré l'identité des appellations, consacrer deux sections à ce sujet.

La proportion des écrits de langue française et de langue anglaise est une donnée significative pour plusieurs rubriques. L'orientation professionnelle, par exemple, compte parmi les disciplines professionnelles enseignées dans les universités de langue française, tandis que la « Vocational Guidance » n'apparaît pas au programme des institutions de langue anglaise. Le « Nursing » est une profession reconnue depuis longtemps au Canada anglais comme étant de niveau universitaire; dans le Québec, les « gardes-malades » ne poursuivent leur formation à l'université que depuis peu d'années; d'ailleurs, nous n'avons pas trouvé d'équivalent français à l'expression « Nursing ». La religion, le journalisme, le droit, plusieurs autres rubriques se prêteraient à des comparaisons fructeuses du même ordre au sujet de la fréquence relative des références de langue anglaise et des références de langue française.

Il va sans dire que la présente bibliographie de l'enseignement supérieur au Canada a mis à contribution d'autres bibliographies publiées antérieurement sur le sujet ou des sujets connexes. Elle a cependant trouvé la plus large part de ses matériaux parmi les articles publiés dans plus de 150 périodiques canadiens. La liste de ces bibliographies et de ces périodiques apparaît à la fin de l'introduction. L'on y indique pour quelle période de publication l'on a dépouillé les périodiques en question et les sigles qui permettent de les identifier dans la bibliographie proprement dite. S'il s'agit d'un article paru dans un périodique non canadien, l'on a indiqué, entre parenthèses, à la suite du nom de la revue, le pays où celle-ci est publiée.

Les compilateurs n'ont pas utilisé deux sources importantes de renseignements sur l'enseignement supérieur au Canada : l'*Encyclopedia Canadiana* et les notices nécrologiques qui apparaissent dans les procès-verbaux de la Société Royale du Canada. Celles-ci contiennent de précieuses indications sur la vie et les œuvres d'un grand nombre de personnes intimement liées à l'évolution de nos universités. On trouve aussi dans l'*Encyclopedia Canadiana* des articles (ordinairement accompagnés d'une bibliographie) sur toutes les institutions universitaires, les professions et beaucoup d'autres sujets : l'éducation des adultes, les collèges classiques, les bibliothèques, etc.

Au-delà de 100 bibliothécaires, professeurs ou présidents d'université ont participé à la préparation de cet ouvrage. Autant que possible, chaque chapitre et chaque section ont été soumis à la critique d'une autorité dans la matière : un physicien a revu la liste de références portant sur la physique, le bibliothécaire de l'Université de Montréal a examiné la section consacrée à son Université; un doyen de faculté de pharmacie a également parcouru la section qui le concernait directement. Si la liste des références présentées sous chaque rubrique est relativement satisfaisante et représente convenablement l'ensemble de la littérature sur le sujet, elle le doit, dans une large mesure, au grand nombre d'additions que ces collaborateurs ont suggérées.

Les compilateurs sont parfaitement conscients que leur bibliographie de l'enseignement supérieur au Canada, comme toutes les bibliographies d'ailleurs, n'est certes pas complète. Elle est même déjà désuète puisqu'elle s'arrête à décembre 1958. Aussi l'on projette de publier de temps à autre des suppléments qui en corrigeront les lacunes et la maintiendront à jour autant possible. A cette fin, les auteurs prient instamment les lecteurs éventuels de leur communiquer à l'adresse des éditeurs (University of Toronto Press) toutes les erreurs et omissions qu'ils auront notées.

Les compilateurs désirent exprimer leur plus vive gratitude à Miss Annabel Connell et à Mademoiselle Annette Faucher qui ont largement contribué à la préparation des six versions préliminaires et de la version finale de l'ouvrage. Ils remercient également leurs collègues du Comité que la Conférence canadienne des Universités a chargé d'étudier l'évolution de l'enseignement supérieur au Canada et qui est présidé par Monsieur le Doyen F. Stiling; ils remercient enfin Miss Francess Halpenny de University of Toronto Press qui a guidé et orienté la publication de cet ouvrage, ainsi que Miss Connell qui a préparé l'index des auteurs cités.

R. S. H.
A. T.

Introduction to Supplement

THE 1965 SUPPLEMENT to *A Bibliography of Higher Education in Canada* adds close to 3,000 entries to the approximately 4,000 listed in the original volume. The same editorial procedure has been followed with respect to the reporting and arrangement of entries, and with one minor exception the same criteria have been applied in the selection of the entries themselves. The exception is a relaxing of the rule against the inclusion of articles of less than five pages in length; this rule still applies but on this occasion exceptions have been more freely admitted, particularly in the sections devoted to individual institutions, academic disciplines, and professional fields.

The main purpose of the supplement is to provide a full list of books, articles, pamphlets, and theses bearing on all aspects of higher education in Canada for the five-year period 1959–63. The terminal date for entries in *A Bibliography* was December 31, 1958. The present volume extends the coverage forward into 1964. So far as *complete* coverage is concerned, the terminal date is December 31, 1963; all the journals listed on pages xxvi–xxxi have been systematically searched up to this date—but not beyond. The 1964 entries—and there are a good number of them—are items known to the editor or reported to him by the specialists who have checked the various sections. The result is even for the first half of 1964 a partial and somewhat haphazard collection but it seemed pointless not to list significant 1964 items which were at hand. It should be emphasized, however, that the 1964 coverage is not complete. There will be many more 1964 entries in the next Supplement.

The Supplement has also provided an opportunity to list items of the period prior to December 1958 which were omitted from *A Bibliography*. The number of new entries for this earlier period is approximately 1,000.

A number of new sections have been introduced. This has been in part necessitated by the proliferation of degree-granting institutions. Since 1958 charters have been granted to Brock, Guelph, Lakehead, Laurentian, Notre Dame, Simon Fraser, Trent, Waterloo, Waterloo Lutheran, and York. The obvious importance and the likelihood of imminent independence from the university with which each is currently associated have suggested the advisability of providing separate sections for two others: Brandon College (affiliated with the University of Manitoba), and the Calgary Campus of the University of Alberta. Two institutions have changed their names since the publication of *A Bibliography* and therefore appear under a new guise: Assumption University, now the University of Windsor, and Université St.-Joseph, now Université de Moncton.

Sections have also been provided for two fields which in *A Bibliography* were included within Medicine: "Physical and Occupational Therapy" and "Public Health, Hygiene, and Preventive Medicine." The increasing complexity of the problems involved in the control and financing of higher education in Canada has led to the inclusion of sections on University Finance and University Government. In *A Bibliography* items on university finance were included under "History and Organization: General"; items on university government, under "The Professor." Such items have been re-listed in the Supplement under the appropriate heading. A section has also been assigned to Community Colleges—Institutes of Technology, Etc., in view of the expansion of post-secondary education in institutions other than degree-granting universities and colleges.

As with *A Bibliography*, the chief source for the entries has been a systematic search of Canadian periodical literature. The files of the 183 journals listed on pages xxvi–xxxi have been examined; these include 66 not covered in the preparation of *A Bibliography*. The majority of the new journals have commenced publication since December 31, 1958, but there are a significant number which have longer histories. In the case of the latter, the search of the files has gone back to the commencement of publication.

The issues of *Canadiana*, the National Library of Canada's monthly record of publications of "Canadian origin and interest," have also been searched for the five-year period 1959–63 as have a number of special bibliographies published since 1958. These bibliographies are listed on page xxv.

The publication of a Supplement at this time is warranted by the number of relevant entries which have accrued in a five-year period, and it can be assumed that a second Supplement will be published about 1970. Work on the next volume has in fact already begun; over 100 entries have been collected in the time which has elapsed between submission of the final manuscript and actual publication of this book. These cards are now filed under the appropriate section (Acadia University, Psychology, University Finance, etc.) in the editor's office, and there will be additional cards filed regularly in that office as they are collected. A list of the entries currently filed under any section can be obtained at any time by writing to:

> Dr. Robin S. Harris
> Professor of Higher Education
> University of Toronto
> Toronto 5, Ontario.

I am anxious to express my gratitude to the approximately 70 librarians and professors who have checked and in every case added entries to the tentative list prepared for their institution, academic discipline, or professional field. The co-operation of the staff of the University of Toronto Library has been thorough and good-humoured.

In particular, I must emphasize the important role played in this undertaking by my three research assistants. M. Alfred Dufour of L'Université Laval has been responsible for the searching of the French-language journals and for identifying and examining French-language bibliographies. Mrs. Carol Tomarken of the University of Toronto, who began by searching some of the English-language journals, has gone on to assume effective responsibility for liaison with our seventy consultants and for the preparation of the final manuscript. Mrs. Constance Allen has assisted Mrs. Tomarken in the preparation of the manuscript and has prepared the index.

Finally, the volume has come under the editorial guidance of Miss Francess Halpenny of the University of Toronto Press, a statement which speaks for itself.

R.S.H.

Introduction à Supplément

LE SUPPLÉMENT 1965 de la *Bibliographie de l'Enseignement Supérieur au Canada* ajoute environ 3,000 ouvrages aux 4,000 titres présentés dans le premier volume. La présentation des titres a été faite selon les mêmes principes, et l'on a utilisé, à une exception près, les mêmes critères pour le choix des titres à présenter. L'exception est d'avoir suivi moins systématiquement la règle qui refusait tout article de moins de cinq pages. Cette règle n'est pas abolie, mais on a admis des exceptions plus nombreuses, surtout sous les rubriques des institutions particulières, des disciplines académiques et des professions.

Ce Supplément a pour objet de mettre à la disposition des chercheurs une liste complète des livres, articles, brochures et thèses où il est question des divers aspects de l'enseignement supérieur au Canada, et qui ont paru entre 1959 et 1963. La première *Bibliographie* avait présenté une liste des ouvrages parus avant le 31 décembre 1958 ; le présent volume donne les titres parus entre 1959 et 1964. La bibliographie est complète pour la période qui se termine le 31 décembre 1963 ; tous les périodiques dont la liste se trouve en pages xxvi–xxxi ont été systématiquement dépouillés jusqu'à cette date, mais non au-delà. Les items datés 1964, assez nombreux, sont des ouvrages connus de l'auteur de cette bibliographie, ou qui lui ont été signalés par les spécialistes chargés de vérifier les divers chapitres du Supplément. Il s'ensuit que, même pour la première moitié de 1964, la liste est partielle et peu systématique ; mais il a semblé inutile d'exclure les items importants de 1964 dont on avait connaissance. Il faut souligner toutefois que l'index 1964 est loin d'être complet. Le prochain Supplément donnera des titres beaucoup plus nombreux pour l'année 1964.

Le présent Supplément a également fourni l'occasion d'inclure des titres qui datent d'avant décembre 1958 et qui furent omis lors de la première *Bibliographie* : il y en a environ mille.

Plusieurs nouvelles rubriques paraissent dans ce Supplément. C'est la prolifération des universités qui les a d'abord rendues nécessaires ; depuis 1958 on a vu la création des Universités Brock, Guelph, Lakehead, Laurentian, Notre Dame, Simon Fraser, Trent, Waterloo, Waterloo Lutheran et York. De plus on a décidé de consacrer des rubriques à deux autres collèges dont l'importance est déjà évidente et qui, selon toute probabilité, seront bientôt indépendants des universités auxquelles ils sont actuellement affiliés : il s'agit de Brandon College, affilié à l'Université du Manitoba, et du « Calgary Campus » de l'Université de l'Alberta. Deux universités ont changé de nom depuis la parution de la *Bibliographie*, par conséquent leurs rubriques ont été modifiés : Assumption University est devenue l'Université de Windsor, et l'Université St.-Joseph est devenue l'Université de Moncton.

Des rubriques nouvelles ont été ajoutées pour deux sujets qui avaient été groupés sous le titre « Médecine » dans la *Bibliographie* : il s'agit de « Thérapeutique Physique et Professionelle », et de « Santé Publique, Hygiène et Médecine Préventive ». La complexité croissante des problèmes associés à la direction et au financement des universités a rendu nécessaire la création de nouvelles rubriques sur les « Finances Universitaires » et le « Gouvernement des Universités ». Dans la *Bibliographie*, les ouvrages traitant des problèmes financiers étaient placés sous la rubrique « Histoire et Organisation : généralités » ; les ouvrages sur le gouvernement des universités venaient sous la rubrique « Le Professeur ». Dans le Supplément, ces items ont été reportés sous la rubrique appropriée. On a aussi consacré une rubrique aux « Community Colleges », Instituts de Technologie, afin de reconnaître l'expansion de l'enseignement supérieur dans des institutions autres que les universités et les collèges.

Comme il en a été de la *Bibliographie*, la source principale de ce Supplément provient du dépouillement systématique des revues et journaux canadiens. On a examiné chaque numéro des 183 périodiques dont la liste se trouve en pages xxvi–xxxi; cette liste comprend d'ailleurs 66 périodiques dont il n'est pas rendu compte dans la *Bibliographie*. La plupart des nouveaux périodiques ont commencé à paraître après le 31 décembre 1958, mais certains remontent à une date antérieure. Pour ces derniers, tous les numéros, depuis le premier, ont été dépouillés.

On a en outre compulsé chaque numéro de *Canadiana* (relevé mensuel des publications d'« origine canadienne ou d'intérêt canadien » édité par la Bibliothèque Nationale du Canada), ayant paru entre 1959 et 1963, ainsi qu'un certain nombre de bibliographies spécialisées parues depuis 1958. La liste de ces bibliographies se trouve en page xxv.

Le grand nombre de titres accumulés depuis cinq ans justifie ce Supplément, et il est à présumer qu'un deuxième Supplément paraîtra en 1970. A vrai dire, la préparation du prochain Supplément a déjà commencé ; pendant les mois écoulés entre la soumission du texte définitif et la parution du présent livre, plus de 100 nouveaux titres ont été relevés. Les fiches son actuellement conservées sous la rubrique appropriée (Acadia University, Psychologie, Finances Universitaires, etc.) dans le bureau de l'éditeur du Supplément; d'autres fiches seront ajoutées régulièrement. Une liste des titres classés sous chaque rubrique est toujours à la disposition des chercheurs ; il suffit d'en demander la communication par lettre adressée à :

> Dr. Robin S. Harris
> Professor of Higher Education
> University of Toronto
> Toronto 5, Ontario.

Je tiens à exprimer ma reconnaissance à quelque 70 bibliothécaires et professeurs qui, au cours de leur révision, n'ont pas manqué d'ajouter des titres aux listes provisoires préparées pour leurs institutions, disciplines académiques et professions respectives. La collaboration du personnel de la Bibliothèque de l'Université de Toronto a été entière et amicale.

Je voudrais souligner en particulier l'importance du travail de mes trois collaborateurs. M. Alfred Dufour de l'Université Laval s'est chargé du dépouillement des périodiques de langue française et de la recherche des bibliographies rédigées en français. Mrs. Carol Tomarken de l'Université de Toronto, qui avait commencé par le dépouillement de certains périodiques de langue anglaise, s'est par la suite chargée de faire la liaison entre nos soixante-dix correspondants et de préparer l'état définitif du manuscrit. Mrs. Constance Allen a aidé Mrs. Tomarken dans la préparation du manuscrit et a préparé l'index.

Enfin, la publication de cet ouvrage a été guidée et orientée par Miss Francess Halpenny de la University of Toronto Press, de qui l'éloge n'est plus à faire ici.

R.S.H.

Sources

I: BIBLIOGRAPHIES

1951 Canadian Bibliographic Centre. *Canadian Graduate Theses in the Humanities and Social Sciences, 1921–1946.* Ottawa: King's Printer. Pp. 194.

1959 Eels, W. C. "Canada" in *American Dissertations on Foreign Education* (Washington: Committee on International Relations, National Education Association of the United States), 31–44.

1960 Gagné, A. *Catalogue des thèses de l'école des gradués de l'Université Laval, 1940–1960.* Québec: L'Auteur, Séminaire du Sacré-Cœur. Pp. 76.

Gagné, A. *Répertoire des thèses des facultés ecclésiastiques de l'Université Laval, 1935–1960.* Québec: L'Auteur, Séminaire du Sacré-Cœur. Pp. 19.

Tanghe, R. *Bibliography of Canadian Bibliographies/Bibliographie des bibliographies canadiennes.* Toronto: U. of T. Press. Pp. 206. *Supplement 1960–61.* Toronto: U. of T. Press. Pp. 24. 1962. *Second Supplement 1962–63.* Toronto: U. of T. Press. Pp. 27. 1964.

1961 Arès, R. « Bibliographie sur l'éducation économique au Canada français », *Instr. Publ.* V, 766–68.

Desrochers, E. « Bibliographie sommaire sur la profession de bibliothécaire », *Bull. Bibl.* VII, 18–25.

Parker, F. *Canadian Education: Bibliography of 131 Doctoral Dissertations.* Austin: Univ. of Texas. Pp. 9.

1962 Dussault, C. « Bibliographie du service social canadien-français », *Serv. Soc.* X, no 3, et XI, no 1, 122–41.

National Library of Canada. *Canadian Theses/Thèses canadiennes, 1960/61.* Ottawa: Queen's Printer. Pp. 89.

Parker, F. "Canadian Education: A Bibliography of Doctoral Dissertations," *Education Office Gazette* II, no. 3, 23–29.

1963 National Library of Canada. *Canadian Theses/Thèses canadiennes, 1961/62.* Ottawa: Queen's Printer. Pp. 89.

Stott, M. M. and C. Verner. *A Trial Bibliography of Research Pertaining to Adult Education.* Vancouver: Extension Department, Univ. of British Columbia. Pp. 29.

1964 Canada, Bureau of Statistics. *A Bibliographical Guide to Canadian Education.* 2nd ed. Ottawa: Queen's Printer. Pp. 55.

1959–63 "Recent Publications Relating to Canada" in each issue of *Canadian Historical Review.*

1959–63 « Répertoire bibliographique » dans chaque livraison de *Culture.*

II: CANADIAN JOURNALS : PERIODIQUES CANADIENS

The journals have been searched for the years indicated. Journals not included in *A Bibliography of Higher Education in Canada* are indicated by an asterisk.

Abbreviation	Title	Dates
Act. Méd.	Action Médicale	1959–63
Act. Nat.	Action Nationale	1959–63
Act. Univ.	Action Universitaire	1959–63
Act. Econ.	Actualité Economique	1959–63
Agr.	Agriculture	1959–63
ACFAS	Annales de l'A.C.F.A.S.	1959–63
Alta. Hist. Rev.*	Alberta Historical Review	1963
Alta. Law Rev.*	Alberta Law Review	1955–63
Alta. Lib. Assoc. Bull.*	Alberta Library Association Bulletin	1963
Alta. Med. Bull.*	Alberta Medical Bulletin	1935–63
App. Therapeutics*	Applied Therapeutics	1959–63
Arch.	Architecture	1959–63
Assoc. Ing. For.	Association des Ingénieurs Forestiers du Québec	1959–63
Bien-être*	Bien-être Social Canadien	1949–63
B.C. Lib. Q.*	British Columbia Library Quarterly *Supersedes* British Columbia Library Association Bulletin	1958–63
Bull. Bibl.*	Bulletin de l'Association Canadienne des Bibliothécaires de Langue Française	1957–63
Bull. ACFAS*	Bulletin de l'A.C.F.A.S.	1959–63
Bull. Féd. Coll.	Bulletin de la Fédération des Collèges Classiques	1959–63
Bull. Inf. Cath.	Bulletin des Infirmières Catholiques du Canada	1959–63
Bull. Univ. Laval	Bulletin de l'Université Laval	1959–63
Bus. Q.	Business Quarterly	1959–63
Cah. Acad. Can.-Fr.	Cahiers de l'Académie Canadienne-Française	1959–63
Cah. Dix	Cahiers des Dix	1959–63
Cah. Droit	Cahiers de Droit	1959–63
Cah. Géog.	Cahiers de Géographie de Québec	1959–63
Cah. Hôtel-Dieu	Cahiers de l'Hôtel-Dieu de Québec	1959–63
Cah. Hist.*	Cahiers d'Histoire	1947–63
Cah. Inst. Soc. Pop.	Cahiers de l'Institut Social Populaire	1959–63
Cah. Nouv.-Fr.	Cahiers de Nouvelle-France *Superseded by* Nouv.-Fr.	1959–60
Cah. Nursing	Cahiers du Nursing Canadien *Supersedes* La Garde-Malade	1959–63

Abbreviation	*Title*	*Dates*
Can. Mental Health*	Canada's Mental Health	1953–63
Can. Arch.*	Canadian Architect	1956–63
Can. Army Jour.*	Canadian Army Journal	1947–63
Can. Art*	Canadian Art	1943–63
Can. Assoc. Med. Students & Internes Jour.	Canadian Association of Medical Students and Internes Journal	1959–63
C.A.U.T. Bull.	Canadian Association of University Teachers Bulletin	1959–63
Can. Bar Assoc. Papers*	Canadian Bar Association Papers	1957–63
Can. Bar Jour.	Canadian Bar Journal	1959–63
Can. Bar Rev.	Canadian Bar Review	1959–63
Can. Bus.*	Canadian Business	1938–58
Can. Cath. Hist. Assoc., Annual Rept.	Canadian Catholic Historical Association, Annual Report	1959–63
Can. Chart. Acc.*	Canadian Chartered Accountant	1917–63
Can. Chem. & Process Ind.	Canadian Chemistry and Process Industries	1959–63
Can. Church Hist. Soc. Jour.*	Canadian Church Historical Society Journal	1950–63
Can. Consulting Eng.*	Canadian Consulting Engineer	1959–63
Can. Doctor*	Canadian Doctor	1935–63
Can. Ed.	Canadian Education *Superseded by* Can. Ed. Research Digest	1959–60
Can. Ed. Research Digest*	Canadian Education and Research Digest	1961–63
Can. For.*	Canadian Forum	1959–63
Can. Geog.	Canadian Geographer	1959–63
Can. Geog. Jour.	Canadian Geographical Journal	1959–63
Can. Hist. Assoc., Annual Rept.	Canadian Historical Association, Annual Report	1959–63
Can. Hist. Rev.	Canadian Historical Review	1959–63
Can. Home Econ. Jour.	Canadian Home Economics Journal	1959–63
Can. Hosp.*	Canadian Hospital	1924–63
Can. Jour. Agric. Econ.	Canadian Journal of Agricultural Economics	1959–63
Can. Jour. Bot.	Canadian Journal of Botany	1959–63
Can. Jour. Chem. Eng.*	Canadian Journal of Chemical Engineering	1957–63
Can. Jour. Chem.	Canadian Journal of Chemistry	1959–63
Can. Jour. Comp. Med.*	Canadian Journal of Comparative Medicine and Veterinary Science	1937–63
Can. Jour. Econ. Pol. Sci.	Canadian Journal of Economics and Political Science	1959–63
Can. Jour. Maths.	Canadian Journal of Mathematics	1959–63

Abbreviation	Title	Dates
Can. Jour. Occup. Therapy°	Canadian Journal of Occupational Therapy	1933–63
Can. Jour. Phys.	Canadian Journal of Physics	1959–63
Can. Jour. Psych.	Canadian Journal of Psychology	1959–63
Can. Jour. Pub. Health	Canadian Journal of Public Health	1959–63
Can. Jour. Theol.	Canadian Journal of Theology	1959–63
Can. Jour. Zool.	Canadian Journal of Zoology	1959–63
Can. Lib. Assoc. Bull.	Canadian Library Association Bulletin	1959–63
Can. Math. Bull.°	Canadian Mathematical Bulletin	1958–63
Can. Med. Assoc. Jour.	Canadian Medical Association Journal	1959–63
Can. Mod. Lang. Rev.	Canadian Modern Language Review	1959–63
Can. Music Jour.°	Canadian Music Journal	1956–62
Can. Nuclear Tech.°	Canadian Nuclear Technology	1962–63
Can. Nurse	Canadian Nurse	1959–63
Can. Pharm. Jour.	Canadian Pharmaceutical Journal	1959–63
Can. Physiotherapy Assoc. Jour.°	Canadian Physiotherapy Association Journal	1944–63
Can. Psych. Assoc. Jour.°	Canadian Psychiatric Association Journal	1956–63
Can. Psychologist	Canadian Psychologist *New Series commences 1960*	1959
Can. Surveyor	Canadian Surveyor	1959–63
Chem. Can.	Chemistry in Canada	1959–63
Chitty's Law Jour.°	Chitty's Law Journal	1950–63
Cité Libre	Cité Libre	1959–63
Coll. et Fam.	Collège et Famille	1959–63
Comm. Jour.	Commerce Journal	1959–63
Continuous Learning	Continuous Learning *Supersedes* Food for Thought	1962–63
Culture	Culture	1959–63
Curr. Law & Soc. Prob.°	Current Law and Social Problems	1936–63
Dalhousie Med. Jour.°	Dalhousie Medical Journal *Publication suspended 1942–53*	1936–63
Dalhousie Rev.	Dalhousie Review	1959–63
Design Eng.°	Design Engineering	1955–63
Dialogue°	Dialogue	1962–63
Ed. Record Prov. Quebec	Educational Record of the Province of Quebec	1959–63
Eng. Jour.	Engineering Journal	1959–63
Ens. Sec.	Enseignement Secondaire	1959–63
Et. Slav.	Etudes Slaves et Est-européennes	1959–63
Executive°	Executive	1959–63

Abbreviation	Title	Dates
Fam.-Coll.	Famille-Collège	1959–63
Food for Thought	Food for Thought	1959–61
	Superseded by Continuous Learning	
Food in Can.*	Food in Canada	1941–63
For. Chron.	Forestry Chronicle	1959–63
For. et Cons.	Forêt et Conservation	1959–63
Industrial Can.*	Industrial Canada	1900–63
Inf. Méd.	Information Médicale et Para-medic	1959–63
Ing.	L'Ingénieur	1959–63
Instr. Publ.	Instruction Publique	1959–63
	Supersedes Enseignement Primaire	
Jour. Can. Dent. Assoc.	Journal of the Canadian Dental Association	1959–63
Jour. Ed.*	Journal of Education of the Faculties and Colleges of Education: Vancouver and Victoria	1957–63
Jour. Mus. Can.	Journal Musical Canadien	1959–63
Laënnec Méd.	Laënnec Médical	1959–63
Laval Méd.	Laval Médical	1959–63
Laval Théol. Philos.	Laval Théologique et Philosophique	1959–63
Liberté*	Liberté	1959–63
McGill Law Jour.*	McGill Law Journal	1952–63
Maintenant*	Maintenant	1962–63
	Supersedes Revue Dominicaine	
Man. Bar News*	Manitoba Bar News	1928–63
Man. Med. Rev.*	Manitoba Medical Review	1921–63
Med. Grad.*	Medical Graduate	1955–63
Med. Services Jour.*	Medical Services Journal	1959–63
Mém. S.R.C.	Mémoires de la Société Royale du Canada	1959–63
Mod. Lang. Jour.	Modern Language Journal	1959–63
Montréal Méd.*	Montréal Médical	1949–63
Music Across Can.*	Music Across Canada	1963
Nat. Can.	Le Naturaliste Canadien	1959–63
N.C.C.U.C. Proc.	Proceedings of the National Conference of Canadian Universities and Colleges	1959–63
Nouv.-Fr.	Nouvelle-France	1960–63
N.S. Med. Bull.*	Nova Scotia Medical Bulletin	1922–63

Abbreviation	Title	Dates
Ont. Coll. Pharm. Bull.*	Ontario College Pharmacy Bulletin	1952–63
Ont. Hist.	Ontario History	1959–63
Ont. Jour. Ed. Research	Ontario Journal of Educational Research	1959–63
Ont. Lib. Rev.	Ontario Library Review	1959–63
Ont. Med. Rev.*	Ontario Medical Review	1934–63
Orient.	Orientation	1959–63
Osgoode Hall Law Jour.*	Osgoode Hall Law Journal	1958–63
Pharmacien	Le Pharmacien	1959–63
Phoenix	Phoenix	1959–63
Physics in Canada	Physics in Canada	1959–63
Plant Admin. Eng.*	Plant Administration and Engineering	1941–63
Prêtre*	Prêtre Aujourd'hui	1951–63
Proc. Geol. Assoc. Can.	Proceedings of the Geological Association of Canada	1959–63
Proc. R.S.C.	Proceedings of the Royal Society of Canada	1959–63
Queen's Q.	Queen's Quarterly	1959–63
Relations	Relations	1959–63
Relations Ind.	Relations Industrielles	1959–63
Rev. Barr.	Revue du Barreau	1959–63
Rev. Can. Biol.	Revue Canadienne de Biologie	1959–63
Rev. Can. Géog.	Revue Canadienne de Géographie	1959–63
Rev. Can. Urb.	Revue Canadienne d'Urbanisme	1959–63
Rev. Desjardins*	Revue Desjardins	1935–63
Rev. Dom.	Revue Dominicaine Superseded by Maintenant	1959–61
Rev. Droit	Revue du Droit	1959–63
Rev. Hist.	Revue d'Histoire de l'Amérique Française	1959–63
Rev. Lég.	Revue Légale	1959–63
Rev. Méd. Univ. Montréal	Revue Médicale de l'Université de Montréal	1959–63
Rev. Notariat	Revue du Notariat	1959–63
Rev. Pharm.	Revue de Pharmacie: Professionnelle et Pratique	1959–63
Rev. Univ. Laval	Revue de l'Université Laval	1959–63
Rev. Univ. Ottawa	Revue de l'Université d'Ottawa	1959–63

Abbreviation	*Title*	*Dates*
Rev. Univ. Sherbrooke°	Revue de l'Université de Sherbrooke	1960–63
R. Arch. Inst. Can. Jour.	Royal Architectural Institute of Canada Journal	1959–63
R. Astron. Soc. Jour.	Royal Astronomical Society of Canada Journal	1959–63
Sask. Bar Rev.°	Saskatchewan Bar Review	1936–63
Sask. Hist.	Saskatchewan History	1959–63
Sch. Prog.°	School Progress	1932–63
Sci. Eccl.	Sciences Ecclésiastiques	1959–63
Sem. Rel. Québec	Semaine Religieuse de Québec	1959–63
Semaines Sociales	Semaines Sociales du Canada	1959–63
Séminaire°	Le Séminaire	1948–63
Serv. Soc.	Service Social	1959–63
Soc. Worker	The Social Worker	1932–63
Soc. Can. Ed. Adultes	Société Canadienne d'Education des Adultes	1959–63
Synthèse	Synthèse	1959–63
Thémis	Thémis	1959–63
Tor. Ed. Q.°	Toronto Education Quarterly	1961–63
Trans. R.C.I.	Transactions of the Royal Canadian Institute	1959–63
Trans. R.S.C.	Transactions of the Royal Society of Canada	1959–63
Union Méd.	Union Médicale du Canada	1959–63
U.B.C. Law Rev.°	University of British Columbia Law Review	1959–63
U.N.B. Law Sch. Jour.°	University of New Brunswick Law School Journal	1947–63
Univ. Tor. Law Jour.°	University of Toronto Law Journal	1935–63
Univ. Tor. Q.	University of Toronto Quarterly	1959–63
Vie Fr.°	Vie Française	1946–63
Vieil Esch.	Le Vieil Escholier de Laval	1959–63

PART I

Background
Contexte Socio-Culturel

1

CANADIAN CULTURE
CULTURE CANADIENNE

1809 Viger, D. B. *Considérations sur les effets qu'ont produit en Canada, la conservation des établissements du pays, les mœurs, l'éducation, etc. de ses habitants ; et les conséquences qu'entraineroient leur décadence par rapport aux intérêts de la Grande Bretagne.* Montréal. Pp. 51.

1838 Bettridge, W. *A Brief History of the Church in Upper Canada.* London. Pp. 143.

1855 Hogan, J. S. *Canada: An Essay.* Montreal. Pp. 110.
Taché, J. C. *Esquisse sur le Canada.* Paris. Pp. 180.

1858 Bibaud, F. M. U. M. *Tableau historique des progrès matériels et intellectuels des Canadiens-français.* Montréal. Pp. 50.

1877 Paquin, L.-P. *Essai sur le droit social chrétien.* Ottawa. Pp. 393.

1901 Bruce, G. "Early Red River Culture," *Transactions of the Historical & Scientific Society of Manitoba,* no. 57. Pp. 16.

1903 Committee of the Executive of the Twentieth Century Fund. *Historic Sketches of the Pioneer Work and the Missionary, Educational and Benevolent Agencies of the Presbyterian Church in Canada.* Toronto. Pp. 128.

1905 Savaète, A. *Voix canadiennes—vers l'abîme.* Paris, 1905–22. 12 vols.

1916 Fauteux, A. *Les Bibliothèques canadiennes, étude historique.* Montréal. Pp. 45.

1927 Asselin, A. « Les Canadiens français et le développement économique du Canada », *Action Française* XVII, 305–26.
Vallée, A. *Un Biologiste canadien, Michel Sarazin (1659–1739) : sa vie, ses travaux et son temps.* Québec: Proulx. Pp. 291.

1928 Royal Commission on the Fisheries of the Maritime Provinces and the Magdalen Islands. *Report* . . . . Ottawa: King's Printer. Pp. 125.

1930 Chown, S. D. *The Story of Church Union in Canada.* Toronto: Ryerson. Pp. 156.

1935 Blanchard, R. *L'Est du Canada français, Province de Québec.* Paris: Masson. 2 vols.

1937 Morin, V. « Les Origines de la Société Royale », *Cah. Dix* II, 157–98.

1938 Asselin, O. *L'Industrie dans l'économique du Canada français.* Montréal: Ecole Sociale Populaire. Pp. 32.

Hudon, T. *L'Institut Canadien de Montréal et l'affaire Guibord.* Montréal: Beauchemin. Pp. 172.

1939   Angers, F.-A. « La Position économique des Canadiens français dans le Québec ». *Act. Econ.* XIV, 401–26.

Montpetit, E. *La Conquête économique.* I, *Les Forces essentielles.* II, *Etapes.* III, *Perspectives.* Montréal: Valiquette, 1939–42. 3 vols.

1943   Morin, V. « L'Odyssée d'une société historique [Société Historique de Montréal] », *Cah. Dix* VIII, 13–54.

1945   Edwards, C. E. « La Survivance de la culture française en Nouvelle-Ecosse ». Unpublished M.A. thesis, McGill Univ.

1947   Bruchési, J. « L'Institut Canadien de Québec », *Cah. Dix* XII, 93–144.

Kistler, R. B. "Religion, Education, and Language as Factors in French-Canadian Cultural Survival." Unpublished doct. dissertation, New York Univ.

1948   Canada, Dominion Bureau of Statistics. *The Maritime Provinces in their Relation to the National Economy of Canada: A Statistical Account of their Social and Economic Condition.* Ottawa: King's Printer. Pp. 227.

1950   Audet, T.-A. « Etudes médiévales et culture canadienne », *Rev. Dom.* LVI, 66–79.

1955   Cooper, J. I. "Irish Immigration and the Canadian Church Before the Middle of the 19th Century," *Can. Church Hist. Soc. Jour.* II (May), 1–16.

Léger, J.-M. *Notre Situation économique, Progrès ou stagnation ?* Montréal: L'Action Nationale. Pp. 60.

Parenteau, R. « Quelques raisons de la faiblesse économique de la nation canadienne-française », *Act. Nat.* XLV, 316–31.

1956   Roy, A. « Visiteurs français de marque à Québec (1800–1850) », *Cah. Dix* XXI, 223–35.

Trudel, M. *Histoire de l'Eglise canadienne sous le régime militaire.* I, *Les Problèmes.* II, *Les Institutions.* Québec: Presses Univ. Laval, 1956–57. 2 vols.

Walsh, H. H. *The Christian Church in Canada.* Toronto: Ryerson. Pp. 355.

1957   Frye, N. *Culture and the National Will.* Ottawa: Carleton Univ. Press. Pp. 16.

Hulliger, J. *L'Enseignement social des Evêques canadiens de 1891 à 1950.* Montréal: Fides. Pp. 373.

Kesterton, W. H. "A History of Canadian Journalism 1752– circa 1900," *Canada Year Book, 1957–58,* 920–34.

Roy, A. « Visiteurs français de marque à Québec (1850–1885) », *Cah. Dix* XXII, 213–26.

1958   Bissell, C. T., ed. *Our Living Tradition.* Toronto: U. of T. Press and Carleton Univ. Press. Pp. 149.

Brunet, M. « Les Canadiens après la conquête : les débuts de la résistance passive », *Rev. Hist.* XII, 170–207.

McLuhan, M. "Knowledge, Ideas, Information, and Communication—A Canadian View" in G. Z. F. Bereday, ed., *The Year Book of Education* (London: Evans Brothers Limited), 225–32.

1959 Aiken, H. G. J., and J. J. Deutsch *et al. The American Economic Impact on Canada.* Durham: Duke Univ. Press. Pp. 176.

Allen, P. « Les Carrières des affaires réclament l'élite des jeunes Canadiens français d'aujourd'hui », *Act. Nat.* XLVIII, 263–71.

Angers, F.-A. « Le Problème économique au Canada français », *Act. Nat.* XLVIII, 171–98.

Arès, R. « Les Cultures et l'état », *Act. Nat.* XLVIII, 392–401.

Arès, R. « Le Problème des cultures au Canada », *Act. Nat.* XLVIII, 366–78.

Bissell, C. T. "American Studies in Canadian Universities," *Queen's Q.* LXVI, 384–87.

Caves, R. E. and R. H. Holton. *The Canadian Economy: Prospect and Retrospect.* Harvard Economic Studies CXII. Cambridge: Harvard Univ. Press. Pp. 676.

Clark, A. H. *Three Centuries and the Island: A Historical Geography of Settlement and Agriculture in Prince Edward Island, Canada.* Toronto: U. of T. Press. Pp. 287.

Cooper, L. *Radical Jack: The Life of the First Earl of Durham.* London: Cresset. Pp. 309.

Frémont, D. *Les Français dans l'Ouest canadien.* Winnipeg: Liberté. Pp. 162.

Irving, J. A. *The Social Credit Movement in Alberta.* Toronto: U. of T. Press. Pp. 369.

Kesterton, W. H. "A History of Canadian Journalism circa 1900–1958," *Canada Year Book, 1959,* 883–902.

Lanctôt, G. *Histoire du Canada.* I, *Des Origines au Régime Royal.* II, *Du Régime Royale au Traité d'Utrecht, 1663–1713.* III, *Du Traité d'Utrecht au Traité de Paris, 1713–1763.* Montréal: Beauchemin. 3 vols. (*Voir* 1963, Lanctôt.)

Lebel, M. « Réflexions sur le travail intellectuel », *Rev. Univ. Laval* XIV, 306–20.

LeFebvre, F. « Vocation à l'étude », *Rev. Univ. Ottawa* XXIX, 129–65.

McConica, J. K. "Kingsford and Whiggery in Canadian History," *Can. Hist. Rev.* XL, 108–20.

McDougall, R. L., ed. *Our Living Tradition.* Second & Third Series. Toronto: U. of T. Press and Carleton Univ. Pp. 223.

McDougall, R. L. "The University Quarterlies," *Can. For.* XXXVIII, 253–55.

Massey, V. *Speaking of Canada.* Toronto: Macmillan. Pp. 244.

Moir, J. S. *Church and State in Canada West: Three Studies in the Relation of Denominationalism and Nationalism, 1841–1867.* Toronto: U. of T. Press. Pp. 223.

Morin, V. *Cent vingt-cinq ans d'œuvres sociales et économiques : réhabilitation historique.* Montréal: Editions des Dix. Pp. 52.

Pilon, J.-G. « Situation de l'édition au Canada français », *Rev. Univ. Laval* XIII, 503–508.

Reid, J. H. S., K. McNaught, and H. S. Crowe, eds. *A Source-book of Canadian History: Selected Documents and Personal Papers.* Toronto: Longmans, Green. Pp. 472.

Rich, E. E. *The History of the Hudson's Bay Company.* London: Hudson's Bay Record Society. 2 vols.

Rioux, M. « Sur le développement socio-culturel du Canada français », *Contributions à l'Etude des Sciences de l'Homme* IV, 144–62.

Smith, A. R. "Quebec Society under the French Regime," *Ed. Record Prov. Quebec* LXXV, 129–56.

Theubet, L. « L'Homme et le spécialiste », *Rev. Univ. Ottawa* XXIX, 220–31.

Underhill, F. H., ed. *The Canadian Northwest; Symposium Presented to the Royal Society of Canada in 1958/ L'Avenir du Nord-Ouest canadien ; Colloque présenté à la Société Royale du Canada en 1958.* Studia Varia Series 3. Toronto: U. of T. Press. Pp. 104.

Woodcock, G. "The New France: The French-Canadian Dream," *History Today* [U.K.] IX, 522–31.

1960 Allen, P. *et al. Le Québec économique.* St. Hyacinthe: Alerte. Pp. 166.

Angers, P. *Problèmes de culture au Canada français.* Montréal : Beauchemin. Pp. 116.

Brebner, J. B. *Canada: A Modern History.* With a final chapter by Donald C. Masters. Ann Arbor: Univ. of Michigan Press. Pp. 554.

Cooper, J. I. *The Blessed Communion: The Origin and History of the Diocese of Montreal 1760–1960.* Montreal: Archives' Committee of the Diocese of Montreal. Pp. 266.

Dansereau, P. « Lettre à un séminariste sur l'aliénation des intellectuels », *Cité Libre* XI, 14–18.

Desbiens, J.-P. *Les Insolences du Frère Untel.* Montréal : Editions de l'Homme. Pp. 158. (*Voir* 1962, J.-P. Desbiens.)

Drolet, A. « Le Médecin dans le roman canadien-français », *Laval Méd.* XXIX, 220–31.

Fergusson, C. B. "Mechanics' Institutes in Nova Scotia," *Bull. Public Archives Nova Scotia,* no. 14. Pp. 47.

Graham, J. F. "Economic Development of the Atlantic Provinces," *Dalhousie Rev.* XL, 50–60.

Hamelin, J. *Economie et société en Nouvelle-France.* Cahiers de l'Institut d'Histoire, Université Laval, no 3. Québec: Presses Univ. Laval. Pp. 137.

Hayne, D. M. « Les Lettres canadiennes en France », *Rev. Univ. Laval* XV, 223–30, 328–33, 420–26, 507–14, 716–25; XVI, 140–48.

Kallmann, H. *A History of Music in Canada, 1534–1914.* Toronto: U. of T. Press. Pp. 311.

Lamontagne, R. « La Contribution scientifique de la Galissonière au Canada », *Rev. Hist.* XIII, 509–24.

Lanctôt, J. *et al. Prise de conscience économique.* Montréal: Conseil d'Expansion Economique. Pp. 176.

Lebel, M. « Ce que les Canadiens français ont fait de leur héritage depuis 1760 », Rev. Univ. Laval XV, 334–44.

Lévesque, A. La Dualité culturelle. Montréal: Lévesque. Pp. 256.

Pilon, J.-G. « Situation de l'écrivain canadien de langue française », Rev. Univ. Laval XV, 55–65.

Smith, A. "John Strachan and Early Upper Canada," Ont. Hist. LII, 159–72.

Smith, C. "Federal Contributions to Education for Adults and Certain Agencies of Cultural Diffusion: An Analytical Survey of Developments in Canada from 1920 to 1960." Unpublished M.A. thesis, Univ. of British Columbia.

Underhill, F. H. In Search of Canadian Liberalism. Toronto: Macmillan. Pp. 282.

Wade, M., ed. Canadian Dualism: Studies of French-English Relations. Toronto: U. of T. Press. Pp. 428.

1961 Angers, P. L'Enseignement et la société d'aujourd'hui. Montréal: Éditions Sainte-Marie. Pp. 46.

Association Canadienne des Educateurs de Langue Française. Avenir du Canada et culture française ; travaux du XIVe Congrès. Montréal : Centre de Psychologie et Pédagogie. Pp. 311.

Benoit, P. Lord Dorchester. Figures canadiennes, no 5. Montréal : Editions HMH. Pp. 203.

Best, H. « L'Etat culturel du Canada, à la cession », Rev. Univ. Laval XV, 836–42.

Blishen, B. R. et al., eds. Canadian Society: Sociological Perspectives. Toronto: Macmillan. Pp. 622.

Clark, S. D., ed. Urbanism and the Changing Canadian Society. Toronto: U. of T. Press. Pp. 150.

Côté, J. « L'Instruction des données », Rev. Hist. XV, 344–78.

Cronmiller, C. R. A History of the Lutheran Church in Canada, I. Kitchener: Lutheran Church Supplies. Pp. 288.

De Corte, M. « La Crise des élites », Rev. Univ. Laval XV, 491–502.

Falardeau, J.-C. Roots and Values in Canadian Lives. Toronto: U. of T. Press. Pp. 62.

Frégault, G. « L'Église et la société canadienne au début du XVIIIe siècle », Rev. Univ. Ottawa XXXI, 351–79, 517–42.

Gaudron, E. « Notre Public et son élite intellectuelle », Culture XXII, 99–108.

Goodwin, C. D. W. Canadian Economic Thought; The Political Economy of a Developing Nation, 1814–1914. Durham: Duke Univ. Press. Pp. 214.

Gosselin, P.-E. et al. « La Vie économique au Canada français », Instr. Publ. V, 707–64.

Haskin, J. « Le Niveau culturel des colonies anglaises d'Amérique du Nord lors de la guerre de Sept Ans (1760) », Rev. Univ. Laval XV, 726–35.

Ministère du Travail, Direction de l'économique et des recherches. Le Canada et la migration des travailleurs intellectuels 1946–1960. Ottawa : Imprimeur de la Reine. Pp. 52.

Morton, W. L. *The Canadian Identity.* Toronto: U. of T. Press. Pp. 125.

Oliver, M. K., ed. *Social Purpose for Canada.* Toronto: U. of T. Press. Pp. 472.

Poisson, J. « Francophobie, chauvinisme culturel américain et assimilation », *Act. Nat.* L, 819–35, 941–52.

Pouliot, L. « L'Institut Canadien de Montréal et l'Institut National », *Rev. Hist.* XIV, 481–86.

Rumilly, R. *Le Problème national des Canadiens français.* Montréal : Fides. Pp. 146.

Waite, P. B. "Edward Whelan Reports from the Quebec Conference," *Can. Hist. Rev.* XLII, 23–45.

1962 Clark, S. D. *The Developing Canadian Community.* Toronto: U. of T. Press. Pp. 248.

Desbiens, J.-P. *The Impertinences of Brother Anonymous.* Montréal: Harvest House. Pp. 126. (*Voir* 1960, Desbiens, J.-P.)

Firth, E. G., ed. *The Town of York, 1793–1815: A Collection of Documents of Early Toronto.* Toronto: U. of T. Press. Pp. 368.

Forsey, E. A. "Canada: Two Nations or One," *Can. Jour. Econ. Pol. Sci.* XXVIII, 485–501.

Garigue, P. « Organisation sociale et valeurs culturelles canadiennes-françaises », *Can. Jour. Econ. Pol. Sci.* XXVIII, 189–203.

Groulx, L. *Le Canada français missionnaire.* Montréal : Fides. Pp. 532.

Irving, J. A., ed. *Mass Media in Canada.* Toronto: Ryerson. Pp. 236.

Lamb, W. K. "The National Library of Canada," *Can. Geog. Jour.* LXIV, 124–26.

Langois, J. « Le Rôle de la philosophie dans la culture canadienne », *Dialogue* I, 117–28.

Lebel, M. « L'Instituteur du Québec et l'instituteur de France », *Rev. Univ. Laval* XVI, 795–806.

Lebel, M. « Le Rôle primordial des bibliothèques dans un pays au XXᵉ siècle », *Instr. Publ.* VI, 591–601.

MacRae, C. F., ed. *French Canada Today: Report of the Mount Allison Summer Institute.* Sackville: Mount Allison Bookstore. Pp. 115.

Manning, H. T. *The Revolt of French Canada 1800–1835.* Toronto: Macmillan. Pp. 426.

Marion, S. « Libéralisme canadien-français d'autrefois et d'aujourd'hui », *Cah. Dix* XXVII, 9–45.

Ouellet, F. « Les Fondements historiques de l'option séparatiste dans le Québec », *Can. Hist. Rev.* XLIII, 185–203.

Société Saint-Jean Baptiste de Montréal. *L'Education nationale suivie de l'enquête sur le problème national des Canadiens français du Québec.* Montréal : Action Nationale. Pp. 179.

1963 Bonenfant, F. et al. *Cri d'alarme... la civilisation scientifique et les Canadiens français.* Québec : Presses Univ. Laval. Pp. 142.

Carrington, P. *The Anglican Church in Canada.* Toronto: Collins. Pp. 320.

Dumont, F. *et al. Les Univers sociaux.* Montréal : Institut Canadien d'Education des Adultes. Pp. 68.

Garigue, P. *L'Option politique du Canada français.* Ottawa : Lévrier. Pp. 74.

Gosselin, P.-E. *L'Empire français d'Amérique.* Québec : Ferland. Pp. 144.

Lanctôt, G. *A History of Canada.* Translated into English by J. Hambleton. Cambridge: Harvard Univ. Press. Pp. 393. (*See* 1959, Lanctôt.)

Lebel, M. *D'Octave Crémazie à Alain Grandbois.* Québec : Editions de l'Action. Pp. 285.

LeBlanc, E. *Les Acadiens.* Montréal : Editions de l'Homme. Pp. 126.

MacNutt, W. S. *New Brunswick: A History, 1784–1867.* Toronto: Macmillan. Pp. 496.

Morton, W. L. *The Kingdom of Canada: A General History from Earliest Times.* Toronto: McClelland and Stewart. Pp. 556.

Matthews, R. "The New University: An Old Role," *Can. For.* XLIII, no. 508, 35–36.

Myers, B. R. *North of the Border: A Story Resulting from Two Years in Canada.* New York: Vintage. Pp. 214.

Overseas Institute of Canada. *Canada's Participation in Social Development Abroad.* Ottawa: The Institute. Pp. 76.

Pichette, C. « Les Canadiens-français dans l'économie canadienne », *Rev. Univ. Sherbrooke* III, 199–216.

Reid, L. "CBC TV 1952–62: A Decade of Achievement," *Can. Geog. Jour.* LXV, 76–89.

Roy, P.-E. *Les Intellectuels dans la cité.* Montréal : Fides. Pp. 85.

Royal Commission on Government Organization. *Report.* . . . Ottawa: Queen's Printer. 5 vols.

Scott, P. D. "Our University Machinery," *Can. For.* XLII, 272–75.

Trudel, M. *Histoire de la Nouvelle-France.* Montréal : Fides. Pp. 307.

1964 Carrière, G. « Nos Archives et la Société Canadienne d'Histoire de l'Eglise Catholique », *Rev. Univ. Ottawa* XXXIV, 73–96.

2

CANADIAN EDUCATION
L'ENSEIGNEMENT AU CANADA

1824 Lower Canada House of Assembly. *Report of the Special Committee of the House of Assembly Appointed to Enquire into the State of Education in the Province.* Quebec. Pp. 240.

1829 Strachan, J. *A Letter to the Rev. A. N. Bethune, on the Management of Grammar Schools.* York. Pp. 45.

1830 Perrault, J. F. « Plan raisonné d'éducation générale et permanente, le plus propre à faire la prospérité du Bas Canada, en égard à ses circonstances actuelles », *Transactions of the Literary and Historical Society of Quebec* II, 317–25.

1857 Hodgins, T., ed. *The Canada Educational Directory and Calendar for 1857–58.* Toronto. Pp. 144.

Nicholls, J. H. "The End and Object of Education," *Journal of Education, Lower Canada* (April), 62–64.

1864 Dawson, J. W. *On . . . Protestant Education in Lower Canada.* Montreal. Pp. 20.

Snodgrass, W. *The Sacredness of Learning.* Kingston. Pp. 15.

1870 Dawson, J. W. *Science Education Abroad: Being the Annual University Lecture of the Session 1870–71.* Montreal. Pp. 15.

1876 Chauveau, P.-J.-O. *L'Abbé Jean Holmes et ses conférences de Notre-Dame.* Québec. Pp. 33.

Marling, A., ed. *The Canada Educational Directory and Year Book for 1876. . . .* Toronto. Pp. 224.

1881 Paquin, L.-P. *Conférences sur l'instruction obligatoire.* Québec. Pp. 156.

1884 Willoughby, J. *Progress of Education in Nova Scotia during Fifty Years.* Halifax. Pp. 140.

1889 Dawson, J. W. *Educated Women: The Substance of an Address Delivered before the Delta Sigma Society of McGill University, December 1889.* Montreal. Pp. 14.

1893 Millar, J. *The Educational System of the Province of Ontario, Canada.* Toronto. Pp. 114.

1901 Millar, J. *Education for the Twentieth Century.* Toronto. Pp. 7.

Millar, J. *The Educational Demands of Democracy.* Ottawa. Pp. 11.

1907 Coleman, H. T. J. *Public Education in Upper Canada.* New York. Pp. 120.

Gosselin, A.-H. *Le Docteur Labrie, un bon patriote d'autrefois.* Québec. Pp. 274.

1909 Hodgins, J. G. *What We Owe to the United Empire Loyalist in the Matter of Education*. Toronto. Pp. 11.

1910 Hodgins, J. G. *The Establishment of Schools and Colleges in Ontario, 1792–1910*. Toronto. 3 vols.

1917 Barnes, A. "The History of Education in Newfoundland." Unpublished doct. dissertation, New York Univ.

1918 Anderson, J. T. M. *The Education of the New-Canadian*. Toronto. Pp. 271.

Foght, H. W. *A Survey of Education in the Province of Saskatchewan*. Regina. Pp. 183.

Robinson, G. C. "A Historical and Critical Account of Public Secondary Education in the Province of Ontario, Canada, 1792–1916." Unpublished doct. dissertation, Harvard Univ.

1919 Barber, D. A. "The Educational System of British Columbia." Unpublished M.A. thesis, Univ. of Washington.

1920 Eames, F. "Pioneer Schools of Upper Canada," *Ontario Historical Society, Papers and Records* XVIII, 91–103.

McCrimmon, A. L. *The Educational Policy of the Baptists of Ontario and Quebec*. Toronto: McMaster Univ. Pp. 35.

1921 Jones, T. W. "Education and Industry, Their Development and Cooperation." Unpublished M.A. thesis, McGill Univ.

1924 Ryan, W. M. "The Educational System of the Province of Quebec." Unpublished M.A. thesis, Catholic Univ. of America.

1926 Hathaway, E. J. "Early Schools of Toronto," *Ontario Historical Society, Papers and Records* XXIII, 312–27.

1930 Henderson, E. "Some Reminiscences of Upper Canada College from 1854 to 1857," *Ontario Historical Society, Papers and Records* XXVI, 457–60.

1931 Groulx, L. *L'Enseignement français au Canada : dans le Québec*. Montréal : Action Canadienne-française. Pp. 327.

1932 Pakenham, W. "Education in Canada" in E. Percy, ed., *The Year Book of Education* (London: Evans Brothers Limited), 663–84.

1933 "Provincial Summaries" in E. Percy, ed., *The Year Book of Education* (London: Evans Brothers Limited), 519–26.

1934 Hans, N. "Canada" in E. Percy, ed., *The Year Book of Education* (London: Evans Brothers Limited), 87–90.

McQueen, J. "The Development of the Technical and Vocational Schools of Ontario." Unpublished M.A. thesis, Columbia Univ.

1935 "Canada: (I) Dominion; (II) The Provinces; (III) Statistics" in E. Percy, ed., *The Year Book of Education* (London: Evans Brothers Limited), 46–59.

L'Education sociale. Montréal : Bellarmin. Pp. 326.

Groulx, L. *et al*. *L'Education nationale*. Montréal : Lévesque. Pp. 212.

MacPherson, W. E. "Canada" in E. Percy, ed., *The Year Book of Education* (London: Evans Brothers Limited), 252–59.

Percival, W. P. *Why Educate?* Toronto: Dent. Pp. 179.

1936 Robbins, J. E. "Canadian Education Viewed in the Light of Social Needs" in E. Percy, ed., *The Year Book of Education* (London: Evans Brothers Limited), 601–17.

Scott, W. L. "Sir Richard Scott, 1825–1913," *Can. Cath. Hist. Assoc., Annual Rept.*, 46–71.

1937   Cunningham, K. S. "The Education of the Adolescent" in H. V. Usill, ed., *The Year Book of Education* (London: Evans Brothers Limited), 170–85.

Ikin, A. E. "Educational Endowments in the Dominion of Canada" in E. Percy, ed., *The Year Book of Education* (London: Evans Brothers Limited), 294–307.

MacLaurin, D. L. "The History of Education in the Crown Colonies of Vancouver Island and British Columbia and in the Province of British Columbia." Unpublished doct. dissertation, Univ. of Washington.

1938   Ault, A. E. "Examinations in Canada" in H. V. Usill, ed., *The Year Book of Education* (London: Evans Brothers Limited), 154–71.

Rumilly, R. *Mgr LaFlèche et son temps.* Montréal : Simpson. Pp. 425.

1939   Hardy, J. H. "Teachers' Organizations in Ontario: An Historical Account of Their Part in Ontario Educational Development, and Their Influence on the Teacher and Teaching, 1840–1938." Unpublished doct. dissertation, Univ. of Toronto.

Morrow, R. L., ed. *Conference on Educational Problems in Canadian-American Relations held at the University of Maine, June 21–23, 1938: Proceedings.* Orono: Univ. of Maine Press. Pp. 256.

Schaefer, C. S. "Education in Canada." Unpublished M.A. thesis, Indiana Univ.

1940   Gibson, G. D. "Jesuit Education of the Indians in New France." Unpublished doct. dissertation, Univ. of California.

Stanley, C. "Canada: Too Much Trust in 'Civics' " in F. H. Spencer, ed., *The Year Book of Education* (London: Evans Brothers Limited), 382–91.

1942   Spragge, G. W. "The Cornwall Grammar School under John Strachan, 1803–1812," *Ontario Historical Society, Papers and Records* XXXIV, 63–84.

1944   De Grandpré, A. *Propos d'un éducateur.* Montréal : Librairie Saint-Viateur. Pp. 167.

1946   Baird, N. B. "Educational Finance and Administration for Ontario." Unpublished doct. dissertation, Univ. of Toronto.

1947   Kistler, R. B. "Religion, Education and Languages as Factors in French-Canada Cultural Survival." Unpublished doct. dissertation, New York Univ.

1948   Lazerte, M. E. "Canada" in G. B. Jeffery, ed., *The Year Book of Education* (London: Evans Brothers Limited), 156–63.

1950   Carlton, S. "Egerton Ryerson and Education in Ontario." Unpublished doct. dissertation, Univ. of Pennsylvania.

McCoffrey, C. F. "The Catholic High School of Montreal," *Can. Cath. Hist. Assoc., Annual Rept.*, 53–64.

Parsey, J. M. "The History and Status of Correspondence Education in Canada." Unpublished M.Ed. thesis, Univ. of Manitoba.

Phillips, C. E. "Canada" in G. B. Jeffery, ed., *The Year Book of Education* (London: Evans Brothers Limited), 309–43.

1951 Bilodeau, C. "Quebec" in G. B. Jeffery, ed., *The Year Book of Education* (London: Evans Brothers Limited), 395–402.

Seeley, J. K. "Education and Morals" in G. B. Jeffery, ed., *The Year Book of Education* (London: Evans Brothers Limited), 386–94.

Spragge, G. W. "Elementary Education in Upper Canada, 1820–1840," *Ont. Hist.* XLIII, 107–22.

1952 Doherty, H. A. "An Inquiry into the Comparative Ability of the Canadian Provinces to Finance Education." Unpublished M.A. thesis, Univ. of Alberta.

Stewart, F. K. "Canada" in G. B. Jeffery, ed., *The Year Book of Education* (London: Evans Brothers Limited), 252–74.

1953 Lazerte, M. E. "Canada" in R. K. Hall, ed., *The Year Book of Education* (London: Evans Brothers Limited), 229–49.

1954 De Grandpré, M. *Une Figure d'éducation, Le Père Alphonse de Grandpré, Clerc de Saint-Viateur, 1883–1942.* Joliette, Québec : Les Clercs de St. Viateur. Pp. 91.

1955 Calder, D. G. *Seventy Years of Progress in Education: An Abbreviated Historical Outline of the Department of Education, Province of Saskatchewan, 1884–1954.* Regina: Department of Education. Pp. 43.

1956 *Education/1. A Collection of Essays on Canadian Education 1954–1956.* Toronto: Gage. Pp. 89.

Frecker, G. A. *Education in the Atlantic Provinces.* Toronto: Gage. Pp. 112.

Smith, F. P. "Early Schools in Kingston," *Historic Kingston* V, 25–29.

1957 Oki, J. A. P. "The Administration of Education in Canada." Unpublished M.A. thesis, Carleton Univ.

1958 Althouse, J. G. *Addresses: A Selection of Addresses by the Late Chief Director of Education for Ontario, Covering the Years 1936–56.* Edited by K. B. McCool. Toronto: Gage. Pp. 243.

Audet, L.-P. « L'Éducation au temps de Mgr de Laval », *Société Canadienne l'Eglise Catholique Rapport, 1957–58.* 59–78.

Croskery, G. G. and G. Nason, eds. *Addresses and Proceedings of the Canadian Conference on Education, Held at Ottawa, February 16–20, 1958.* Ottawa: Montreal Press. Pp. 591.

Flower, G. E. and F. K. Stewart, eds. *Leadership in Action: The Superintendent of Schools in Canada.* Toronto: Gage. Pp. 392.

Harris, R. S. "The Conference on Education," *Can. For.* XXXVIII, 9–10.

Swift, W. H. *Trends in Canadian Education.* Toronto: Gage. Pp. 94.

1959 Audet, L.-P. « La Querelle de l'instruction obligatoire », *Cah. Dix* XXIV, 133–50.

Booth, C. W. "Some Basic Aims and Recent Trends in Secondary Education," *Can. Ed.* XIV, 35–50.

Canadian Education Association. "Developments in Education in Canada 1957–1958; a Report by the C.É.A. for the International Conference on Public Education," *Can. Ed.* XIV, no. 2, 16–25.

Education/2. A Collection of Essays on Canadian Education 1956–1958. Toronto: Gage. Pp. 100.

Genest, J. « Rockefeller, Conant et l'éducation », *Relations* XIX, 149–51.

Harris, R. S. "Egerton Ryerson" in R. L. McDougall, ed., *Our Living Tradition.* Second & Third Series (Toronto: U. of T. Press and Carleton Univ.), 244–67.

Humble, A. H. *The Crisis in Canadian Education.* Toronto: Ryerson. Pp. 21.

Lloyd, W. S. *The Role of Government in Canadian Education.* Toronto: Gage. Pp. 98.

Moir, J. S. "The Origins of the Separate School Question in Ontario," *Can. Jour. Theol.* V, 105–18.

Ontario Department of Education. "The Carnegie Study of Identification and Utilization of Talent in High School and College," *Ont. Jour. Ed. Research* I, 149–54.

Robinson, E. W. "The History of Frontier College, 1899–1954." Unpublished M.A. thesis, Univ. of Toronto.

Ross, M. G. "The Role of the School in a Changing Society," *Can. Ed.* XIV, 12–23.

Royal Commission on Education in Alberta. *Report.* . . . Edmonton: Queen's Printer. Pp. 451.

Royal Commission on Education in Manitoba. *Report.* . . . Winnipeg: Queen's Printer. Pp. 284.

St. John, J. B. *Spotlight on Canadian Education: Background to the Canadian Conference on Education, 1958.* Toronto: Gage. Pp. 111.

Sissons, C. B. *Church and State in Canadian Education: An Historical Study.* Toronto: Ryerson. Pp. 414.

Wallace, R. H., ed. *The Superintendent as Educational Leader.* Toronto: Ryerson. Pp. 62.

1960　Audet, L.-P. « Création du Conseil de l'instruction publique dans le Bas-Canada 1856–1960 », *Mém. S.R.C.* Sect. I, 1–29.

Audet, L.-P. « La Surintendance de l'éducation et la loi scolaire de 1841 », *Cah. Dix* XXV, 147–69.

Begin, E. *François de Laval.* Québec : Presses Univ. Laval. Pp. 225.

Cameron, D. R. *Teacher Certification in Canada.* Ottawa: Canadian Teachers' Federation. Pp. 213.

Canadian Education Association. "Developments in Education in Canada, 1958–1959—A Report Prepared by the CEA for the International Conference on Public Education," *Can. Ed.* XV, no. 2, 3–16.

Commonwealth Education Conference, Oxford, 15–28 July 1959. *Report.* . . . Ottawa: Queen's Printer. Pp. 65.

Desbiens, J.-P. *Les Insolences du Frère Untel.* Montréal : Editions de l'Homme. Pp. 158. (*Voir* 1962, Desbiens, J.-P.)

Education/3. A Collection of Essays on Canadian Education 1958–1960. Toronto: Gage. Pp. 140.

Fairley, M., ed. *The Selected Writings of William Lyon Mackenzie, 1824–1837.* Toronto: Oxford. Pp. 383.

Fédération des Collèges Classiques. *Problèmes d'éducation.* Document no 11. Montréal: La Fédération. Pp. 36.

Filion, G. *Les Confidences d'un commissaire d'écoles.* Montréal: Editions de l'Homme. Pp. 122.

Gingras, P.-E. « Bilan 1959–60 », *Act. Nat.* XLIX, 741–52.

Guillet, E. C. *In the Cause of Education: Centennial History of the Ontario Educational Association, 1861–1960.* Toronto: U. of T. Press. Pp. 472.

Lloyd, W. S. *The Role of Government in Canadian Education.* Toronto: Gage. Pp. 98.

Lussier, I. *L'Education catholique et le Canada français/Roman Catholic Education and French Canada.* Toronto: Gage. Pp. 82.

MacKinnon, F. *The Politics of Education: A Study of the Political Administration of the Public Schools.* Toronto: U. of T. Press. Pp. 187.

Potvin, D. « L'Instruction publique sous le régime français », *Nouvelle-France* XV, 202–205.

Prang, M. "Clerics, Politicians, and the Bilingual Schools Issue in Ontario, 1910–1917," *Can. Hist. Rev.* XLI, 281–307.

Royal Commission on Education in British Columbia. *Report. . . .* Victoria: Queen's Printer. Pp. 460.

Smith, A. "John Strachan and Early Upper Canada 1799–1814," *Ont. Hist.* LII, 159–73.

Stewart, F. K. "An Organizational Problem in Canadian Education," *Can. Ed.* XV, 17–23.

Trudel, J.-P. « Réflexions sur l'éducation et la culture », *Coll. et Fam.* XVII, 160–65.

Wright, H. E. " 'Five-Score and Seventeen Years Ago'—The High School of Montreal 1843," *Jour. Ed.* no. 4, 12–20.

1961 Angers, F.-A. « Le Problème des structures », *Coll. et Fam.* XVIII, no 1–2, 35–44.

Angers, F.-A. « La Singulière Théorie du désengagement », *Act. Nat.* LI, 35–50.

Angers, P. *L'Enseignement et la société d'aujourd'hui.* Montréal: Editions Sainte-Marie. Pp. 46.

Association canadienne des éducateurs de langue française. *Avenir du Canada et culture française ; travaux du XIVᵉ congrès.* Québec: ACELF. Pp. 176.

Barbeau, V. « Le Profit d'être plus homme », *Cah. Acad. Can.-Fr.*, 135–47.

Barrett, H. O., ed. *The Status of the Secondary School Teacher in Ontario.* A symposium prepared by the Ontario Secondary School Teachers' Federation. Toronto: Gage. Pp. 132.

Campeau, L. « Les Principes de l'enseignement au Canada français », *Relations* XXI, 89–92.

Canadian Education Association. "Developments in Education in Canada, 1959–60," *Can. Ed. Research Digest* I, no. 1, 7–15.

Caverhill, A. "A History of St. John's School and Lower Canada College." Unpublished M.A. thesis, McGill Univ.

Dhillon, P. S. "An Historical Study of Aims of Education in Ontario, 1800–1900." Unpublished M.A. thesis, Univ. of Toronto.

Drummond, I. M. "Employment and Education: Prospects for the Sixties," *Can. For.* XLI, 193–95.

Durand, S.-M. *Pour ou contre l'éducation nouvelle ; essai de synthèse pédagogique.* Québec : Pélican. Pp. 203.

Erskine, J. S. "Politics and Education in Nova Scotia," *Dalhousie Rev.* XLI, 5–14.

Gagnon, A. « Education et l'édification de la Cité » *Instr. Publ.* V, 363–76.

Huot, P. et L. Garneau. « L'Education au Québec », *Rev. Univ. Sherbrooke* I, 129–38.

Jackson, R. W. B. *Educational Research in Canada Today and Tomorrow.* Toronto: Gage. Pp. 145.

Joly, J.-M. "Recent Educational Developments in Quebec," *Can. Ed. Research Digest* I, 21–39.

Klass, A. A. "What is a Profession?" *Can. Bar. Jour.* IV, 466–73.

Lacoste, P. « La Réforme du Conseil de l'Instruction publique », *Cité Libre* XII, 5–10.

Lambert, M. « La Fin de l'éducation », *Rev. Univ. Sherbrooke* I, 65–84.

Léger, P.-E. *Réflexions pastorales sur notre enseignement.* Montréal : Fides. Pp. 30.

Léger, P.-E. *Responsabilités actuelles du laïcat.* Montréal : Fides. Pp. 16.

Marzolf, A. D. "Alexander Cameron Rutherford and his Influence on Alberta's Educational System." Unpublished M.A. thesis, Univ. of Alberta.

Minville, E. « Education sociale et civique », *Cah. Acad. Can.-Fr.*, 97–112.

O'Bready, M. « Education, garantie de l'avenir », *Rev. Univ. Sherbrooke* I, 163–70.

Ouellet, F. « L'Enseignement primaire : responsabilité des églises ou de l'état? (1801–1836) », *Recherches Sociographiques* II, 171–88.

Pigott, A. V. "Public Education and Employment," *Food for Thought* XXI, 206–11.

Porter, J. "Social Class and Education" in M. K. Oliver, ed., *Social Purpose for Canada* (Toronto: U. of T. Press), 103–29.

Reid, J. H. S. and C. Bilodeau. "Education" in J. T. Saywell, ed., *Canadian Annual Review for 1960* (Toronto: U. of T. Press), 243–52, 253–60.

Robinson, E. W. "The History of the Frontier College." Unpublished M.A. thesis, McGill Univ.

Shutt, G. M. *The High Schools of Guelph: Being the Story of Wellington District Grammar School, Guelph Grammar School, Guelph High School, and Guelph's Collegiate Institutes.* Toronto: U. of T. Press. Pp. 138.

Sutherland, K. "Reflections on Education in Saskatchewan," *Universities Review* [U.K.] XXXIV, 21–26.

Université de Montréal, Association des Professeurs. *La Crise de l'enseignement au Canada.* Montréal : Editions du Jour. Pp. 123.

Wormsbecker, J. H. "The Development of Secondary Education in Vancouver." Unpublished doct. dissertation, Univ. of Toronto.

1962 Association des Bibliothécaires du Québec. *A Brief Submitted to the Royal Commission of Inquiry on Education/Mémoire soumis à la Commission Royale d'Enquête sur l'Enseignement.* Montréal : L'Association. Pp. 91.

Association des Religieuses Enseignantes du Québec. *Mémoire à la Commission Royale d'Enquête sur l'Enseignement.* Québec : L'Association. Pp. 192.

Audet, L.-P. « Urgel-Eugène Archambault instituteur (1851–1859) », *Cah. Dix* XXVII, 135–76 ; XXVIII, 219–54.

Bassett, J. *et al.* "The Future of Grade 13: A Symposium," *Tor. Ed. Q.*, no. 3, 2–9.

Boisvert, R. « Education et orientation », *Rev. Univ. Sherbrooke* II, 223–32.

Bouvier, E. « Les Responsabilités d'une université catholique », *Rev. Univ. Sherbrooke* III, 3–8.

"Canada: Educational Development 1961–62," *Can. Ed. Research Digest* II, 73–98.

Cheal, J. E., H. C. Melsness, and A. W. Reeves. *Educational Administration: The Role of the Teacher.* Toronto: Macmillan. Pp. 277.

Crawford, K. G. *Provincial Grants to Canadian Schools.* Toronto: Canadian Tax Foundation. Pp. 259.

Desbiens, J.-P. *Les Insolences du Frère Untel.* Montréal : Editions de l'Homme. Pp. 158. (*Voir* 1962, Desbiens, J.-P.)

Frye, N., ed. *Design for Learning.* Toronto: U. of T. Press. Pp. 148.

Harris, R. S. "The Second Canadian Conference on Education," *Can. For.* XLII, 1–3.

Howsam, R. B. "Canada" in T. L. Reller and E. L. Morphet, eds., *Comparative Educational Administration* (Englewood, N.J.: Prentice-Hall), 132–50.

Hunte, K. D. "The Development of the System of Education in Canada East, 1841–1867; an Historical Survey." Unpublished M.A. thesis, McGill Univ.

Hurtubise, R. « La Confessionnalité de notre système scolaire et les garanties constitutionnelles », *Rev. Notariat* LXV, 167–84.

Labarrère, P. A. *P.-J.-O. Chauveau.* Collection Classiques Canadiens, no 24. Montréal : Fides. Pp. 96.

Lacoste, P. «Réforme et confessionnalité », *Cité Libre* XIII, 16–20.

Lamarche, J.-A. « Mémoire de la 'Fierté Française' à la Commission Royale d'Enquête sur l'Enseignement », *Temps Présent* V, 57–84.

Lebel, M. « P.-J.-O. Chauveau, humaniste du dix-neuvième siècle », *Mém. S.R.C.* Sect. I, 1–10. (*Voir aussi Rev. Univ. Laval* XVII, 32–42.)

Légaré, H. F.   *La Fin première de l'éducation.* Montréal : Fides. Pp. 31.

Lemieux, E.   « Les Ecoles doivent-elles être confessionnelles ?» *Sem. Rel. Québec* LXXIV, 567–73.

Lessard, V.   « L'Instruction obligatoire dans la province de Québec de 1875 à 1943 ». Thèse de doctorat, Univ. d'Ottawa.

Morel, A. *et al. Justice et paix scolaire.* Montréal : Editions du Jour. Pp. 173.

« Nos Educateurs ont-ils perdu le Nord ? » *Act. Nat.* LII, 11–27.

Parenteau, H.-A.   *Les Robes Noires dans l'école.* Montréal : Editions du Jour. Pp. 170.

Paton, J. M.   *The Role of Teachers' Organizations in Canadian Education.* Toronto: Gage. Pp. 89.

Patterson, R. S.   "F. W. G. Haultain: Educational Statesman of the Canadian West," *Alberta Journal of Educational Research* VIII, 85–93.

Price, F. W., ed.   *The Second Canadian Conference on Education: A Report.* Toronto: U. of T. Press. Pp. 414.

Purdy, J. D.   "John Strachan and Education in Canada." Unpublished doct. dissertation, Univ. of Toronto.

Reeves, A. W., J. H. M. Andrews, and F. Enns.   *The Canadian School Principal.* Toronto: McClelland and Stewart. Pp. 311.

Reid, J. H. S. and C. Bilodeau.   "Education" in J. T. Saywell, ed., *Canadian Annual Review for 1961* (Toronto: U. of T. Press), 269–79, 280–87.

Roberts, G. D. and F. W. Price, general eds.   *Conference Studies* 1–9. Ottawa: Canadian Conference on Education.
1. C. E. Phillips, ed. *The Aims of Education.* Pp. 59.
2. J. M. Paton.   *The Professional Status of Teachers.* Pp. 76.
3. L. S. Beattie.   *The Development of Student Potential.* Pp. 63.
4. J. P. Kidd and D. C. Williams.   *New Development in Society.* Pp. 49.
5. W. J. McCordic.   *Financing Education.* Pp. 61.
6. J. R. Kidd.   *Continuing Education.*Pp. 104.
7. C. P. Collins, ed.   *Research & Education.* Pp. 53.
8. H. J. A. Brown.   *The Citizen & Education.* Pp. 61.
9. A. V. Pigott.   *Education and Employment.* Pp. 81.

Ruel, P. H.   « Civisme, responsabilité de l'éducation », *Rev. Univ. Sherbrooke* II, 189–98.

Société Saint-Jean-Baptiste de Montréal.   « Mémoire de la SSJB de M. sur l'éducation nationale », *Act. Nat.* LI, 761–929.

Story, G. M.   *Education and Renascence; an Address to the Halifax Teachers' Union, Halifax, Nova Scotia, 9th March, 1962.* St. John's: Memorial Univ. of Newfoundland. Pp. 18.

Tremblay, A.   "The Role of Research in Education," *Ont. Jour. Ed. Research* IV, 161–67.

Tremblay, J.   *Scandale au D.I.P. : l'affaire Guérin, ou le Frère Untel avait raison.* Montréal : Editions du Jour. Pp. 124.

Whitworth, F. E.   *Skills for Tomorrow.* Ottawa: Canadian Conference on Education. Pp. 67.

1963 Angers, F.-A. *et al.* « Manifeste de l'Action Nationale (le Rapport Parent) », *Act. Nat.* LIII, 1–148.

Angers, F.-A. « La Querelle des structures », *Act. Nat.* LII, 565–75.

Angers, P. *Réflexions sur l'enseignement.* Montréal : Bellarmin. Pp. 204.

Audet, L.-P. *Educateurs : parents, maîtres.* Québec. Editions de l'Action. Pp. 145.

Baker, H. S. "Re-Examining the Purposes of Education," *Can. Ed. Research Digest* III, 181–93.

Beattie, K. *Ridley: The Story of a School.* St. Catharines: Ridley College. 2 vols.

Campeau, L. « L'Autorité du ministre dans le bill 60 », *Act. Nat.* LIII, 354–63.

"Canada: Report on Educational Developments, September 1962– June 1963," *Can. Ed. Research Digest* III, 71–84.

Cheal, J. E. *Investment in Canadian Youth: An Analysis of Differences among Canadian Provincial School Systems.* Toronto: Macmillan. Pp. 167.

Commission Royale d'Enquête sur l'Enseignement dans la Province de Québec. *Rapport...* Québec : Imprimeur de la Reine, 1963–65, 3 vols./Royal Commission of Inquiry on Education in the Province of Quebec. *Report....* Quebec : Queen's Printer, 1963–65, 3 vols.

Craig, G. M. "Religion and Education in the 1820's and 1830's" in *Upper Canada: The Formative Years, 1784–1841* (Toronto: McClelland and Stewart), 165–88.

De Grandpré, M. *Pour un Ministère de l'éducation vraiment moderne.* Document no 25. Montréal: Fédération des Collèges Classiques. Pp. 136.

Dion, G. et P. Saucier. « Le Bill 60 », *Maintenant,* 260–66.

Downey, L. W. and L. R. Goodwin, eds. *The Canadian Secondary School: An Appraisal and a Forecast.* Toronto: Macmillan. Pp. 125.

Education/4 A Collection of Essays on Canadian Education 1960– 1962. Toronto: Gage. Pp. 135.

"Education Services" in J. G. Glassco (Chairman), *Royal Commission on Government Organization, Report* III (Ottawa: Queen's Printer), 137–71.

Fédération des Collèges Classiques. *Notre Réforme scolaire* : I, *Les Cadres généraux* ; II, *L'Enseignement classique.* Montréal: Centre de Psychologie et de Pédagogie. 2 vols.

Genest, J. « Croire en la liberté », *Coll. et Fam.* XX, 245–56.

Genest, J. «Rentabilité en éducation », *Coll. et Fam.* XX, 195–202.

Gérin-Lajoie, P. *Pourquoi le Bill 60.* Montréal : Editions du Jour. Pp. 142.

Godbout, A. « Les Franco-Ontariens et leurs écoles, de 1781 à 1844 », *Rev. Univ. Ottawa* XXXIII, 245–68, 472–79.

Hunte, K. D. "The Educational System of Canada East, 1867– 1873." Unpublished doct. dissertation, McGill Univ.

Hurtubise, P. « Mgr de Charbonnel et Mgr Guigues, o.m.i. : la lutte en faveur des écoles séparées à la lumière de leur correspondance (1850–1856) », *Rev. Univ. Ottawa* XXXIII, 38–61.

Labarrère-Paulé, A. *Les Laïques et la presse pédagogique au Canada-français au XIXᵉ siècle.* Québec : Presses Univ. Laval. Pp. 185.

Laycock, S. R. *Special Education in Canada.* Toronto: Gage. Pp. 187.

Lebel, M. *Propos inédits et interdits sur l'éducation.* Québec : Imprimerie Franciscaine Missionnaire. Pp. 49.

Maltais, R. « Notre Nord en Amérique », *Act. Nat.* LII, 457–64.

Martin, J.-M. « Education et Etat », *Culture* XXIV, 236– 49.

Nason, G. "The Historical Development of the Canadian Teachers' Federation." Unpublished doct. dissertation, Univ. of Toronto.

Parent, A.-M. « Notes sur la conception catholique de l'éducation », *Rev. Univ. Laval* XVIII, 90–110.

Reid, J. H. S. and A. Gauthier. "Education" in J. T. Saywell, ed., *Canadian Annual Review for 1962* (Toronto: U. of T. Press), 260–69, 270–80.

Scarfe, N. V. "Some Problems of English and Canadian Education," *Can. Ed. Research Digest* III, 235–50.

Semaines Sociales du Canada. *L'Education, problème social.* Montréal : Bellarmin. Pp. 236.

Skinner, A. "Philosophy of Education in Canada," *Can. Ed. Research Digest* III, 251–61.

Thompson, F. "Reflections upon Education in the Midland District, 1810–1816," *Historic Kingston* XI, 8–20.

Tremblay, A. *Aurons-nous des écoles neutres ?* Cap-de-la-Madeleine : Editions Notre Dame du Cap. Pp. 32.

Yetnikoff, S. *Jewish Education in Quebec: A Recommended Solution.* Montreal: Northern Printing and Lithographing Co. Pp. 24.

1964   "Canada: Report on Developments in Education 1963–64," *Can. Ed. Research Digest* IV, 77–88.

De Grandpré, M. *L'Enseignement catholique dans un système scolaire national.* Document no 27. Montréal : Fédération des Collèges Classiques. Pp. 220.

Dupré, V. *Le Sens de l'éducation.* Sherbrooke: Editions Paulines. Pp. 202.

Hamilton, F. A. (Chairman). *Report of the Grade 13 Study Committee, 1964: Submitted to the Honourable William G. Davis, Minister of Education, June 26, 1964.* Toronto: Ontario Department of Education. Pp. 35.

Rowe, F. *The Development of Education in Newfoundland.* Toronto: Ryerson. Pp. 225.

Walker, F. A. *Catholic Education and Politics in Ontario: A Documentary Study.* Toronto: Nelson. Pp. 507.

Whitworth, F. E. *Education and the Expanding Economy.* Edmonton: Educational Society of Edmonton. Pp. 14.

Wittenberg, A. I. "How Not to Reform the Curriculum," *Can. For.* XLIII, 270–72.

PART II

Higher Education in Canada
L'Enseignement Supérieur au Canada

3

HISTORY AND ORGANIZATION
HISTOIRE ET ORGANISATION

A. GENERAL : GENERALITES

1790 Committee of the Council on the Subject of Promoting the Means of Education. *Report.* . . . Quebec. Pp. 26.

Hubert, J. F. « Réponse de l'évêque de Québec aux observations de monsieur le coadjuteur sur un écrit adressé le 18 novembre dernier à l'honorable William Smith, président d'un comité appointé par son Excellence pour considérer l'état de l'éducation en cette Province et les moyens de la promouvoir » in *Mandements des Evêques de Québec* II, 414–21.

1857 Hodgins, T. ed. *The Canada Educational Directory and Calendar for 1857–58.* Toronto. Pp. 144.

1860 Langton, J. *University Question.* Toronto. Pp. 90.

1876 Marling, A., ed. *The Canada Educational Directory and Year Book for 1876.* . . . Toronto. Pp. 224.

1878 Drapeau, S. *Histoire des institutions de charité, de bienfaisance et d'éducation au Canada.* Ottawa. 2 vols.

1884 Dawson, J. W. *Report on the Higher Education of Women.* Presented to the Corporation of McGill University, October 1884. Montreal. Pp. 14.

1894 Dawson, J. W. *An Ideal College for Women: An Address Delivered before the Delta Sigma Society of McGill University, December 1894.* Montreal. Pp. 16.

1896 Ross, G. W. *The Universities of Canada, Their History and Organization, with an Outline of British and American University Systems.* Toronto. Pp. 440.

1899 Bryce, G. *University Education.* Winnipeg. Pp. 8.

MacGregor, J. G. *On the Utility of Knowledge-making as a Means of Liberal Training.* Halifax. Pp. 24.

1903 Cooke, C. K., ed. "Official Report of the Allied Colonial Universities Conference Held at Burlington House on July 9, 1903. . . ," *Empire Review* [U.K.] VI, 65–128.

1905 Peterson, W. *The Place of a University in a Commercial City.* Montreal. Pp. 11.

1912 Congress of the Universities of the Empire. *Congress of the Universities of the Empire, 1912, Report of Proceedings.* London. Pp. 464.

1914 Craick, W. A. "University Development in Western Canada,"

Canadian Magazine of Politics, Science, Art and Literature XLII, 421–28.

1920 Cody, H. J. "The Recent Commission on University Finance," *Canadian Club of Toronto Addresses* XVIII, 178–91.

Falconer, R. A. *Idealism in National Character: Essays and Addresses.* New York: Hodder and Stoughton. Pp. 216. Includes: "The Conflict of Educational Ideas Arising out of the War," 39–65; "A School of Virtue, Learning and Urbanity," 66–93; "The Canadian Universities and the War," 175–95.

Gauthier, G. *La Mission de l'Université.* Montréal: L'Action Française. Pp. 32.

1921 Congress of the Universities of the Empire. *Second Congress of the Universities of the Empire, 1921, Report of Proceedings.* London: Bell. Pp. 452.

1926 Congress of the Universities of the Empire. *Third Congress of the Universities of the Empire, 1926, Report of Proceedings.* London: Bell. Pp. 270.

Gray, W. H. "A Comparative Study of the Entrance Requirements of American and Canadian Universities." Unpublished M.A. thesis, Univ. of Chicago.

1931 Congress of the Universities of the Empire. *Fourth Congress of the Universities of the Empire, 1931, Report of Proceedings.* London: Bell. Pp. 260.

1936 Congress of the Universities of the British Empire. *Fifth Quinquennial Congress of the Universities of the British Empire.* London: Bell. Pp. 262.

Needler, G. H. *The Secondary School and University.* Toronto: Ontario Educational Association. Pp. 7.

1948 Gilmour, G. P. *Higher Education in the Canadian Democracy.* Hamilton: McMaster Univ. Press. Pp. 20.

Stearn, C. H. *University and Community in the Canadian Democracy.* Hamilton: McMaster Univ. Pp. 19.

1949 Gelley, T. F. "Khaki University," *Food for Thought* IX, no. 7, 29–34.

Woods, H. D., ed. *The Universities and Industrial Relations.* Montreal: Southam Press. Pp. 70.

1951 Congress of the Universities of the British Commonwealth. *Sixth Congress of the Universities of the British Commonwealth, 1948, Report of Proceedings.* London: Bell. Pp. 237.

1953 MacKenzie, N. A. M. *The Freedom of a University in a Free Society.* Fredericton: Univ. of New Brunswick. Pp. 16.

1954 Congress of the Universities of the Commonwealth. *Seventh Congress of the Universities of the Commonwealth, 1953, Report of Proceedings.* Cambridge: Cambridge University Press. Pp. 296.

1956 Thomas, L. G. "The Church of England and Higher Education in the Prairie West before 1914," *Jour. Can. Church Hist. Soc.* III, 1-11.

1958 Alberta Department of Education, Joint Committee to Coordinate High School and University Curricula. *Report of the Matriculation*

Study Sub-Committee, February, 1958. Edmonton: Alberta Dept. of Educ. Pp. 53.

Duchemin, L. A., ed. *The Challenge to our Universities.* Sackville: Mount Allison Univ. Bookstore. Pp. 108.

Mealing, S. "The Enthusiasm of John Graves Simcoe," *Can. Hist. Assoc. Annual Report.* 50–62.

Morrison, H. W. *Oxford Today and the Canadian Rhodes Scholarships.* Published for a Commission appointed by the Canadian Association of Rhodes Scholars. Toronto: Gage. Pp. 71.

1959 Armstrong, H. S. *Academic Administration in Higher Education: A Report on Personnel, Policies, and Procedures Current in some Universities and Colleges in Canada and the U.S.* Ottawa: Canadian Universities Foundation. Pp. 98.

Bissell, C. T. "American Studies in Canadian Universities," *Queen's Q.* LXVI, 384–87.

Congress of the Universities of the Commonwealth. *Eighth Congress of the Universities of the Commonwealth, 1953, Report of Proceedings.* Cambridge: Cambridge University Press. Pp. 100.

Falardeau, J.-C. « Les Chaînes de Prométhée », *Liberté* I, 69–78.

Falardeau, J.-C. « L'Université au XXᵉ siècle », *Vieil Esch.* XI, no 2, 4–7.

Fleming, W. G. *Research into the Utilization of Academic Talent.* Toronto: Department of Educational Research, Ontario College of Education, Univ. of Toronto. Pp. 26.

Moir, J. S. *Church and State in Canada West: Three Studies in the Relation of Denominationalism and Nationalism, 1848–1867.* Toronto: U. of T. Press. Pp. 223.

Scully, E. "Higher Education for Every Man," *Rev. Univ. Ottawa* XXIX, 322–30.

Sheffield, E. F. "Our Booming College Campuses," *Can. Bus.* XXXII, 26–35.

Underhill, F. H. "The University and Politics," *Queen's Q.* LXVI, 217–25.

University of Toronto, Ontario College of Education, Department of Educational Research. "The Carnegie Study of Identification and Utilization of Talent in High School and College," *Ont. Jour. Ed. Research* I, 149–54.

Wittenberg, A. I. « La Spécialisation : service ou trahison de la culture ? » *Rev. Univ. Laval* XIV, 37–55.

1960 Caron, M. « Qu'est-ce qu'une université catholique ? » *Relations* XX, 316–19.

Commonwealth Education Conference, Oxford, 15–28 July 1959. *Report. . . .* Ottawa: Queen's Printer. Pp. 65.

Décarie, V. et al. « Nouvelles universités ou consolidation des universités existantes ? » *Act. Univ.* XXVII, 5–7.

Kerr, A. E. "Importance of the Imponderables in University Education," *Atlantic Advocate* L, 75–78:

« Liberalités gouvernementales et responsabilités institutionnelles en éducation », *Relations* XX, 86–87.

McGregor, M. F., ed.   *The Proceedings of an Academic Symposium Held at the University of British Columbia, Tuesday, September 23 to Friday, September 26, 1958.* Vancouver: Univ. of British Columbia. Pp. 152.

Mitchener, R. D.   "The Development of the National Conference of Canadian Universities, 1911–1959," *Culture* XXI, 46–77.

Mitchener, R. D.   "Junior Colleges in Canada," *Junior College Journal* [U.S.] XXX, 400–12.

Poisson, J.   « Nos Universités sont-elles françaises ? » *Act. Nat.* XLIX, 433–47, 566–75, 618–25, 725–40; L, 14–22, 148–54, 220.

Robarts, J., E. E. Bouvier, R. Winters, and W. H. Johns.   "The Creation of New Universities," *N.C.C.U.C. Proc.*, 20–37.

Sheffield, E. F.   "Canadian Government Aid to Universities," *Vestes, The Australian University Review* III, (2), 20–25.

1961   Angers, P.   « La Place des arts et des sciences dans l'Université », *Relations* XXI, 19–21.

« Les Anglo-Montréalais et le problème des universités », *Relations* XXI, 14–15.

Bernier, R.   « Conditions nouvelles de notre progrès universitaire », *Relations* XXI, 31–34.

Bernier, R.   « Notre avenir universitaire », *Relations* XXI, 3–6.

Bissell, C. T.   "The University and the Intellectual," *Queen's Q.* LXVIII, 1–14.

Cable, K. J.   "Church, State and University in the British Empire, 1783–1860: A Study of the Foundation of Universities in the British Colonies of Settlement." Unpublished doct. dissertation. Harvard Univ.

Canada, External Aid Office. *Technical Co-operation Program, Statistical Summary from 1950 to 30 June, 1961.* Ottawa: External Aid Office. Pp. 18.

Daniells, R.   *The University and the Impending Crisis.* Fredericton: Univ. of New Brunswick. Pp. 13.

Gérin-Lajoie, P.   « La Fonction de l'université », *N.C.C.U.C. Proc.*, 124–32.

Kirkconnell, W.   "The Universities of Canada" in J. Foster, ed., *Commonwealth Universities Yearbook 1961* (London: Association of Universities of the British Commonwealth), 105–12.

Lane, G.   « L'Eglise et l'université », *Relations* XXI, 37–40.

Lebel, M.   *Quelques Considérations sur le rôle de l'université au XXᵉ siècle.* Québec : Presses Univ. Laval. Pp. 30.

Leddy, J. F.   "The Importance of Obtaining a University Education," *Saskatchewan Bulletin* XXVII (April), 14–16.

Lefebvre, J.-J.   « Les Canadiens aux universités étrangères, 1760–1850 », *Mém. S.R.C.* Sect. I, 21–38.

Lesage, J.   « L'Université, l'état, la culture », *Rev. Univ. Laval* XV, 587–93.

MacKinnon, F.   "The University: Community or Utility?" *C.A.U.T. Bull.* X, 4–11.

Mitchener, R. D.   "On Determining the Seniority of Canadian Universities," *Dalhousie Rev.* XLI, 222–32.

« A propos des universités », *Coll. et Fam.* XVIII, 131–39.

Reid, J. H. S.   "The Canadian Universities," *Improving College and University Teaching* [U.S.] IX, 4–5.

Ross, M. G.   "Trends in Canadian Higher Education," *Improving College and University Teaching* [U.S.] IX, 6–8.

Sheffield, E. F.   *University Development: The Past Five Years and the Next Ten.* Ottawa: Canadian Universities Foundation. Pp. 19.

Stanley, G. and G. Sylvestre, eds.   *Canadian Universities Today: Symposium Presented to the Royal Society of Canada in 1960.* Toronto: U. of T. Press. Pp. 97.

Université de Montréal, Association des Professeurs.   *L'Université dit non aux Jésuites.* Editions de l'Homme. Pp. 151.

Wilson, K.   "Some Factors in the Development of Canadian Universities prior to Confederation." Unpublished M.Ed. thesis, Univ. of Manitoba.

1962   Andrew, G. C., I. Lussier, and D. Dunton.   "Canadian Types of Institutions of Higher Education: Their Characteristics, Roles and Special Problems—The University: A Symposium," *N.C.C.U.C. Proc.*, 20–38.

Boisvert, R.   « Education et Orientation », *Rev. Univ. Sherbrooke* II, 223–32.

Commission Royale d'Enquête sur l'Enseignement Supérieur au Nouveau-Brunswick. *Rapport...* Fredericton. Pp. 122./Royal Commission on Higher Education in New Brunswick. *Report. . . .* Fredericton. Pp. 118.

Dean, B.   "What is a University for?" *Can. Bar. Jour.* V, 280–89.

Decary, P., J. G. Morden, and W. J. Cousins.   "Canadian Types of Institutions of Higher Education, Their Characteristics, Roles and Special Problems—The College: A Symposium," *N.C.C.U.C. Proc.*, 39–57.

Dobbs, K. R. E.   "Calgary Report: The West's Awake." *Saturday Night* LXXVII (January 6, 1962), 32–34.

Dunton, D. and D. Patterson, eds.   *Canada's Universities in a New Age: Proceedings of the Conference held by the N.C.C.U.C., at Ottawa November 13–15, 1961.* Ottawa: N.C.C.U.C. Pp. 167.

Eddison, R. F.   "Opportunities for University Education," *Dalhousie Rev.* XLI, 466–72.

Lebel, M.   « Le Mirage des Etats-Unis et de la Russie dans l'enseignement supérieur au Canada », *Rev. Univ. Laval* XVI, 495–511.

Macdonald, J. B.   *Higher Education in British Columbia and a Plan for the Future.* Vancouver: Univ. of British Columbia. Pp. 118.

MacKenzie, N. A. M.   "Universities, Colleges and Federal Grants," *Dalhousie Rev.* XLII, 5–17.

Owen, D. R. G.   "The Presuppositions of the University," *Can. Jour. Theol.* VIII, 137–46.

Pirlot, P.   « L'Idée universitaire et son contexte social », *Rev. Univ. Laval* XVI, 395–404.

Rogers, R.   "Higher Education: Crisis and Contribution," *C.A.U.T. Bull.* X, 5–10.

Sheffield, E. F.   *Enrolment in Canadian Universities and Colleges to 1970–71 (1961 Projection)*. Ottawa: Canadian Universities Foundation. Pp. 15./*Inscriptions aux universités et collèges canadiens jusqu'à 1970–1971 (prévisions faites en 1961)*. Ottawa : Fondation des Universités Canadiennes. Pp. 15.

Underhill, F. H.   "How Good are Our Universities?" with reply "Our University Machinery," by P. D. Scott, and rejoinder "The New University: An Old Role," by R. Matthews. *Can. For.* XLII, 199–201, 273–75; XLIII, 35–36.

The University in Canadian Life/L'Université dans la vie canadienne. Ottawa: National Federation of Canadian University Students, National Seminar/Fédération Nationale des Etudiants des Universités Canadiennes, Séminaire national. Pp. 89.

Vachon, L.-A.   *Unité de l'université*. Québec : Presses Univ. Laval. Pp. 67.

Vanderkamp, J. R.   *University Study in Canada: A Guide for Students from Other Countries who are Planning to Study at Canadian Universities or Colleges*. Ottawa: Canadian Universities Foundation. Pp. 52.

1963   Andrew, G. C.   "The N.C.C.U.C. and C.U.F.—Their Roles and Relationships," *C.A.U.T. Bull.* XII, no. 1, 30–34.

Bouvier, E.   « L'Université et la planification », *Rev. Univ. Sherbrooke* III, 135–44.

Bowman, M. J.   "Educational Shortage and Excess,"*Can. Jour. Econ. Pol. Sci.* XXIX, 446–61.

Canadian Universities Foundation.   *Brief to the Prime Minister of Canada*. Ottawa: The Foundation. Pp. 20.

Commission Royale d'Enquête sur l'Enseignement dans la Province de Québec. *Rapport...* Québec : Imprimeur de la Reine, 1963–65, 3 vols./Royal Commission of Inquiry on Education in the Province of Quebec. *Report. . . .* Quebec: Queen's Printer, 1963–65, 3 vols.

Parmi les mémoires présentés par la Commission se trouve les suivants :

McGill University.   *Brief Presented to the Royal Commission on Education*, November 1961, English and French texts. Montreal: McGill University Press, 1961. Pp. 114.

Université de Montréal.   *Mémoire à la Commission Royale d'Enquête sur l'Enseignement*, juillet 1962. Montréal Université de Montréal. Pp. 120.

Université Laval.   *Mémoire de l'Université Laval à la Commission Royale d'Enquête sur l'Enseignement*, juin 1962. Québec : Presses Universitaires Laval. Pp. 185.

Angers, R. P.   *Réflexions sur l'enseignement*. Montréal : Les Editions Bellarmin, 1963. Pp. 197. (Annexe au Mémoire de la

Compagnie de Jésus soumis à la Commission Royale d'Enquête sur l'Enseignement, 1962).

La Crise de l'enseignement au Canada français. Mémoire présenté à la Commission Royale d'Enquête sur l'Enseignement par l'Association des professeurs de l'Université de Montréal, novembre, 1961. Montréal : Les Editions du Jour, 1961. Pp. 123.

Notre Réforme scolaire. Mémoire à la Commission Royale d'Enquête sur l'Enseignement par la Fédération des Collèges Classiques. Montréal : Centre de Psychologie et de Pédagogie, 1962. Pp. 206.

Committee of Presidents of Provincially Assisted Universities and Colleges of Ontario. *Post-Secondary Education in Ontario, 1962–1970; Report of the Presidents of the Universities of Ontario to the Advisory Committee on University Affairs.* Toronto: U. of T. Press. Pp. 44.

Committee of Presidents of Provincially Assisted Universities and Colleges of Ontario. *The Structure of Post-Secondary Education in Ontario; Supplementary Report No. 1, June 1963.* Toronto: U. of T. Press. Pp. 30.

Entr'aide Universitaire Mondiale du Canada. *Le Rôle de la science et de la culture dans le développement des nations ; rapport sur le séminaire de 1962, Pologne, juin–juillet–août 1962.* Toronto: Entr'aide Universitaire. Pp. 87.

Frye, N. *The Changing Pace in Canadian Education.* Montreal: Association of Alumni, Sir George Williams Univ. Pp. 10.

Harris, R. S. "Canadian Higher Education: A Documentary History?" *Univ. Tor. Q.* XXXII, 319–24.

Harris, R. S. "Higher Education in Canada," *Dalhousie Rev.* XLII, 423–36.

Jackson, R. W. B. *The Problem of Numbers in University Enrolment.* Paper presented at the Canadian Education Association 40th Convention. Toronto: Canadian Education Association and Department of Educational Research, Ontario College of Education, Univ. of Toronto. Pp. 53.

LeMire, E. D. "The Year-Round Campus: Some Problems and Sources," *C.A.U.T. Bull.* XII, no. 2, 39–46.

Macdonald, J. B. "New Dimensions: Higher Education in the Years Ahead," *Jour. Ed.,* no. 8, 3–14.

MacDonald, W. R. "The Training of College Teachers: A Survey in the Atlantic Provinces," *Can. Ed. and Research Digest* III, 221–29.

Mitchener, R. D. "Why not a University Centre for the Study of Higher Education?" *C.A.U.T. Bull.* XII, no. 2, 36–38.

Myers, B. R. *North of the Border: A Story Resulting from Two Years in Canada.* New York: Vintage. Pp. 214.

Reid, J. H. S. "The Evolution of Canadian University Organization," *C.A.U.T. Bull.* XI, no. 6, 3–24.

Smith, J. P. "The University and Society," *C.A.U.T. Bull.* XI, no. 5, 4–26.

Thompson, W. T. "The Number of University Teachers: Needs and Prospects," *C.A.U.T. Bull.* XII, no. 2, 16–22.

Vachon, L.-A. *Apostolat de l'Universitaire Catholique.* Québec : Presses Univ. Laval. Pp. 85.

Vachon, L.-A. *Communauté universitaire.* Québec : Presses Univ. Laval. Pp. 121.

Webb, D. C. *Year-Round Operation of Universities and Colleges: A Preliminary Research Report on the Practices and Problems of Year-Round Calendar Systems, with Particular Reference to the Canadian Scene.* Montreal: Canadian Foundation for Educational Development. Pp. 73.

1964   Balsdon, J. P. V. D., E. N. Griswold, J. A. Corry, and H. D. Hicks. *The University and the Modern State.* Papers delivered at a symposium on February 1st, 1964, in honour of the Inauguration of Henry Davies Hicks . . . as the President and Vice-Chancellor of Dalhousie University together with the Address of Dr. Hicks to Convocation. Toronto: Copp Clark. Pp. 46.

Belshaw, C. S. *Anatomy of a University.* Vancouver: Univ. of British Columbia. Pp. 67.

Bronowski, J. *et al. Imagination and the University.* The Frank Gerstein Lectures, January and February 1963. Toronto: U. of T. Press. Pp. 15.

Canadian Association of University Teachers. *Final Report of Committee on Year-Round Operation of Universities. C.A.U.T. Bull.* XIII, special issue, September 1964, 3–32.

Congress of the Universities of the Commonwealth. *Ninth Congress of the Universities of the Commonwealth.* London: Clark. Pp. 276.

Drummond, I. M. "The Robbins Commission and the Canadian Scene," *Can. For.* XLIII, 265–68.

Hamilton, F. A. (Chairman). *Report of the Grade 13 Study Committee, 1964: Submitted to the Honourable William G. Davis, Minister of Education, June 26, 1964.* Toronto: Department of Education. Pp. 35.

Hamlin, D. L. B. *International Studies in Canadian Universities.* Ottawa: Canadian Universities Foundation. Pp. 120. *Bound with*: Lalande, G. *L'Etude des relations internationales et de certaines civilisations étrangères au Canada.* Ottawa : Fondation des Universités Canadiennes. Pp. 100.

Maheux, A. « Notes sur les éléments d'une somme de la vie universitaire », *Rev. Univ. Laval* XVIII, 643–47.

Masters, D. C. "Patterns of Thought in Anglican Colleges in the Nineteenth Century," *Journal of the Canadian Church Historical Society* VI, 54–68.

Nicol, E. P., ed. *Guideposts to Innovation: Report of a President's Committee on Academic Goals.* Vancouver: Univ. of British Columbia. Pp. 67.

Ontario Council of University Faculty Associations. "University Education in Ontario—A Brief prepared for Presentation to the Prime Minister of Ontario," *C.A.U.T. Bull.* XII, 10–41.

Reid, J. H. S. "Origin and Portents," in G. Whalley, ed., *A Place of Liberty* (Toronto: Clarke, Irwin), 3–25.
Scarfe, N. V. "The Modern University," *Can. Ed. Research Digest* IV, 102–6.
Walker, F. A. *Catholic Education and Politics in Ontario: A Documentary Study.* Toronto: Nelson. Pp. 507.
Wittenberg, A. I. *General Education as a Challenge for Creative Scholarship.* Toronto: York Univ. Pp. 45.

B. THE INSTITUTIONS : LES INSTITUTIONS

ACADIA UNIVERSITY

1933 Chute, A. C. *The Religious Life of Acadia.* Wolfville: Acadia Univ. Pp. 249.
1935 Patterson, F. W. *Acadia University as a Business Enterprise: An Address to the Wolfville Men's Forum, Jan. 6, 1935.* Wolfville: Acadia Univ. Pp. 8.
1950 Knaplund, P. "James Stephen on Nova Scotian College Charters 1840–41," *Dalhousie Rev.* XXIX, 395–401.
1953 O'Grady, W. E. "The Fathers and Higher Education." Unpublished B.D. thesis, Acadia Univ.
1954 Cochran, O. D. "The Development of Theological Education at Acadia University." Unpublished B.D. thesis, Acadia Univ.
MacGregor, S. E. "Dr. V. B. Rhodenizer: A Bibliographical and Critical Sketch." Unpublished M.A. thesis, Acadia Univ.
1961 Acadia University. *Department of Biology, Acadia University, 1910–1960.* Wolfville: Acadia Univ. Pp. 565.
Hiltz, J. E. and N. Morse. *The Acadia University Institute 1955–1961.* Wolfville: Acadia University Institute. Pp. 24.
Small, C. W. "New Chemistry Building at Acadia," *Chem. Can.* XIII, no. 3, 41.
Smith, E. C. *Department of Biology, Acadia University, 1910–1960.* Kentville: Kentville Publ. Co. Pp. 44.

UNIVERSITY OF ALBERTA

1909 Alexander, W. H. "The University of Alberta," *University of Toronto Monthly* X, 16–20.
1935 Rankin, A. C. "The Provincial Medical School—the University of Alberta Faculty of Medicine," *Alta. Med. Bull.* I (July), 7–11.
1945 Brown, H. P. "The Story of a Building," *New Trail* III, 151–56.
1946 Gordon, R. K. "Assiniboia Hall, 1913–19," *New Trail* IV, 173–74.
1949 Revell, G. "The Medical Faculty—University of Alberta," *New Trail* VII, 170–77.

1954   Cameron, D.   "Banff School of Fine Arts," *Can. Geog. Jour.* XLVIII, 207–15.

Corbett, E. A.   *Henry Marshall Tory—Beloved Canadian.* Toronto: Ryerson. Pp. 241.

1955   Bowker, W. F.   "The Faculty of Law of the University of Alberta," *New Trail* XIII, 54–57.

1956   Collins, R. J.   "Campus that Covers a Province," *Maclean's* LXIX (February 18, 1956), 26–28, 31–32.

1958   Lister, R. C.   *My Forty-Five Years on the Campus.* Edmonton: Univ. of Alberta Printing Department. Pp. 75.

1959   Flock, D. L.   "Petroleum Research at University of Alberta," *Oil in Canada* XII, 36–40.

Irving, J. A.   *The Social Credit Movement in Alberta.* Toronto: U. of T. Press. Pp. 369.

1960   Alexander, W. H.   "In the Beginning," *Alta. Hist. Rev.* VIII, 15–20.

Johns, W. H.   "The Creation of New Universities," *N.C.C.U.C. Proc.*, 33–37.

1961   Birss, F. W., S. G. Davis, and H. E. Gunning.   "New Facilities for Chemistry at the University of Alberta, Edmonton," *Chem. Can.* XIII, no. 12, 40–42.

Marzolf, A. D.   "Alexander Cameron Rutherford and His Influence on Alberta's Educational System." Unpublished M.A. thesis, Univ. of Alberta.

1963   Peel, B. B.   "Library Planning at the University of Alberta," *Can. Lib. Assoc. Bull.* XIX, 359–63.

University of Alberta.   *Opening of the New Education Building, May 30, 1963.* Edmonton: Univ. of Alberta. Pp. 20.

BISHOP'S UNIVERSITY

1857   Bishop's University.   *Historical Sketch of the University of Bishop's College, Established at Lennoxville, C.E., Showing its Origin, Progress and Present Condition.* Montreal. Pp. 26.

1860   Nicholls, J. H.   "Address Delivered before Convocation of University of Bishop's College, Lennoxville . . . June 27, 1860" in *Bishop's University Calendar, 1895–96,* x–xxiv.

1862   Bishop's University.   *Proceedings of the Annual Convocation of the University of Bishop's College, Lennoxville, held on the 26th Day of June, 1862, with the Addresses then Delivered, a List of the Degrees Conferred and of the Prizes Awarded in the Junior Department.* Montreal. Pp. 18.

1863   Bishop's University.   *Proceedings of the Annual Convocation of the University of Bishop's College, Lennoxville, held on Thursday, the 25th Day of June, 1863, with the Addresses then Delivered, a List of the Degrees Conferred, and the Prizes Awarded in the Junior Department.* Montreal. Pp. 39.

1872   Bishop's University.   *Report on the Financial & Educational Position of the College, at 31st December, 1871.* Montreal. Pp. 19.

1896 Canada Medical Record. "The Dental Profession and Bishop's College," *Canada Medical Record* XXIV, 241–45.
1962 Bishop's University. *A Brief Submitted to the Royal Commission of Inquiry on Education in the Province of Quebec by Bishop's University, 1962*. Lennoxville: Bishop's Univ. Pp. 124.
1963 Masters, D. C. "G. J. Mountain: Frontier Bishop," *Can. Hist. Assoc., Annual Rept.*, 89–101.

BRANDON COLLEGE

1957 Morton, W. L. *One University: A History of the University of Manitoba*. Toronto: McClelland and Stewart. Pp. 200.
1962 McKenzie, A. E., ed. *History of Brandon College, Inc.* Brandon. Privately Printed. Pp. 48.
1964 Fox, W. S. *Sherwood Fox of Western*. Toronto: Burns and MacEachern. Pp. 250 (esp. 50–57, 71–80).

UNIVERSITY OF BRITISH COLUMBIA

1941 Hill, F. W. "Philosophy at the University of British Columbia," *Culture* II, 494–96.
1954 "Canada's Eleventh Medical School Graduates First Student Doctors," *Can. Doctor* XX, no. 7, 35–39.
1956 Macdonald, J. B. *A Prospectus on Dental Education for the University of British Columbia*. Vancouver: Univ. of British Columbia. Pp. 105.
1958 Rose, W. J. "Slavonic Studies in the University of British Columbia," *Slavonic and East European Review* XXXVII [U.K.], 246–53.
 Wales, B. E. "The Development of Adult Education in British Columbia." Unpublished doct. dissertation, Oregon State College.
1959 Brown, J. B. "Physics at the University of British Columbia," *Jour. Ed.* no. 3, 38–43.
1961 Eagles, B. A. "Agricultural Extension at U.B.C. Past and Present" in Seminar on Agricultural Extension in British Columbia, *Proceedings* (Vancouver: Univ. of British Columbia), 9–23.
 Robinson, J. L. "Geography at the University of British Columbia," *Can. Geog.* XIV, 46–47.
 Peake, F. A. "Theological Education in British Columbia," *Can. Jour. Theol.* V, 251–63.
 Lusztig, P. A. and J. Haskett. "A Look at Two Canadian Business Schools," *Can. Bus.* XXXIV, 96–102.
 Selman, G. R. "The Extension Programme of the University of British Columbia," *B.C. Lib. Q.* XXIV, 11–16.
1962 Macdonald, J. B. *Excellence and Responsibility*. Vancouver: Univ. of British Columbia. Pp. 44.
 Macdonald, J. B. *Higher Education in British Columbia and a Plan for the Future*. Vancouver: Univ. of British Columbia. Pp. 119.

"The School of Librarianship: The University of British Columbia," *Alta. Lib. Assoc. Bull.* IX, no. 2, 16–19.

Williams, D. H. "The Department of Continuing Medical Education, University of British Columbia: A First Progress Report—the Organizational Phase," *Can. Med. Assoc. Jour.* LXXXVI, 639–44.

1963 Detwiller, L. F. "University of British Columbia Health Sciences Centre," *Can. Hosp.* XL, 35–38.

Selman, G. R. "A History of the Extension and Adult Education Services of the University of British Columbia." Unpublished M.A. thesis, Univ. of British Columbia.

1964 Nicol, E. P., ed. *Guideposts to Innovation: Report of a President's Committee on Academic Goals.* Vancouver: Univ. of British Columbia. Pp. 67.

University of British Columbia. *The Challenge of Growth.* Vancouver: Univ. of British Columbia. Pp. 11.

BROCK UNIVERSITY

1963 Brock University, Founders' Committee. *Statement of the Chairman of the Founders' Committee Regarding the Site Selected as the Home of Brock University.* St. Catharines: The University. Pp. 23.

1964 Edinborough, A. "How to Create a Home-Town College," *Saturday Night* LXXIX (December 1964), 18–21.

Hart, J. "Brock University," *Sch. Prog.* XXXIII, no. 7, 41–43.

Mitchelson, E.-E. *The Story of Brock University to Date.* St. Catharines: The University. Mimeo. Pp. 20.

UNIVERSITY OF ALBERTA, CALGARY

1951 Weston, P. E. "The History of Education in Calgary." Unpublished M.A. thesis, Univ. of Alberta.

1960 Johns, W. H. "The Creation of New Universities," *N.C.C.U.C. Proc.*, 33–37.

1961 Armstrong, D. A. "New University Campus at Calgary," *Chem. Can.* XIII, no. 4, 18, 23.

1962 Dobbs, K. R. E. "Calgary Report: The West's Awake," *Saturday Night* LXXVII (January 6, 1962), 32–34.

Potter, G. T. "Building the University at Calgary," *Sch. Prog.* XXXI, no. 7, 37–39.

Scarlett, E. P. "The Chancellor's Chair," *New Trail* XX, 7–9.

Simon, F. "History of the Alberta Provincial Technical Institute of Technology and Art." Unpublished M.A. thesis, Univ. of Alberta.

1963 Peel, B. B. "Library Planning at the University of Alberta," *Can. Lib. Assoc. Bull.* XIX, 359–63.

Weston, P. E. "A University for Calgary," *Alta. Hist. Rev.* XI, 1–11.

1964 Ryder, D. E. "The Library, University of Alberta, Calgary," *Alta. Lib. Assoc. Bull.* XI, 6–9.

CARLETON UNIVERSITY

1951   Sheffield, E. F.   "Shaping University Extension Policy," *Food for Thought* XI, no. 6, 31–33.
1960   "Carleton University, Ottawa," *Can. Arch.* V, 43–63.
       Gibson, J. A.   "The Shape of Universities to Come," *Sch. Prog.* XXIX, no. 4, 34–36.
       Gifford, H.   "The Carleton University Library Building," *American Library Association Bulletin* LIV, 478–80.
       Holmes, J. M.   "The Modern Look–Carleton University," *Chem. Can.* XII, no. 5, 39–42.
1963   "Carleton University Campus on the Move," *Ottawa Journal*, February 15, 1963, [special 12-page supplement].
       Gifford, H.   "The MacAdam Library of Carleton University," *College and Research Libraries* [U.S.] XXXIV, 43–46.

LES COLLÈGES CLASSIQUES

1875   Séminaire de St. Hyacinthe.   *Catalogue des élèves du Séminaire de St. Hyacinthe depuis 1818.* St. Hyacinthe. Pp. 88.
1876   Sulte, B. et C. Tanguay.   *Le Collège de Rimouski, qui l'a fondé?* Ottawa. Pp. 40.
1884   Lanjuere, A.   *Vie de Monsieur Olier, fondateur du Séminaire Saint-Sulpice et de la colonie de Montréal.* Montréal. Pp. 239.
       Séminaire de St. Hyacinthe.   *Souvenir de la réunion générale des élèves du Séminaire de St. Hyacinthe, les 30 juin et juillet 1884.* St. Hyacinthe. Pp. 103.
1894   Dionne, N.-E.   *Vie de C.-F. Painchaud, prêtre, curé, fondateur du Collège de Sainte Anne de la Pocatière.* Québec. Pp. 440.
1898   Collège Ste-Marie.   *Souvenir des fêtes jubilaires du Collège Sainte-Marie de Montréal, 1848–1898.* Montréal. Pp. 243.
1903   Sylvain, R.-P.   *De la fondation du Collège de Rimouski et de son fondateur.* Rimouski. Pp. 94.
1908   Gosselin, D.   *Les Etapes d'une classe au Petit Séminaire de Québec 1859–1868.* Québec. Pp. 291.
1912   Dionne, N.-E.   *Une Dispute grammaticale en 1842 : le G. V. Demers vs. le G. V. Maguire précédée de leur biographie.* Québec. Pp. 229.
       Gauthier, H.   *La Compagnie de Saint-Sulpice au Canada.* Montréal. Pp. 150.
       Monet, D.   *Régions nos comptes à propos de la question de Monnoir.* St. Jean. Pp. 28.
1914   Dugas, A.-C.   *Gerbes de souvenirs ou mémoires, épisodes, anecdotes et réminiscences du Collège Joliette, franc et sincère.* Montréal. 2 vols.
1925   Mercier-Gouin, L.   « Le Vieux Collège de Québec » in *Les Jésuites de Québec, fêtes du 3ième Centenaire* (Québec : Action Sociale), 103–14.

1926 Gauthier, H.   *Sulpitiana*. Montréal : Bureau des Œuvres Paroissiales de St. Jacques. Pp. 277.

1937 Maurault, O.   « Une Révolution collégiale à Montréal il y a cent ans », *Cah. Dix* II, 35–44.

1942 Bernier, A.   "The Contribution of the Schools of Sainte-Anne-de-la-Pocatière to Catholic Education in the Province of Quebec." Unpublished M.A. thesis, Catholic Univ. of America.

1944 Maurault, O. *et al. Figures nicolétaines*. Ottawa : Société Canadienne d'Histoire de l'Église Catholique. Pp. 196.

1954 De Grandpré, M.   *Une Figure d'éducation : Le Père Alphonse de Grandpré, Clerc de Saint-Viateur, 1883–1942*. Joliette : Les Clercs de St.-Viateur. Pp. 91.

1957 Duval, R.   "The Roman Catholic Colleges of Quebec" in G. Z. F. Bereday, ed., *The Year Book of Education* (London: Evans Brothers Limited), 270–85.

1958 Gagnon, F.   « Motivation des élèves qui fréquentent le collège », *Ens. Sec.* XXXVIII, 69–78.

      « Le Séminaire de Rimouski : esquisse historique », *Ens. Sec.* XXXVIII, 2–8.

1959 Larivière, F.   « La Réforme des programmes à Laval », *Relations* XIX, 261–62.

      Provost, H.   « Documents pour une histoire du Séminaire de Québec », XIII, 460–73, 563–67, 665–69, 755–62, 854–59, 936–49; XIV, 83–91, 179–84, 275–81, 378–81, 468–73, 572–74, 759–64, 847–55, 940–46; XV, 93–99, 190–95, 284–87, 367–87, 967–70, 948–53; XVI, 86–89, 187–90, 272–78, 380–84, 476–81, 580–85, 677–79, 968–72; XVII, 178–81, 382–85, 472–73; XVIII, 768–75, 868–73, 962–70.

      Tessier, A.   « Fondation du Collège de Trois-Rivières (1860) », *Cah. Dix* XXIV, 169–88.

1960 Chenier, A.   « La Profession de bibliothécaire et les collèges », *Coll. et Fam.* XVII, 240–45.

      Dugas, G.   « Perspectives en éducation », *Nouv.-Fr.* XIV, 130–33.

      Gingras, P.-E.   « L'Education : Bilan 1959–1960 », *Act. Nat.* XLIX, 811–18.

      Hamel, J.-F.   « Le Rôle d'un ancien collège », *Ens. Sec.* XL, no 2, 37–44.

      Maurault, O.   « Galerie de portraits des supérieurs du Collège de Montréal », *Cah. Dix* XXV, 191–217.

      Parmeton, G.   *Le Séminaire Saint-Joseph de Trois-Rivières, foyer de patriotisme*. Trois-Rivières: Education du Centenaire. Pp. 8.

      Plante, G.   « L'Université Sainte-Marie », *Relations* XX, 313–16.

1961 Desrochers, E.   *Programme pour une bibliothèque collégiale*. Montréal : Association Canadienne des Bibliothécaires de Langue française. Pp. 82.

      Drolet, A.   « La Bibliothèque du Collège des Jésuites », *Rev. Hist.* XIV, 487–544.

      Gadbois, L.   « Qualifications des professeurs au cours collégial ; collèges affiliés à l'Université de Montréal, 1960–61 », *Bull. Féd. Coll.* VI, (6), 7–8.

Gay, P. « Brève Histoire du Collège Saint-Alexandre », *Ens. Sec.* XL, no 3, 3–6.

Genest, J. « Brève Histoire des Collèges et des Universités », *Coll. et Fam.* XVIII, 1–2, 72–77.

Joly, R. *Les Bibliothèques d'élèves au cours classique.* Québec : Presses Univ. Laval. Pp. 202.

Lebel, M. *Quelques Considérations sur le rôle de l'université au XXe siècle.* Québec : Presses Univ. Laval. Pp. 30.

« Nos Libertés et nos collèges classiques menacés », *Act. Nat.* L, 593–600.

Poulin, J.-P. « Cinquante ans de service aux 'Pays d'en haut' » [Séminaire St. Joseph de Mt. Laurier]. *Ens. Sec.* XL, no 4, 3–6.

Tremblay, M. « L'Externat classique Saint Jean-Eudes », *Ens. Sec.* XL, no 5, 7–10.

1962 Decary, P. « Le Collège classique », *N.C.C.U.C. Proc.*, 39–46.

Notre réforme scolaire : Mémoire à la Commission Royale d'Enquête sur l'Enseignement par la Fédération des Collèges Classiques. Montréal : Centre de Psychologie et de Pédagogie. Pp. 206.

Savard, P. « Les Débuts de l'enseignement de l'histoire et de la géographie au Petit Séminaire de Québec (1765–1830) », *Rev. Hist.* XV, 508–25; XVI, 43–62, 188–212.

Slattery, T. P. *Loyola and Montreal: A History.* Montreal: Palm. Pp. 319.

Tremblay, A., F. Bourque, and R. Chiasson, "Trends in Education" in C. F. MacRae, ed., *French Canada Today* (Sackville: Mount Allison Bookstore), 60–78.

1963 Provost, H. « Historique du Séminaire de Québec », *Rev. Univ. Laval* XVII, 591–99.

Provost, H. « Le Séminaire de Québec, premier logement, premier esprit », *Rev. Univ. Laval* XVII, 788–97.

1964 Provost, H. « Le Petit Séminaire de Québec devenu 'collège' », *Rev. Univ. Laval* XVIII, 787–800.

DALHOUSIE; KING'S COLLEGE

1819 McCulloch, T. *The Nature and Uses of a Liberal Education Illustrated.* Halifax. Pp. 24. (Only known copy in Nova Scotia Public Archives.)

1922 Thibeau, P. W. "Education in Nova Scotia before 1811." Unpublished doct. dissertation, Catholic Univ. of America.

1936 Lydekker, J. W. *The Life and Letters of Charles Inglis 1759–87.* London: Society for Promoting Christian Knowledge. Pp. 272.

1937 Harris, R. V. *Charles Inglis: Missionary, Loyalist, Bishop (1734–1816).* Toronto: General Board of Religious Education. Pp. 186.

1938 McKinnon, C. *Reminiscences.* Toronto: Ryerson. Pp. 236.

1950 Knaplund, P. "James Stephen on Nova Scotian College Charters 1840–41," *Dalhousie Rev.* XXIX, 395–401.

1954 Thomas, M. E., ed. "The Memoirs of William Cochran, sometime Professor of Columbia College, New York, and at King's College,

Windsor, Nova Scotia," *New York Historical Society Quarterly* XXXVIII, 55–83.

1958   "Fifty Years of Dental Education Commemorated by Dalhousie Faculty Opening," *Jour. Can. Dent. Assoc.* XIV, 659–65.

1959   Kinghorn, A. M.   "King's College, Halifax, the Overseas Commonwealth's Oldest University," *Aberdeen University Review* XXXVIII, 24–25.

Nicholls, G. V. V.   "A Course on Legal Research and Writing," *Univ. Tor. Law Jour.* XIII, 88–92.

Steeves, L. C.   "The Dalhousie Post Graduate Program: An Experience in Continuing Medical Education," *Journal of Medical Education* [U.S.] XXXIV, 236–38.

1960   Irving, J. A.   "The Achievement of Thomas McCulloch" in M. M. Ross, ed., *The Stepsure Letters* (Toronto: McClelland and Stewart), 150–56.

1963   Blakeley, P. R.   "King's—A Living Tradition," *Atlantic Advocate* LIII, 45–52.

Dalhousie University. *Aims and Practices of University Education at Dalhousie University; a Report of an Inter-Faculty Symposium, December 1962.* Halifax: Dalhousie Univ. Pp. 96.

Kerr, A. E.   *The Post War Years, 1945–1963: President's Convocation Address May 16, 1963 and Highlights of the Development of the Period, by Faculties.* Halifax: Dalhousie Univ. Pp. 49.

1964   Balsdon, J. P. V. D., E. N. Griswold, J. A. Corry, and H. D. Hicks. *The University and the Modern State.* Papers delivered at a symposium on February 1st, 1964, in honour of the Inauguration of Henry Davies Hicks . . . as the President and Vice-Chancellor of Dalhousie University together with the Address of Dr. Hicks to Convocation. Toronto: Copp Clark. Pp. 46.

UNIVERSITY OF GUELPH

1905   Cappon, J.   "Sir William Macdonald and Agricultural Education," *Queen's Q.* XII, 315–22.

1921   Zavitz, C. A.   "History and Development of the O.A.C.," *Ontario Agricultural College Review* XXXIV, 1–8.

1924   Ontario Agricultural College. *Half Century of the College.* Guelph: Ontario Agricultural College. Pp. 28.

Stevenson, O. J.   "From a Humble Beginning to One of the Finest Agricultural Colleges in the World—A Half Century of Progress in Science and Farming," *Guelph Evening Mercury,* June 7, 1924.

1934   Ontario Agricultural College. *Diamond Jubilee of the College.* Guelph: Ontario Agricultural College. Pp. 17.

1937   Madill, A. J.   *A History of Agricultural Education in Ontario.* Rev. ed. Toronto: U. of T. Press. Pp. 316.

1946   Jones, R. L.   *History of Agriculture in Ontario 1613–1880.* Toronto: U. of T. Press. Pp. 420.

1948 Galbraith, J. K. "Horse and Buggy Type Teaching at O.A.C. instead of Scientific Research," *Saturday Night*, April 24, 1948; "Defence from Politics is Needed in O.A.C.," *ibid.*, May 8, 1948.

1950 Benson, L. R. "An O.A.C. Student in the 1880's," *Ont. Hist.* XLII, 67–80.

Chapman, E. "Mrs. Adelaide Hoodless," *Food for Thought* XI, no. 2, 15–20.

1956 Rowles, E. C. "A Brief History of Some Early Canadian Developments in Home Economics," Unpublished doct. dissertation, Teachers' College, Columbia Univ.

1959 Penrose-FitzGerald, C. P. "The New Medical-Surgical Building at the Ontario Veterinary College," *Can. Jour. Comp. Med.* XXIII, 180–85.

1962 Gattinger, F. E. *A Century of Challenge—A History of the Ontario Veterinary College.* Toronto: U. of T. Press. Pp. 224.

Gattinger, F. E. "Veterinary Instruction at Queen's and O.A.C.," *Canadian Veterinarian Journal* III, 174–77.

Jones, T. L. "The Ontario Veterinary College is One Hundred Years Old," *Canadian Veterinarian Journal* III, 194–99.

LAKEHEAD COLLEGE OF ARTS, SCIENCE & TECHNOLOGY

1963 Braun, H. S. and D. W. Morgan. *Lakehead College: Origin and Growth.* Port Arthur: Lakehead College of Arts, Science & Technology. Pp. 12.

Taylor, Lieberfeld, and Heldman (Canada) Limited. *Report to the Lakehead College of Arts, Science & Technology.* Pp. 277.

LAURENTIAN UNIVERSITY : UNIVERSITÉ LAURENTIENNE

1960 Bouvier, E. "The Creation of New Universities," *N.C.C.U.C. Proc.*, 26–28.

Bouvier, E. « L'Université Laurentienne de Sudbury », *Relations* XX, 120–23.

L'UNIVERSITÉ LAVAL

1857 Chauveau, P.-J.-O. "The Colleges of Canada: Laval University," *Journal of Education, Lower Canada* I, 53–56, 69–72, 85–89, 109–14, 125–28, 141–45.

1864 Université Laval. *Mémoire présenté par le Séminaire de Québec à NN.SS. les évêques de la province assemblés à Trois-Rivières.* Québec. Pp. 30.

1872   Rédaction de Franc-Parleur. *Réponse au second factum intitulé :
« Suite aux remarques de l'Université Laval ».* Montréal. Pp. 17.

      Sainte-Foi, Abbé [A. Pelletier]. *Les Quatre Lettres—Croquis de
topographie universitaire.* Montréal : Pp. 20.

1880   D'Orsonnens, d'O. *Mémoire du Dr d'Odet d'Orsonnens à leurs
Eminentissimes Cardinaux de la S.C. de la Propagande, relati-
vement aux difficultés survenues entre l'Ecole de Médecine et de
Chirurgie de Montréal et l'Université Laval.* Rome. Pp. 162.

1881   Trudel, F.-X. *Réplique aux plaidoyers de M. M. Hamel et Lacoste.*
Rome. Pp. 190.

      Université Laval. *Questions sur la succursale de l'Université Laval à
Montréal.* (2me édition—avec appendice). Québec. Pp. 44.

1882   Paquin, E. *La Conscience catholique outragée et les droits de l'in-
telligence violés par les deux principaux défenseurs de l'Université
Laval, sa Grâce Monseigneur Taschereau, Archevêque de Québec
et sa Grandeur Mgr Fabre, Evêque de Montréal. Ouvrage réservé
pour le public canadien et pour Notre Très Saint Père le Pape.*
Montréal. Pp. 23.

1883   Oudesse, E.-P. *Le Triomphe des idées catholiques (Victoria) sur le
libéralisme (Laval).* Montréal. Pp. 23.

1884   Duclos, R. P. et T. Lafleur. *La Vraie Source du mal ou encore la
question de l'Université Laval.* Montréal. Pp. 48.

1890   Gosselin, A.-H. *Vie de Mgr de Laval.* Québec. 2 vols.

1891   Proulx, J.-B. *Les Quatre Mémoires sur la question universitaire
présentés à son Eminence le Cardinal Simeoni, préfet de la S.C. de
la Propagande.* Montréal. Pp. 339.

1905   Roy, J.-E. *Souvenirs d'une classe au Séminaire de Québec (1867–
1877).* Lévis. Pp. 41.

      Savaète, A. *Voix canadiennes—vers l'abîme.* Paris, 1905–22, 12
vols. [en particulier II, III, IV, VI, IX, X].

1938   Rumilly, R. *Mgr La Flèche et son temps.* Montréal: Simpson. Pp.
425.

1940   Donnay, J. D. H. "The New School of Mines" in A. Ewart, ed.,
University of Toronto Studies, Geological Series No. 44 (Toronto:
U. of T. Press), 21–29.

1941   Université Laval. *L'Inauguration de l'Ecole des Mines de l'Université
Laval.* Québec : Univ. Laval. Pp. 73.

1943   Université Laval, Faculté de Droit Canonique. *La Faculté de Droit
canonique de Laval et les vingt-cinq ans de Code pro-bénédictin.*
Québec : Presses Univ. Laval. Pp. 17.

1946   Lebel, M. *Le Rôle et l'avenir de la Faculté des Lettres de Laval.*
Québec : Univ. Laval. Pp. 8.

      Yon, A. *L'Abbé H.-A. Verreau éducateur—polémiste-historien.*
Montréal : Fides. Pp. 208.

1948   Université Laval. *Faculté des Sciences Sociales 1938–1948 : déjà...
10 ans de vie.* Québec : Univ. Laval. Pp. 68.

      Université Laval. *Pour mieux connaître Laval : Manuel des orateurs.*
Québec : Comité de l'aide à Laval. Pp. 78.

1951   Lussier, D. « La Faculté des Sciences Sociales », *Rev. Univ. Laval*
VI, 272–90.

Pouliot, A. « La Faculté des Sciences », *Rev. Univ. Laval* VI, 378–82.

Vandry, F. « L'Université Laval et le service social », *Serv. Soc.* I, no 1, 38–39.

1952 Lebel, M. « La Faculté des Lettres de Laval », *Rev. Univ. Laval* VI, 449–64.

Maheux, A. "Centenary of the Faculty of Medicine of Laval University," *Can. Doctor* XVIII, no. 8, 44–48.

Maheux, A. « La Fête patronal de l'université », *Rev. Univ. Laval* VI, 582–87.

Maheux, A. « Le Séminaire de Québec en 1848 », *Rev. Univ. Laval* VI, 701–709, 795–801.

1955 Provost, H. « Documents pour une histoire du Séminaire de Québec », *Rev. Univ. Laval* IX, 362–70, 456–65, 552–62, 645–54, 743–52, 848–55, 938–48; X, 176–83, 262–72, 365–70, 468–77, 573–78, 662–70, 772–75, 856–67, 955–59; XI, 79–86, 173–80, 261–71, 355–63, 449–59, 555–62, 652–59, 743–50, 836–40; XII, 69–83, 179–86, 276–83, 368–73, 467–73, 565–70, 650–60, 753– 60, 851–58, 939–47; XIII, 171–80, 270–81, 366–76, 460–73, 563–67, 665–69, 755–62, 854–59, 936–49; XIV, 83–91, 179–84, 275–81, 378–81, 468–73, 572–74, 759–64, 847–55, 940–46; XV, 93–99, 190–95, 284–87, 367–87, 967–70, 948–53; XVI, 86–89, 187–90, 272–78, 380–84, 476–81, 580–85, 677–79, 968–72; XVII, 178–81, 382–85, 472–73; XVIII, 768–75, 868–73, 962–70.

1956 Hamelin, L.-E. « Documents relatifs à la fondation d'un centre de recherches dans l'Ungava par l'Université Laval », *Act. Nat.* XLV, 592–612

1957 Provost, H. « Les Origines éloignées du Séminaire de Québec », *Can. Cath. Hist. Assoc., Annual Rept., 1955–56*, 25–31.

1959 Blais, J. E. « Monseigneur Camille Roy : Témoin d'une époque littéraire », *Société Canadienne d'Histoire de l'Eglise Catholique, Rapport Annuel*, 51–56.

Falardeau, J.-C. « Lettre à mes étudiants à l'occasion des 20 ans de la Faculté des Sciences Sociales de Québec », *Cité Libre* X, no 23, 4–14.

Fortier, J.-M. « François de Laval », *Rev. Hist.* XIII, 18–29.

Larivière, F. « La Réforme des programmes à Laval », *Relations* XIX, 261–62.

Lavallée, J.-G. « Monseigneur Antoine Racine et la question universitaire canadienne (1875–1892) », *Rev. Hist.* XII, 80–107, 247–61, 372–86, 485–516.

Provost, H. « Le Séminaire de Québec dans le plan de Mgr de Laval », *Société Canadienne d'Histoire de l'Eglise Catholique, Rapport Annuel*, 19–30.

Sainte-Louise de Morillac Frenette, Sister. "An Integrated Curriculum for Laval University Collegiate School Nursing," *Cah. Hôtel-Dieu* V, 432–42.

1960 Begin, E. *François de Laval*. Québec : Presses Univ. Laval. Pp. 225.

Commission du Programme de la Faculté des Arts de l'Université Laval. *Rapport...* Québec : Univ. Laval. Mimeo. 3 vols.

Genest, J. « Le Nouveau Programme de Laval », *Relations* XX, 178–79.

Maheux, G. "Half a Century in Retrospective: 1910–1960," *For. et Cons.* XXVI, no. 8, 17–18.

Rousseau, L. Z. "Survey Education at Laval University," *Can. Surveyor* XV, 61–64.

Université Laval. *Cinquantenaire de l'enseignement des sciences forestières à l'Université Laval, 1910–1960.* Québec : Presses Univ. Laval. Pp. 39.

1961 Hamelin, L.-E. « Fonctions du Centre d'Etudes Nordiques de l'Université Laval », *Mém. S.R.C.* LV, Sect. I, 13–20.

Jobin, J.-B. « Evolution de l'enseignement à la Faculté de Médecine de l'Université Laval », *Laval Méd.* XXXII, 423–32.

Rousseau, L. Z. "50 Years of Forestry Teaching at Laval," *Pulp and Paper Magazine of Canada* LXII, 227–30.

Tremblay, A. « Projet de réforme de l'enseignement des humanités à l'Université Laval » in G. Stanley and G. Sylvestre, eds., *The Canadian University Today* (Toronto: U. of T. Press), 67–79.

1962 Des Hazards, P. « La Nouvelle Faculté d'Agriculture », *Vieil Esch.* XIV, no 4, 18–20.

Hamelin, L.-E. « Le Centre d'études nordiques de l'Université Laval », *Rev. Univ. Laval* XVI, 736–40.

« Institut de catéchétique de l'Université Laval », *Sem. Rel. Québec* LXXIV, 602–606.

Lebel, M. « 25e Anniversaire de la Faculté des Lettres de l'Université Laval », *Ens. Sec.* XLI, no 4, 41–46.

Provost H. « Le premier livre de comptes du séminaire de Québec », *Rev. Hist.* XVI, 3–36.

Risi, J. « L'Ecole des Gradués », *Vieil Esch.* XIV, no 4, 4–8.

Tremblay, A. "Trends in Education" in C. F. MacRae, ed., *French Canada Today* (Sackville: Mount Allison Bookstore), 60–69.

Université Laval. *Mémoire de l'Université Laval à la Commission Royale d'Enquête sur l'Enseignement.* Québec : Presses Univ. Laval. Pp. 196.

Vachon, L.-A. *Unité de l'université.* Québec : Presses Univ. Laval. Pp. 67.

1963 Baillargeon, N. « La Vocation missionnaire du Séminaire de Québec », *Rev. Univ. Laval* XVII, 495–507.

Besson, A. et M. Lemay. « Le Centre de recherche de la Faculté de Commerce », *Vieil Esch.* XV, no 4, 4–7.

Cloutier, L. « Les Vingt-Cinq Ans de la Faculté des Sciences », *Vieil Esch.* XV, no 3, 10–15.

Gagné, H. « Le Troisième Centenaire du Séminaire de Québec », *Vieil Esch.* XV, no 2, 4–10.

Provost, H. « Historique du Séminaire de Québec », *Rev. Univ. Laval* XVII, 591–99.

1964 Provost, H. « Le Petit Séminaire de Québec devenu 'collège' », *Rev. Univ. Laval* XVIII, 787–800.

Provost, H. « Propos sur l'histoire du Séminaire de Québec », *Rev. Univ. Laval* XVIII, 883–91.

MCGILL UNIVERSITY

1858   Chauveau, P.-J.-O.   "The Colleges of Canada: The McGill University," *Journal of Education, Lower Canada* II, 17–19, 33–35, 81–82, 97–99.

1860   Dawson, J. W.   *James McGill and the Origin of his University.* Montreal. Pp. 14.

1882   Howard, R. P.   "A Sketch of the Life of the Late Dr. G. W. Campbell and a Summary of the Early History of the Faculty," in McGill College, Medical Faculty, *Semi-Centennial Celebration* (Montreal), 1–14.

1884   Dawson, J. W.   *The Higher Education of Women in Connection with McGill University.* Montreal. Pp. 12.

1887   Wood, J.   *Memoir of Henry Wilkes, D.D., LL.D.: His Life and Times.* Montreal. Pp. 280.

1888   Dawson, J. W.   *The Constitution of McGill University, Montreal: Being the Annual University Lecture of the Session 1888–1889.* Montreal. Pp. 11.

       Dawson, J. W.   *The University in Relation to Professional Education: McGill University, Annual Lecture, Session 1887–88.* Montreal. Pp. 12.

1889   McGill University.   *Public Inauguration of the Chancellor, the Hon. D. A. Smith and the Annual Address of the Principal.* Montreal. Pp. 21.

1891   Dawson, J. W.   "Notes on Trees on the Grounds of McGill University," *Canadian Record of Science* IV, 407–33.

1894   Dawson, J. W.   *Thoughts on an Ideal College for Women: An Address Delivered before the Delta Sigma Society of McGill University, December 1894.* Montreal. Pp. 16.

1895   Craik, R.   "Sketch of the History of the Faculty of Medicine" in *Annual Report of the Governors, Principal, and Fellows of McGill University for the Year 1894,* 19–28.

       Dawson, J. W.   *Educational Lectures and Addresses.* Montreal. Pp. 330.

1900   Ami, H. M.   "Sir John William Dawson," *American Geologist* XXVI, 1–48.

1904   Macvicar, J. H.   *Life and Work of Donald Harvey Macvicar, D.D., LL.D.* Toronto. Pp. 351.

       Peterson, W.   *Principal Peterson Reviews the History and Progress of McGill University.* McGill University Annual Lecture. Montreal. Pp. 12.

1905   Peterson, W.   *The Place of the University in a Commercial City.* Montreal. Pp. 11.

1906   Tory, H.   *McGill University in British Columbia.* A statement issued under the authority of the Corporation of the University. Montreal. Pp. 75.

1907   Craik, R.   *Papers and Addresses, by Robert Craik . . . Governor of McGill University.* Montreal: Gazette. Pp. 222.

1915   Peterson, W.   *Canadian Essays and Addresses.* London. Pp. 373. Contains the following: "Inaugural Address as Principal," 155–75;

"Our Seventy-fifth Anniversary," 176–99; "A Sessional Address (1913)," 200–12; "Address . . . at the Opening of the McGill Conservatorium of Music," 352–57; "The Place of the University in a Commercial City," 253–66.

1920   Blackader, A. D. "Montreal Days" in *Sir William Osler, Memorial Number* (Montreal: Canadian Medical Association Journal), 28–34.

McEachran, D. "Osler and the Montreal Veterinary College" in *Sir William Osler, Memorial Number* (Montreal: Canadian Medical Association Journal), 35–38.

1921   Congregational College of Canada. *A Short History and a Plea.* Montreal: Congregational College of Canada. Pp. 31.

1934   Howell, W. B. *F. J. Shepherd–Surgeon: His Life and Times.* Toronto: Dent. Pp. 251.

1939   Oakeley, H. *My Adventures in Education.* London: Williams & Norgate. Pp. 215.

1944   Trott, H. W. *Campus Shadows.* Hemlock, N.Y.: Crosset and Williams. Pp. 371.

1955   Macdonald College. *Macdonald College Semi-Centenary 1905–1955.* Ste Anne de Bellevue, Quebec: Macdonald College. Pp. 54.

1956   McGill University, Osler Society. *W. W. Francis, Tributes from his Friends on the Occasion of the Thirty-fifth Anniversary of the Osler Society of McGill University.* Montreal: The Society. Pp. 123.

1957   McGill University, Institute of Education. *A Century of Teacher Education, 1857–1957.* Montreal: McGill Univ. Pp. 96.

1958   Corbett, E. A. "McGill Men and the Start of the Western Universities," *McGill News* XXXIX, 24–27.

1959   Curry, R. L. *Stephen Leacock; Humorist and Humanist.* New York: Doubleday. Pp. 383.

1960   Hecht, M. "What Luck for McGill's 1949 Commerce Grads?" *Executive* II, no. 3, 30–32.

MacLennan, H., ed. *McGill: The Story of a University.* Toronto: Nelson. Pp. 135.

1961   McGill University. *Brief Presented to the Royal Commission on Education.* Montreal: McGill Univ. Press. Pp. 114.

Stevenson, L. G. "A New Venture at McGill: The Combined Course in Science and Medicine," *Can. Med. Assoc. Jour.* LXXXIV, 697–98.

1962   Adams, C. J. "The Institute of Islamic Studies," *Can. Geog. Jour.* LXV, 34–36.

Eddy, E. B. "Henry Wilkes," *United Church of Canada Committee on Archives Bulletin* XV, 10–21.

Marshall, J. S. "Meteorology at McGill," *Physics in Canada* XVIII, no. 2, 9–16.

Rosevear, A. B. "McGill's Institute of Air and Space Law," *Univ. Tor. Law Jour.* XIV, 257–60.

1963   Collard, E. A. *Montreal Yesterdays.* Toronto: Longmans. Pp. 220.

Howard, O. *The Montreal Diocesan Theological College: A History from 1873 to 1963.* Montreal: McGill Univ. Press. Pp. 141.

Near, H. I. "The Educational Theories of Stephen Leacock." Unpublished doct. dissertation, George Peabody College for Teachers.
Penfield, W. "The University on the Burn-side" in *The Second Career* (Boston: Little, Brown), 153–59.
Snell, J. F. *Macdonald College of McGill University—A History from 1904–1955.* Montreal: McGill Univ. Press. Pp. 259.

MCMASTER UNIVERSITY

1885(?) Wells, J. E. *Life and Labors of Robert Alexander Fyfe.* Toronto. Pp. 466.
1891 Toronto Baptist College. *Memoir of Daniel Arthur McGregor, Late Principal of Toronto Baptist College.* Toronto. Pp. 145.
1947 Frost, R. W. *Concerning McMaster: The University's Past and Present in Facts and Figures.* Hamilton: McMaster Univ. Pp. 15.
Graham, R. P. and L. Cragg. "Department of Chemistry at McMaster University," *Can. Chem. & Process Ind.* XXXI, 822–24.
1949 Stokes, H. W. "McMaster's Swimmingpool Reactor," *Can. Chem. & Process Ind.* XLIII, 104–10.
1960 Davenport, B. "McMaster—The Septuagenarian Youngster," *Executive* II, 26–32.
1961 "Engineering at McMaster," *Chem. Can.* XIII, no. 2, 40–42.
"McMaster University," *Sch. Prog.* XXX, no. 7, 28–36.
Thode, H. G. *Address on the Occasion of the 14th Convocation and His Installation as President and Vice-Chancellor, McMaster University, October 27, 1961.* Hamilton. Mimeo. Pp. 30.
1964 Fox, W. S. "Undergraduate Years" in *Sherwood Fox of Western* (Toronto: Burns and MacEachern), 41–49.

UNIVERSITY OF MANITOBA

1910 Royal Commission on the University of Manitoba. *Report.* . . . Winnipeg: King's Printer. Pp. 92.
1922 Savaète, A. *Mgr Adélard Langevin, archevêque de St.-Boniface : sa vie, ses contrariétés, ses œuvres (Voix canadiennes—vers l'abîme XII).* Paris : A. Savaète. Pp. 540.
1924 *Reports on the College of Agriculture and the University of Manitoba Submitted by the Royal Commission on Education.* Winnipeg: King's Printer. Pp. 62.
1954 Buchwald, H. "The Manitoba Law School: Forty Years," *Man. Bar News* XXVI (October), 77–82.
1956 University of Manitoba, Faculty of Agriculture and Home Economics. *A Record of the Years, Commemorating Fifty Years of Agricultural Education and Endeavour: Golden Jubilee, 1906–1956.* Winnipeg: Univ. of Manitoba. Pp. 88.
1957 Davis, F. M. "The History of the Growth of the Faculty of Education

within the University of Manitoba." Unpublished M.A. thesis, Univ. of Manitoba.

1959   "School of Architecture, University of Manitoba," *R. Arch. Inst. Can. Jour.* XXXVI, 64–87.

1961   Corbett, E. A.   *Sidney Earle Smith.* Toronto: U. of T. Press. Pp. 72.

1962   Bartlett, L. C.   "Post-Graduate Surgical Education at the University of Manitoba," *Journal of Medical Education* [U.S.] XXXVII, 1021–23.

MEMORIAL UNIVERSITY OF NEWFOUNDLAND

1952   Newton, R.   *Report of Robert Newton. . . on His Survey of the Memorial University of Newfoundland Made at the Request of the Board of Regents of the University in March, 1951.* St. John's: Memorial Univ. Board of Regents. Pp. 97.

Pitt, D. G.   "Myth, Memorial and Alma Mater: The Story of the Memorial University of Newfoundland," *Maritime Advocate and Busy East* XLIII, no. 4, 29–36.

1953   Memorial University.   *The Proceedings on the Occasion of the Installation of the Right Honourable Viscount Rothermere of Hemsted as First Chancellor and Raymond Gushue as Second President, October 8th and 9th, 1952.* St. John's: Memorial Univ. Pp. 47.

1961   Harrington, M. F.   "A Century Old Dream Realized in Newfoundland," *Atlantic Advocate* LI (May), 21, 23–31.

Harrington, M. F.   "Memorial University's 'Mammoth Housewarming,'" *Atlantic Advocate* LII (November), 25–32.

Mansfield, M.   *The Official Opening of the New Campus of Memorial University of Newfoundland, October 9th and 10th, 1961.* St. John's: Memorial Univ. Pp. 59.

Seymour, E. A.   "Memorial University of Newfoundland," *Newfoundland Quarterly* LX (Fall), 1–8.

1962   Story, G. M. (Chairman).   *University Government: A Report of the Memorial University of Newfoundland Teachers' Association.* St. John's: Memorial Univ. Pp. 54.

1964   Rowe, F. W.   "Memorial University of Newfoundland" in *The Development of Education in Newfoundland* (Toronto: Ryerson), 177–82.

Whitaker, I. R. (Chairman).   *Brief to the Royal Commission on Bilingualism and Biculturalism.* St. John's: Memorial Univ. Pp. 30.

UNIVERSITÉ DE MONCTON

1898   Poirier, P. *Le Père Lefebvre et l'Acadie.* Montréal. Pp. 311.

1913   Bourgeois, P. F.   *Vie de l'Abbé François-Xavier LaFrance suivi d'une courte notice biographique de l'Abbé François-Xavier Cor-*

mier, premier prêtre né dans la paroisse de Memramcook. Montréal. Pp. 235.

1949   Tremblay, M.   *50 Ans d'éducation catholique et française en Acadie.* Bathurst, New Brunswick : Univ. du Sacré-Cœur. Pp. 326.

1957   Taillon, L. J.   *Au service de l'Ecole acadienne, 20 ans de cours d'été, 1938–57.* Moncton : Univ. St.-Joseph. Pp. 128.

1962   Commission Royale d'Enquête sur l'Enseignement Supérieur au Nouveau-Brunswick. *Rapport...* Fredericton. Pp. 122./Royal Commission on Education in New Brunswick. *Report.* . . . Fredericton. Pp. 118.

1963   Gosselin, P.-E.   « L'Université de Moncton », *Vie Fr.* XVII, 291–93.

1964   Collège St.-Joseph.   *Album Souvenir: Collège St.-Joseph 1864–1964.* Nouveau-Brunswick : Comité du Centenaire, Collège St.-Joseph. Pp. 64.

UNIVERSITÉ DE MONTRÉAL

[1890?]   Fortier, L. E.   *L'Ecole de Médecine.* Montréal. Pp. 16.

1905   Savaète, A.   *Voix Canadiennes—vers l'abîme.* Paris, 1905–22. 12 vols. [*en particulier* II, III, IV, VI, IX, X].

1922   Talbot-Gouin.   *Quatre lettres, de la reconstruction de l'Université de Montréal.* Montréal : Drouin. Pp. 41.

1931   Caron, P. et P. Caron.   *Lettre sur l'université.* Montréal. Pp. 13.

1933   Laureys, H.   "Education for Commerce," *Sch. Prog.* II, no. 2, 7–8, 19.

1940   Léveillé, A.   « La Faculté des sciences de l'Université de Montréal », *Culture* I, 450–57.

1943   Stucher, E.   « La Superbe Université de Montréal » (with translation), *Sch. Prog.* XII, no 1, 15–18.

Université de Montréal.   *Inauguration des nouveaux immeubles de l'Université de Montréal du Mont Royal.* Montréal : Univ. de Montréal. Pp. 32.

1955   Pouliot, L.   *Monseigneur Bourget et son temps.* Montréal : Beauchemin. 2 vols.

1956   Charbonneau, M. L. G.   "The History of the School of Public Health Nursing at the University of Montreal, Canada, 1925–1950." Unpublished M.A. thesis, Catholic Univ. of America.

1958   Garigue, P.   « La Faculté des sciences sociales de l'Université de Montréal », *Culture* XIX, 391–98.

1959   « Ecole Polytechnique—New Engineering Building », *Eng. Jour.* XLII, 43–52.

Larose, A.-F.   « Dix Ans de progrès à la faculté de pharmacie de Montréal », *Rev. Pharm.* XI, 12–13.

Lavallée, J.-G.   « Monseigneur Antoine Racine et la question universitaire canadienne (1875–1892) », *Rev. Hist.* XII, 80–107, 247–61, 372–86, 485–516.

Lefolii, K. "The College Where Joe College Wouldn't Fit," *Maclean's* LXXII, no. 20, 26–27, 60–64.

1960 Collège Ste-Marie. *Mémoire concernant la création de l'Université Sainte-Marie.* Montréal : Collège Ste-Marie. Pp. 31.

Maurault, O. «Galerie de portraits des supérieurs du Collège de Montréal», *Cah. Dix* XXV, 191–217.

Ecole des Hautes Etudes Commerciales. *Contribution des professeurs de l'Ecole des Hautes Etudes Commerciales de Montréal à la vie intellectuelle du Canada..., Catalogue des principaux écrits, octobre 1960.* Montréal : L'Ecole. Pp. 135.

1961 Denis, L. G. « Ecole de Bibliothéconomie de l'Université de Montréal », *Bull. Bibl.* VII, 78–84.

Leduc, J.-R. « Ecole de Bibliothécaires de l'Université de Montréal », *Bull. Bibl.* VII, 37–40.

Picard, R. « L'Université Sainte-Marie », *Tradition et Progrès* IV, no 1, 43–49.

Université de Montréal, Association des Professeurs. *La Crise de l'enseignement au Canada français : mémoire présenté à la Commission Royale d'Enquête sur l'Enseignement par l'association des professeurs de l'Université de Montréal.* Montréal : Les Editions de Jour. Pp. 123.

Université de Montréal, Association des Professeurs. *L'Université dit non aux Jésuites.* Montréal : Editions de l'Homme. Pp. 158.

1962 Beetz, J. « Inauguration de l'Institut de Recherche en Droit Public », *Thémis* XII, 66–68.

Fournier, N. « Pour une meilleure formation des catéchistes », *Vie des Communautés Religieuses* XX, 114–16.

Lamarche, A. *M.-A. Lamarche, O.P.* Collection Classiques Canadiens no 22. Montréal : Fides. Pp. 96.

Rumilly, R. « Monseigneur Laflèche et les ultra-montains », *Rev. Hist.* XVI, 95–101.

Saucier, P. « Un Instrument de formation de premier ordre : l'Ecole Normale Supérieure de Montréal », *Maintenant* I, 266–67.

Slattery, T. P. *Loyola and Montreal.* Montreal : Palm. Pp. 319.

Tanghe, R. *L'Ecole de Bibliothécaires de l'Université de Montréal, 1937–1962.* Montréal : Fides. Pp. 69.

Université de Montréal. *Mémoire à la Commission Royale d'Enquête sur l'Enseignement.* Montréal : Univ. de Montréal. Pp. 122.

1963 Beausoleil, P. *Le Milieu étudiant : ses origines sociales.* Montréal : Association Générale des Etudiants de l'Université de Montréal. Pp. 32.

Patenaude, L. "The Public Law Research Institute at the University of Montreal," *Univ. Tor. Law Jour.* XV, 185–86.

MOUNT ALLISON UNIVERSITY

1875 Stockton, A. A. "University Consolidation," *Maritime Monthly,* 444–45.

1960 Bell, R. P. *An Address Delivered on the Occasion of His Installation as Chancellor of Mount Allison University on October 28, 1960.* Sackville: Mount Allison Univ. Pp. 7.

1962 Commission Royale d'Enquête sur l'Enseignement Supérieur au Nouveau-Brunswick. *Rapport...* Fredericton. Pp. 122./Royal Commission on Education in New Brunswick. *Report. . . .* Fredericton. Pp. 118.

UNIVERSITY OF NEW BRUNSWICK

1919 Raymond, W. O. *The Genesis of the University of New Brunswick with a Sketch of the Life of William Brydone-Jack, A.M., D.C.L. President, 1861–1885.* St. John. Pp. 40. [A considerably expanded version of the article and the same title published 1918 in *Trans. R.S.C.* Sect. II, 95–108.]

1948 McInerney, K. C. "Notes on the Law School History," *U.N.B. Law Sch. Jour.* I, 14–18.

1955 McAllister, G. A. "Some Phases of Legal Education in New Brunswick," *U.N.B. Law Sch. Jour.* VIII (May), 33–50.

University of New Brunswick, Faculty of Forestry. "Cradle of Foresters," *Timber of Canada* XV, no. 6, 40–42.

1956 Gibson, J. M. "Forestry at the University of New Brunswick," *Timber of Canada* XVII, no. 8, 28–31, 34.

1958 McLeod, J. "UNB's Winter Carnival," *Atlantic Advocate* XLVIII, 85, 87–88.

1959 Bailey, A. G. "Creative Moments in the Culture of the Maritime Provinces," *Dalhousie Rev.* XXIX, 231–44.

1960 Konecny, G. "The New Bachelor of Surveying Engineering Curriculum at the University of New Brunswick," *Can. Surveyor* XV, 135–37.

MacLaggan, K. "U.N.B.'s School of Nursing," *Can. Nurse* LVI, 424–26.

1961 Konecny, G. "The Surveying Engineering Course; Thoughts after Completion of the First Term," *Can. Surveyor* XV, 371–75.

Pacey, D. "Bruno Bobak at U.N.B.," *Can. Art* XVIII, 140–42.

1962 Commission Royale d'Enquête sur l'Enseignement Supérieur au Nouveau-Brunswick. *Rapport...* Fredericton. Pp. 122./Royal Commission on Education in New Brunswick. *Report. . . .* Fredericton. Pp. 118.

Dineen, J. O. "A Short History of Engineering Education at the University of New Brunswick," *Eng. Jour.* XLV, 68.

Mackay, C. B. "Cost of Our Universities," *Atlantic Advocate* LII, 17–20.

1963 MacNutt, W. S. *New Brunswick: A History, 1784–1867.* Toronto: Macmillan. Pp. 496.

1964 Mackay, C. B. "U.N.B. Development," *Atlantic Advocate* LIV, 18–19.

NOTRE DAME UNIVERSITY

1962   McLean, M.   "New B.C. College Began in Bake Shop," *Calgary Herald Magazine*, Dec. 1, 1962, 5–6.
1963   Arnett, J.   "Notre Dame's President Just Wants Equal Chance," *Vancouver Sun*, May 18, 1963, 6.
       Pollard, J.   "Modern Education Pioneers Build New Varsity," *Western Weekly* [Ponoka, Alberta], Nov. 20, 1963, 1–3.
1964   "Notre Dame University of Nelson," *Nelson Daily News*, Special Supplement, September 29, 1964. Pp. 16.

NOVA SCOTIA TECHNICAL COLLEGE

1963   "Nova Scotia Tech. Opens New Chemical Engineering Labs," *Chem. Can.* XV, no. 5, 57.

UNIVERSITÉ D'OTTAWA : UNIVERSITY OF OTTAWA

1874   Guigues, J. E. B.   *In Memoriam: The Late Joseph Eugene Bruno Guigues, Bishop of Ottawa*. Ottawa. Pp. 38.
1901   University of Ottawa.   *The New Science Hall of the University of Ottawa*. Ottawa. Pp. 13.
1922   Savaète, A.   *Mgr Adélard Langevin, archevêque de St.-Boniface : sa vie, ses contrariétés, ses œuvres (Voix canadiennes — vers l'abîme XII)*. Paris : A. Savaète. Pp. 540.
1923   Simard, G.   *Tradition et évolution dans l'enseignement classique*. Ottawa : Univ. d'Ottawa Presse. Pp. 33.
1928   Simard, G.   *Un Centenaire : le Père Tabaret, O.M.I. et son œuvre d'éducation*. Ottawa : Univ. d'Ottawa Presse. Pp. 40.
1931   Université d'Ottawa.   *L'Université d'Ottawa, une maison d'enseignement catholique et bilingue*. Ottawa : Univ. d'Ottawa. Pp. 12.
1934   University of Ottawa.   *The University of Ottawa*. Ottawa: Publicity Bureau of the University. Pp. 19.
1945   Morisset, A. M.   *La Bibliothèque de l'Université d'Ottawa, son rôle et ses initiatives*. Montréal : Imprimerie Populaire. Pp. 8.
1954   Creamer, L.   "The Faculty of Medicine of the University of Ottawa," *Can. Doctor* XX, no. 11, 28–32.
1957   Caron, G.   "The Faculty of Law of the University of Ottawa," *Univ. Tor. Law Jour.* XII, 292–95.
1958   Carrière, G.   *Un Grand Educateur : le R. P. Lamoureux (1890–1958), fondateur de l'Ecole Normale de l'Université d'Ottawa*. Ottawa : Séminaire Universitaire, Editions de l'Université. Pp. 136.
       Drouin, P.   « La Bibliothèque médicale de l'Université d'Ottawa », *Bull. Bibl.* IV, no 4, 10–15.
1959   Moir, J. S.   *Church and State in Canada West: Three Studies in the Relation of Denominationalism and Nationalism, 1841–1867*. Toronto: U. of T. Press. Pp. 223.

1960 Carrière, G. *L'Université d'Ottawa, 1848–1861*. Ottawa : L'Université d'Ottawa. Pp. 95.

Cheng, C.-S. "The Main Factors that Led to the Establishment of the University of Ottawa Teachers' College." Thèse de doctorat, Univ. d'Ottawa.

"The Old and the New at Ottawa University," *Chem. Can.* XII, no. 4, 36–39.

1962 Carrière, G. *Bibliographie des professeurs oblats des facultés ecclésiastiques de l'Université d'Ottawa, 1932–1961*. Ottawa : Revue Univ. d'Ottawa. Pp. 54.

1963 Azard, P. and T. G. Feeney. "The Canadian and Foreign Research Centre at the University of Ottawa," *Univ. Tor. Law Jour.* XV, 186–87.

Carrière, G. *Thèses préparées aux facultés ecclésiastiques de l'Université d'Ottawa, 1932–1963*. Ottawa : Revue Univ. d'Ottawa. Pp. 224.

L'École de Psychologie et d'Education de l'Un. d'Ottawa. Ottawa : Revue Univ. d'Ottawa. Pp. 6.

QUEEN'S UNIVERSITY

1885 Grant, G. M. *Inaugural Address Delivered at Queen's University, Kingston, on University Day*. Toronto. Pp. 14.

1887 Grant, G. M. *A Statement Concerning Queen's Submitted to the Founders, the Graduates and Alumni and the Benefactors and Friends of the University*. Kingston. Pp. 8.

1894 Clark, J. M. *The Functions of a Great University*. Toronto. Pp. 17.

1902 Grant, G. M. "Thanksgiving and Retrospect: An Address to the Students of Queen's by the Principal, on January 6th, 1902, in the Convocation Hall of the University," *Queen's Q.* IX, 219–32.

1903 Queen's University. *An Illustrated Sketch of its Foundation, Growth and Present Prospect*. . . . Kingston. Pp. 42.

1904 Macallum, A. B. "The Late Principal Grant and the University Question," *University of Toronto Monthly* V, 67–73.

1905 Charlton, J. "Queen's University—Presbyterian Theological College" in *Speeches and Addresses Political, Literary and Religious* (Toronto), 291–304.

1911 Queen's University. *Queen's 1841–1911: The Making of Queen's*. Kingston. Pp. 40.

1921 Royal Commission on University Finances. *Report*. . . . Toronto: King's Printer. 2 vols.

1944 Pierce, L. A., ed. *Queen's University Art Foundation . . . 1940–1944*. Toronto: Ryerson. Pp. 24.

1954 "Special Centenary Issue," *Can. Med. Assoc. Jour.* LXX, 320–66.

1957 Corry, J. A. "The Queen's University Faculty of Law," *Univ. Tor. Law Jour.* XII, 290–92.

Dorrance, R. L. "The Department of Chemistry, Queen's University,

Kingston, Ontario," *Journal of the Royal Institute of Chemistry* LXXXI, 560–66.
1958 Douglas, A. V. "Astronomy at Queen's University," *R. Astron. Soc. Jour.* LII, no. 2, 82–86.
Watts, R. L. and T. H. B. Symons. "The Residence Hall and the University," *Queen's Q.* LXIV, 552–68.
1959 Moir, J. S. *Church and State in Canada West: Three Studies in the Relation of Denominationalism and Nationalism, 1841–1867.* Toronto: U. of T. Press. Pp. 223.
1960 Plewes, A. C. "Chemical Engineering Training at Queen's," *Chem. Can.* XII, no. 9, 88–92.
1961 Queen's University. *The Installation of James Alexander Corry as Principal of Queen's University at Kingston, Friday, October 20, 1961.* Kingston: Queen's Univ. Pp. 20.
1962 Gattinger, F. E. "Veterinary Instruction at Queen's and O.A.C.," *Canadian Veterinarian Journal* III, 174–77.
1964 Gundy, H. P., ed. "How We Raised the $150,000: A Narrative of the Endowment Campaign of 1878," *Douglas Library Notes* XIII, no. 2, 8–11.
Gundy, H. P., ed. "That Man Grant," *Douglas Library Notes* XIII, no. 2, 2–8.
"Kingston and its Universities," *Chem. Can.* XVI, no. 2, 41–44.
Lower, A. R. M. "Queen's, Yesterday and Today," *Queen's Q.* LXX, 69–75.

ST. FRANCIS XAVIER UNIVERSITY

1939 Timmons, H. P. "An Analysis of the Religio-Cultural Aspects of the Nova Scotia Adult Education Movement." Unpublished M.A. thesis, Catholic Univ. of America.
1940 Kelly, M. G. "The Cooperative Movement and Its Promotion by Catholic Leaders." Unpublished M.A. thesis, Boston Univ.
Sherber, M. E. "The Cooperative Movement of Antigonish, Nova Scotia." Unpublished doct. dissertation, Harvard Univ.
1942 Ward, L. *Nova Scotia: Land of Cooperators.* New York: Sheed and Ward. Pp. 207.
1947 Glasgow, F. J. "The Role of Education and Rural Conferences in the Development of St. Francis Xavier University." Unpublished M.A. thesis, St. Francis Xavier Univ.
1948 MacDonell, M. "The Early History of St. Francis Xavier University," *Can. Cath. Hist. Assoc., Annual Rept.*, 81–90.
1955 Lewack, H. *The Quiet Revolution.* New York: Student League for Industrial Democracy. Pp. 20.
1958 Usbaine, J. "The Antigonish Movement," *Geographical Magazine* [U.K.] XXX, 516–26.
1961 Laidlaw, A. F. *The Campus and the Community: The Global Impact of the Antigonish Movement.* Montreal: Harvest House. Pp. 171.

1962 Truman, H. L. and A. F. Laidlaw. *The Quiet Revolution and Focus on the Antigonish Movement.* Antigonish: Casket Printing and Publishing Co. Pp. 32.
1964 Sister Anselm. *The Antigonish Movement and Social Welfare.* Antigonish: St. Francis Xavier Univ. Press. Pp. 16.

ST. MARY'S UNIVERSITY

1926 Quinan, J. "History of St. Mary's," *Halifax Gazette,* June 24, 1926.
1950 Knaplund, P. "James Stephen on Nova Scotian College Charters 1840–41," *Dalhousie Rev.* XXIX, 395–401.

UNIVERSITY OF SASKATCHEWAN

1946 Basterfield, S. "The Department of Chemistry, Univ. of Saskatchewan," *Can. Chem. & Process Ind.* XXX (November), 46–48.
1954 Appelt, D. C. "Murray Memorial Library," *Can. Lib. Assoc. Bull.* X, 157–59.
1959 Arnott, G. "University of Saskatchewan," *R. Arch. Inst. Can. Jour.* XXXVI, 179–90.
      Clare, J. P. "Precious Alma Mater of the Prairies," *Maclean's* LXXII (February 14, 1959), 18–19, 57–59.
      King, C. *The First Fifty: Teaching, Research and Public Service at the University of Saskatchewan, 1909–59.* Toronto: McClelland and Stewart. Pp. 186.
      Kirk, L. E. "Recollections and Reminiscences—Early Years in the College of Agriculture," *Sask. Hist.* XII, 23–30.
      "Memorial Library, University of Saskatchewan, Saskatoon, Saskatchewan," *R. Arch. Inst. Can. Jour.* XXXVI, 110–12.
      Morton, A. S. *Saskatchewan: The Making of a University.* Toronto: U. of T. Press. Pp. 120.
      Murray, J. W. "The Contest for the University of Saskatchewan," *Sask. Hist.* XII, 1–22.
      Thomas, L. H. *The University of Saskatchewan.* Saskatoon: Univ. of Saskatchewan Bookstore. Pp. 64.
      Turner, A. R. "W. R. Motherwell and Agricultural Education, 1905–18," *Sask. Hist.* XII, 81–96.
      University of Saskatchewan. *Facts about University of Saskatchewan, Saskatoon-Regina.* Regina: Univ. of Saskatchewan. Pp. 14.
1960 Bocking, D. H. "Premier Walter Scott: His Early Career," *Sask. Hist.* XIII, 81–99.
      University of Saskatchewan. *The Installation of John William Tranter Spinks, Fourth President.* Saskatoon: Univ. of Saskatchewan. Pp. 36.
1961 McMurray, G. A. "Psychology at Saskatchewan," *Can. Psych.* IIa, 45–50.
      Spinks, J. W. T. "The Next Fifty," *Improving College and University Teaching* [U.S.] IX, 9–12.

Sutherland, K. "Reflections on Education in Saskatchewan," *Universities Review* [U.K.] XXXIV, 21–26.

1964   Booth, A. D. "Engineering Research in the University of Saskatchewan," *Saskatchewan Engineer* XVIII, 9–11.

Thompson, W. P. "A University in Trouble," *Sask. Hist.* XVII, 81–104.

UNIVERSITÉ DE SHERBROOKE

1959   « Projet de centre universitaire pour Sherbrooke », *Architecture, Bâtiment, Construction* XIV, 212–15.

1961   Larouche, G.-L. « Enfin une nouvelle faculté de médecine », *Union Méd.* XL, 1261–62.

1962   Morrier, B. « L'Université de Sherbrooke, aujourd'hui », *La Presse Magazine du samedi*, 17 novembre 1962.

1964   Struelens, M. « Le Canada à l'heure de l'Afrique », *Rev. Univ. Sherbrooke* IV, 203–10.

SIMON FRASER UNIVERSITY

1963   Board of Assessors, Simon Fraser University Architectural Competition. *Report*. . . . Burnaby: Simon Fraser Univ. Pp. 37.

1964   Baker, R. J. "B.C.'s New Simon Fraser University," *Sch. Prog.* XXXIII, no. 7, 34–35.

Erickson, A. "The Campus in Canada–Simon Fraser University," *Can. Arch.* IX, no. 5, 54–55.

Stainby, D. "Instant University," *Saturday Night* (March), 16–18. (*See also* "Postscript," *ibid.* [June, 1964], 42.)

SIR GEORGE WILLIAMS UNIVERSITY

1941   Sheffield, E. F. "College for Employed Adults: A Survey of the Facilities in Canada for the Formal College Education of Employed Adults and a Study of the Characteristics and Achievements of the Faculty of Arts, Science and Commerce of Sir George Williams College." Unpublished M.A. thesis, McGill Univ.

1949   Norris, K. E. "The College in 1949," *The Quarterly Newsletter* VI, no. 3, 4–6.

1951   "A College's Phenomenal Growth: The Principal's Annual Report," *The Postgrad* VII, no. 4, 11–14.

1956   Hamilton, B. "A Georgiantique Remembers," *The Postgrad* XII, no. 1, 75–76.

Hayes, B. "The Nature of the College," *The Postgrad* XII, no. 1, 110–12, 115.

Hayes, B. "The New Building Opened," *The Postgrad* XII, no. 1, 37, 41.

1960   "Now a University: Year of Great Activity," *The Postgrad* XVI, no. 1, 8, 10, 12, 15–16.

1962   "Professor Thompson on Sir George's Past," *The Postgrad* XVIII, no. 1, 15.

       Rae, R. C. *Installation Address, October 19, 1962.* Montreal: Sir George Williams Univ. Pp. 6.

1963   Kerner, F. "Twenty Years Ago: Footnote to History," *The Postgrad* XIX, no. 1, 14.

UNIVERSITY OF TORONTO

1854   A Graduate of King's College. "Thoughts on University of Toronto— Its Present Condition," *Anglo-American Magazine* IV, 463–66.

1871   Burns, R. F. *The Life and Times of Rev. Robert Burns.* Toronto. Pp. 462.

1883   Ryerson, E. *The Story of My Life.* Edited by J. G. Hodgins. Toronto. Pp. 614.

1887   Dewart, E. H. *University Federation: Considered in its Relation to the Interests of the Methodist Church.* Toronto. Pp. 16.

1891   University of Toronto and University College. *Revenues and Requirements: Report of a Committee Appointed by the Senate of the University of Toronto and also by the Board of Trustees.* Toronto. Pp. 94.

1892   Aylsworth, M. B., ed. *Alumni Souvenir Illustrating Buildings and Faculties of the University of Toronto and Affiliated Arts Colleges.* Toronto. Pp. 49.

       University of Toronto. *The Benefactors of the University of Toronto after the Great Fire of 14th February, 1890.* Toronto. Pp. 58.

1893   Macallum, A. B. *Retrospect, Aspect and Prospect in Medical Science.* The Inaugural Lecture of the University Medical Faculty for 1893. Toronto. Pp. 15.

1894   Loudon, J., M. Hutton *et al. Memorials of Chancellor W. H. Blake, Bishop John Strachan, Professor H. H. Croft and Professor G. P. Young, Presented to the University of Toronto in the University Library, January 13, 1894.* Toronto. Pp. 20.

       Symonds, H. *Trinity University and University Federation.* Peterborough. Pp. 26.

1909   University of Toronto. *Report of the Special Committee to the Board of Governors.* [Appointed to investigate the complaints made by the Hon. S. H. Blake and others with respect to the Department of Religious Knowledge.] Toronto. Pp. 14.

1912   University of Toronto. *The Organization of the University of Toronto.* Toronto. Pp. 20.

1913   Clarke, C. K. *History of the Toronto General Hospital.* Toronto. Pp. 147.

1924   Laughton, S. "The University of Toronto 1856," *Can. Hist. Rev.* V, 132–45.

       Muloch, W. *"The University Act"* (Toronto) *R.S.O.* cap. 279, a

Review of University Legislation and some of its Results. Ottawa: Ottawa Branch, Alumni Association. Pp. 12.

University of Toronto. *The University of Toronto: A Brief Outline of its History and its Administration, with Illustrations of Twenty-five of the University Buildings.* Toronto: U. of T. Press. Pp. 20.

1927   Cody, H. J. "The University of Toronto as a Public Servant," *Canadian Club of Toronto Addresses* XXV, 134–48.

McCorkell, E. J. *et al. St. Michael's College Seventy-Fifth Anniversary.* Toronto: St. Michael's College. Pp. 57.

University of Toronto. *University of Toronto . . . 1827–1927: The First One Hundred Years.* Toronto: U. of T. Press. Pp. 31.

1929   *The Spirit of 29; University of Toronto, Victoria College.* Toronto: United Church Publishing House. Pp. 32.

1930   Henderson, E. "Some Reminiscences of Upper Canada College from 1854–1857," *Ontario Historical Society, Papers and Records* XXVI, 457–60.

Hutton, M. *The Sisters Jest and Earnest.* Toronto: Musson. Pp. 287.

1931   Gwyn, N. B. "Some Details Connected with the Evolution of Medical Education in Toronto," *University of Toronto Medical Journal* VIII, 224–29.

1932   Cody, H. J. "Toronto University and the Public" in *Empire Club Addresses* (Toronto), 274–85.

1933   Glazebrook, G. P. de T. *Sir Edmund Walker.* London: Oxford Univ. Press. Pp. 160.

1938   Gordon, C. W. *Postscript to Adventure: The Autobiography of Ralph Connor.* New York: Farrar & Rinehart. Pp. 430. [*See* especially "University Days," pp. 39–44.]

1939   Carr, H. "The Very Reverend J. R. Teefy, C.S.B., LL.D.," *Can. Cath. Hist. Assoc., Annual Rept.,* 85–95.

1941   Fairclough, H. R. *Warming Both Hands: The Autobiography of . . . .* Palo Alto: Stanford Univ. Press. Pp. 629. [*See* especially pp. 24–127.]

1942   McFall, W. A. "The Life and Times of Dr. Christopher Widmer," *Annals of Medical History* [U.S.] IV, 324–34.

1946   "Ajax Division: University of Toronto," *Sch. Prog.* XIV, no. 4, 29–33.

1947   University of Toronto. *A Brief Sketch of its History and its Organization.* Toronto: U. of T. Press. Pp. 32.

1950   Ellis, R. G. and T. Cowling. "University of Toronto (Faculty of Dentistry)," *Dental Record* [U.K.] LXX, 114–22.

1951   Dow, J. *Alfred Gandier: Man of Vision and Achievement.* Toronto: United Church Publishing House. Pp. 138.

Roy, M. "The Presbyterian Archives Collection of Victoria University," *United Church of Canada Committee on Archives Bulletin* IV, 4–9.

1952   Line, W. *et al. The Veteran at Varsity: An Enquiry Concerning the Impact of the Veteran Student on Policy and Practices in the University of Toronto, 1945–1951.* Toronto: Univ. of Toronto Bookstore. Pp. 49.

Massey, V. *Trinity College Centenary Lecture: Things That Remain.* Toronto: Trinity College. Pp. 16.

Watson, A. *et al.* *Trinity 1852–1952.* Special Centennial Issue of the *Trinity Review.* Toronto: Trinity College. Pp. 186.

1955 Henderson, J. H. L. "John Strachan as Bishop, 1839–1867." Unpublished doct. dissertation, Huron College.

1957 Gallie, W. E. "The University of Toronto Medical School—Fifty Years' Growth," *Med. Grad.* III, no. 2, 6–13.

1958 Benson, N. A. "Edward Johnson," *Can. Music Jour.* II, no. 3, 28–34.

Bruce, H. A. *Varied Operations.* Toronto: Longmans, Green. Pp. 366.

McCorbett, E. J. "Bertram Coghill Alan Windle, F.R.S., F.S.A., K.S.A., M.D., LL.D., Ph.D., Sc.D." *Can. Cath. Hist. Assoc., Annual Rept.*, 53–58

Taylor, T. G. *Journeyman Taylor: The Education of a Scientist.* London: R. Hale. Pp. 352.

1959 Bladen, V. "In Memoriam Sidney Earle Smith, 1897–1959," *Can. For.* XXXIX, 31–32.

Careless, J. M. S. *Brown of the Globe.* Toronto: Macmillan, 1959–63. 2 vols.

Forster, L. "Ernst Stadler and the University of Toronto," *Univ. Tor. Q.* XXIX, 11–20.

Frye, N. *By Liberal Things.* Address on his Installation as Principal of Victoria College, University of Toronto. Toronto: Clarke, Irwin. Pp. 23.

Lorriman, F. R. "The Department of Chemistry, University of Toronto," *Chem. Can.* XI, no. 10, 38–40.

Moir, J. S. *Church and State in Canada West: Three Studies in the Relation of Denominationalism and Nationalism, 1841–1867.* Toronto: U. of T. Press. Pp. 223.

1960 Feasby, W. R. "The Discovery of Insulin," *Medical Library Association Bulletin* [U.S.] XLVIII, 11–20.

Smith, A. "John Strachan and Early Upper Canada," *Ont. Hist.* LII, 159–72.

Symons, T. H. B. *The University in Summer.* Toronto: Univ. of Toronto Library. Pp. 55.

1961 Cameron, D. F. "The Royal Ontario Museum, 1912–1962," *Ont. Hist.* LIII, 193–96.

Corbett, E. A. *Sidney Earle Smith.* Toronto: U. of T. Press. Pp. 72.

Harman, E., ed. *The University as Publisher.* Toronto: U. of T. Press. Pp. 165.

Kidd, J. R. *18 to 80—Continuing Education in Metropolitan Toronto.* Toronto: Toronto Board of Education. Pp. 153.

Parkes, A. E. M. *The Development of Women's Athletics at the University of Toronto.* Toronto: U. of T. Press. Pp. 14.

Sisam, J. W. B. *Forestry Education at Toronto.* Toronto: U. of T. Press. Pp. 116.

Timonin, I. M.   "John Strachan and King's College, Upper Canada, 1799–1843." Unpublished M.A. thesis, Carleton Univ.

1962   Gattinger, F. E.   *A Century of Challenge: A History of the Ontario Veterinary College.* Toronto: U. of T. Press. Pp. 223.

Tough, A. M.   "The Development of Adult Education at the University of Toronto before 1920." Unpublished M.A. thesis, Univ. of Toronto.

1963   Collins, P.   "An Appraisal [Massey College]," *R. Arch. Inst. Can. Jour.* XL, no. 10, 39–48.

Field, A.   "Honourable Edward Blake, 1833–1912," *Western Ontario Historical Notes* XIX, March, 1963, 9–18.

Le Roy, D. J.   "Lash Miller and a History of Chemistry at the University of Toronto." Toronto: Dept. of Chemistry, Univ. of Toronto. Typescript. Pp. 14.

"Massey College," *Can. Arch.* VIII, no. 10, 47–62.

Massey, V.   *What's Past is Prologue: The Memoirs of Vincent Massey.* Toronto: Macmillan. Pp. 540.

Samuel, S.   *In Return.* Toronto: U. of T. Press. Pp. 166.

1964   Bush, D.   "A. S. P. Woodhouse: Scholar, Critic, Humanist" in Millar MacLure and F. W. Watt, eds., *Essays in English Literature from the Renaissance to the Victorian Age* (Toronto: U. of T. Press), 320–34.

TRENT UNIVERSITY

1963   Wills, T.   *A Vision of Trent.* Peterborough: Peterborough Examiner. Pp. 15.

1964   Edinborough, A.   "Canada Gets a Quiet College," *Saturday Night* LXXIX (February 15, 1964), 23–26.

Smith, D.   "Trent University Prepares for First Classes," *Sch. Prog.* XXXIII, no. 7, 39–40.

UNIVERSITY OF VICTORIA

1958   Logan, H. T.   *Tuum Est: A History of the University of British Columbia, 1908–1958.* Vancouver: Univ. of British Columbia. Pp. 268.

UNIVERSITY OF WATERLOO

1958   Dainton, D. G.   "Co-operative Education at Work," *Monetary Times* CXXVI (December), 20–22.

"First Year of Co-operative Engineering Studies Completed," *Eng. Jour.* XLI (September), 108–109.

1959   Batke, T. L.   "Engineering Education at Waterloo," *Chem. Can.* XI, no. 8, 43–46.

"Waterloo's Engineering Students Spend Six Months on the Campus, Six Months on the Job," *Industrial Canada* LX (November), 47–48.

1961   Lewis, D. E. "Lion's Share," *Ont. Lib. Rev.* XLV, 239–40.

Myers, B. R. and J. S. Keeler. "Engineering Education in Canada and the Co-operative Electrical Engineering Program at the University of Waterloo," *IRE Transactions on Education* [U.S.] E-IV, no. 2 (June), 71–79.

1962   Brookes, E. M. "Campus Planning: University of Waterloo," *Building Management* (November), 25–28.

Brookes, E. M. "Problem: Plan for Growth You Can't Predict," *Modern Power and Engineering* LVI, 74–76.

"Earn-as-you-learn," *Star Weekly Magazine* (Sept. 29, 1962), 16–19.

McCaffrey, G. "Canada's Newest Universities Need Executives to Start," *Executive* IV (November), 42–47.

"Success at Waterloo: The Changing Face of Engineering Education," *Can. Consulting Eng.* IV, 61.

"University of Waterloo," *R. Arch. Inst. Can. Jour.* XXXIX (December), 45–54.

Walters, R. H. "Psychology at the University of Waterloo," *Ontario Psychological Association Quarterly* XVI (Summer), 5–9.

Wright, D. T. *The First Five Years of the Co-operative Engineering Programme at the University of Waterloo.* Montreal: Engineering Institute of Canada. Pp. 17.

1963   Adams, J. D. "Waterloo, Ontario: Canada's Pioneer University," *UNESCO Features* [U.S.] no. 145 (May 3, 1963), 16–17.

1964   Batke, T. L. "Graduate Professional Studies in Engineering," *Professional Engineer & Engineering Digest* XXV (June), 35–38.

Brookes, E. M., W. Greer, and D. E. Lewis. "University of Waterloo Arts Library" in *Proceedings of the Library Buildings Institute* (Chicago: American Library Association), 36–45.

University of Waterloo, Faculty of Engineering. *Research in Engineering.* Waterloo: Univ. of Waterloo Press. Pp. 39.

WATERLOO LUTHERAN UNIVERSITY

1953   Talman, J. J. and R. D. Talman. "Waterloo College" in *Western 1878–1953* (London: Univ. of Western Ontario Press), 132–34.

UNIVERSITY OF WESTERN ONTARIO

1944   Trott, H. W. *Campus Shadows.* Hemlock, N.Y.: Crosset and Williams. Pp. 371.

1961   Lusztig, P. A. and J. Haskett. "A Look at Two Canadian Business Schools," *Can. Bus.* XXXIV, 96–102.

Rand, L. C. "The New Faculty of Law at the University of Western Ontario," *Univ. Tor. Law Jour.* XIV, 107–108.

60

1963 Crowfoot, A. H. *This Dreamer: Life of Isaac Hellmuth, Second Bishop of Huron.* Toronto: Copp Clark. Pp. 86.
Talman, J. J. *Huron College, 1863–1963.* London:Huron College. Pp. 102.
1964 Fox, W. S. *Sherwood Fox of Western.* Toronto: Burns and MacEachern. Pp. 250.

UNIVERSITY OF WINDSOR

1920 Assumption University. *Golden Jubilee, Assumption College 1870–1920.* Windsor: Assumption College. Pp. 158.
1958 Dollar, W. F. "Friends of the Library, Assumption University of Windsor," *Can. Lib. Assoc. Bull.* XV, 77–78.
1959 "Assumption University Library, Windsor, Ontario," *R. Arch. Inst. Can. Jour.* XXXVI, 107–109.
Mate, H. V. "Assumption University of Windsor," *Ont. Lib. Rev.* XLIII, 16–18.
1961 Garvey, E. C. "Pluralism in the University: College Affiliations," *Commonweal* [U.S.] LXXIII, 458–62.
1963 Ruth, N. J. "A Dean's Look at a New University," *Assumption University Alumni Times* VIII (Winter), 7–9.

YORK UNIVERSITY

1959 Winters, R. "The Creation of New Universities," *N.C.C.U.C. Proc.*, 29–32.
1961 Howarth, T. "Campus Planning; York University, Toronto," *R. Arch. Inst. Can. Jour.* XXXVIII, 30–34.
Ross, M. G. *The New University.* Toronto: U. of T. Press. Pp. 110.
1962 Moon, B. "Perils and Pleasures of a Brand New University," *Maclean's* LXXV (April 7, 1962), 12–13, 52–54.
"Three-Campus Plan for York University," *Sch. Prog.* XXXI, no. 7, 40–41, 56.
1963 Corbett, E. A. "Atkinson College," *Continuous Learning* II, 22–25.
University Planners, Architects, and Consulting Engineers. *Report on the Master Plan for the York University Campus Prepared for the Board of Governors of York University.* Toronto. Pp. 79.
1964 Johnson, A. C. "York's Plans Crystallizing," *Sch. Prog.* XXXIII, no. 7, 36–38.
Wittenberg, A. I. *General Education as a Challenge for Creative Scholarship.* Toronto: York Univ. Pp. 45.

4

CURRICULUM AND TEACHING
PROGRAMME D'ETUDE ET METHODES
D'ENSEIGNEMENT

A. THE FACULTY OF ARTS AND SCIENCE

1948 Kirkconnell, W. *Liberal Education in the Canadian Democracy.* Hamilton: McMaster Univ. Press. Pp. 18.

1949 Penfield, W. "The Liberal Arts in Canada," *Dalhousie Rev.* XXXVIII, 497–508.

1961 Leddy, J. F. "New Dimensions in the Arts and Science Curriculum," *Improving College and University Teaching* [U.S.] IX, 16–18.

1964 Priestley, F. E. L. *The Humanities in Canada: A Report Prepared for the Humanities Research Council of Canada.* Toronto: U. of T. Press. Pp. 246.

Wittenberg, A. I. *General Education as a Challenge for Creative Scholarship.* Toronto: York Univ. Pp. 45.

B. FACULTE DES ARTS; ENSEIGNEMENT
SECONDAIRE CLASSIQUE

1888 De Foville, P. « Rôle de la faculté des arts dans l'université catholique », *Canada-Français* I, 79–91.

1954 Vanier, P. *Mélanges sur les humanités.* Québec : Presses Univ. Laval. Pp. 264.

1958 Bluteau, A. « Notre cours classique », *Jour. Ed.*, no 2, 53–62.

Dionne, Y.-M. « Essai sur le cours classique », *Ens. Sec.* XXXVIII, no 2, 9–16.

1959 Bertrand, T. and E. Caron. *Faut-il abandonner le cours classique?* Montréal : Thérien Frères. Pp. 155.

Desrochers, E. « Les Normes d'excellence des bibliothèques collégiales », *Coll. et Fam.* XVI, 1–5.

Desrochers, E. « Quelle Bibliothèque nous faut-il ? » *Coll. et Fam.* XVI, 45–50.

Genest, J. « Faut-il abandonner le cours classique ? » *Coll. et Fam.* XVI, 168–71.

Genest, J. « La Place des sciences dans le cours classique », *Coll. et Fam.* XVI, 76–86.

Laliberté, J. « L'Enseignement secondaire qu'il faut à la nation », *Cah. Nouv.-Fr.* X, 116–30.

Prevost, Y. « Nos Collèges classiques demeureront les derniers bastions de resistance contre toute infiltration », *Instr. Publ.* III, 466–70.

1960 Chabot, J. « Collaboration entre la bibliothèque et les collèges classiques », *Bull. Bibl.* VI, 16–20.

Chenier, A. « La Profession de bibliothécaire et les collèges », *Coll. et Fam.* XVII, 240–45.

Commission du Programme de la Faculté des Arts de l'Université Laval. *Rapport...* Québec : Univ. Laval. Mimeo. 3 vols.

Décarie, V. « Fonds publics et enseignement classique », *Cité Libre* XI, 21–25.

Desbiens, J.-P. *Les Insolences du Frère Untel.* Montréal : Editions de l'Homme. Pp. 158. (*Voir* 1962, Desbiens, J.-P.)

"Education at the Secondary and College Level in French-Speaking Quebec," *Can. Ed.* XVI, no. 1, 17–22.

Fédération des Collèges Classiques. *Discours et conférences.* Document no 9. Montréal : La Fédération. Pp. 112.

Fédération des Collèges Classiques. *Les Finissants de juin 1959 dans les collèges classiques.* Document no 8. Montréal : La Fédération. Pp. 92.

Fédération des Collèges Classiques. *Horaires quotidiens suivis dans les collèges.* Montréal : La Fédération. Pp. 100.

Gagné, L. « Les Petits Séminaires pour futurs religieux », *Ens. Sec.* XXXIX, no 5, 4–7.

Genest, J. « L'Enseignement de la géographie au collège », *Coll. et Fam.* XVII, 196–207.

Gingras, P.-E. « Les Collèges classiques en très mauvaises situations », *Act. Nat.* L, 41–46.

Gingras, P.-E. « Une Opinion—que deviendront nos collèges classiques ? » *Act. Univ.* XXVI, no 2, 9–10, 14–18.

Larivière, F. « De l'ancien au nouveau Collège des Jésuites », *Ens. Sec.* no 2, 3–7.

Leman, P.-H. « Le Rôle de l'enseignement secondaire dans notre société », *Coll. et Fam.* XVII, 90–95.

Marchand, P. et J. Panneton. « Ne Intermittant », *Ens. Sec.* XXXIX, no 3, 5–9.

« Revolution au cours classique ? » *Relations* XX, 143–44.

Rourgault, R. « Proposition sur l'essence du 'cours classique' », *Coll. et Fam.* XVII, 180–85.

Tousignant, J.-M., J. Panneton, et G. Boulet. « Le Cours classique dévelope-t-il un humanisme canadien », *Ens. Sec.* XXXIX, no 3, 28–35.

Tousignant, J.-M., J. Panneton, et G. Boulet. « Qualibets », *Ens. Sec.* XXXIX, no 3, 36–41.

1961   Angers, P. « La Place des arts et des sciences dans l'université »,
        Relations XXI, 19–21.
        Beauchemin, J.-M. « Cours classique pour jeunes filles », *Bull.*
        Féd. Coll. VI, no 5, 4–6.
        Beauchemin, J.-M. *Hausse des frais de scolarité dans les collèges*
        classiques. Montréal : Fédération des Collèges Classiques.
        De Dainville, F. « Tradition et adaptation du cours classique »,
        Coll. et Fam. XVIII, 27–34.
        Fédération des Collèges Classiques. *Les Changements d'orienta-*
        tion au sortir du collège classique. Document no 15. Montréal :
        La Fédération. Pp. 46.
        Gagné, L. « Le Cours du collège », *Bull. Féd. Coll.* VI, no 5, 3, 6.
        Genest, J. « L'Accrédition et les collèges classiques », *Coll. et Fam.*
        XVIII, 83–93.
        Genest, J. « Les Objectifs du cours classique », *Coll. et Fam.*
        XVIII, 13–26.
        Gingras, P.-E. « On trame la mort des collèges classiques », *Act.*
        Nat. L, 600–606.
        Gingras, P.-E. « Structure et autonomie du collège classique »,
        Coll. et Fam. XVIII, 50–56.
        Larivière, F. « Le Baccalauréat », *Coll. et Fam.* XVIII, 78–82.
        Minville, E. « Collèges et milieu national », *Coll. et Fam.* XVIII,
        5–12.
        Tanguay, A. « L'Etudiant de nos collèges », *Coll. et Fam.* XVIII,
        58–71.
1962   De Dainville, F. « Tout dépend du maître », *Coll. et Fam.* XIX,
        72–81.
        Desbiens, J.-P. *The Impertinences of Brother Anonymous.* Mont-
        real: Harvest House. Pp. 126. (*See* 1960, Desbiens, J.-P.)
        Fédération des Collèges Classiques. *Notre Réforme scolaire.* I, *Les*
        Cadres généraux. 1962. Pp. 206. II, *L'Enseignement classique.*
        1963. Pp. 254. *Mémoire à la Commission Royale d'Enquête sur*
        l'Education (Commission Parent). Montréal : Centre de Psycho-
        logie et de Pédagogie. 2 vols.
        Fédération des Collèges Classiques. *Le Règlement dans les col-*
        lèges. Document no 17. Montréal : La Fédération. Pp. 109.
        Fédération des Collèges Classiques. *Trois Etudes statistiques sur*
        l'enseignement classique (1961–62). Document no 19. Montréal :
        La Fédération. Pp. 98.
        Genest, J. « Le Collège moderne », *Coll. et Fam.* XIX, 220–28.
        Labarre, P. « Nos Facultés des arts », *Act. Nat.* LI, 466–76.
        Monette, G. « Evolution du processus éducatif dans nos collèges
        classiques », *Coll. et Fam.* XIX, 161–65.
        Savard, M. *Paradoxes... et réalités de notre enseignement secon-*
        daire. Montréal : Centre de Psychologie et Pédagogie. Pp.
        144.
        Tremblay, A. "Trends in Education" in C. F. MacRae, ed., *French*
        Canada Today (Sackville: Mount Allison Bookstore), 60–69.

1963   Association Canadienne des Bibliothécaires de Langue Française.
« Les Bibliothèques de nos collèges », *Coll. et Fam.* XX, 215–23.
Fédération des Collèges Classiques. *Le Collège chrétien.* Document
no 21. Montréal : La Fédération. Pp. 81.
Fédération des Collèges Classiques. *Le Directeur d'élèves.* Docu-
ment no 22. Montréal : La Fédération. Pp. 64.
Fédération des Collèges Classiques. *Les Sanctions en éducation.*
Document no 23. Montréal : La Fédération. Pp. 65.
Fédération des Collèges Classiques. *Le Statut du directeur d'élèves.*
Document no 24. Montréal : La Fédération. Pp. 49.
Gadbois, L.   « Le Baccalauréat commence au foyer », *Bull. Féd.
Coll.* VIII, no 4, 1–15.
Gadbois, L.   « Les Etudiants de l'enseignement classique », *Bull.
Féd. Coll.* VII, no 4, 2–16.
1964   Savard, M.   *Le Directeur des études et le secteur académique.*
Document no 29. Montréal : Fédération des Collèges Classiques.
Pp. 80.

C. THE HUMANITIES : LES HUMANITES

GENERAL : GÉNÉRALITÉS

1932   Wallace, R. C.   *A Liberal Education in a Modern World.* Toronto:
Macmillan. Pp. 114.
1954   Fieldhouse, H. N.   "What Subject or Subjects Today are Best
Fitted to Fulfil the Role Played Previously in the University
Curriculum by the Classics" in *Seventh Congress of the Universi-
ties of the Commonwealth* (Cambridge: Cambridge Univ. Press),
129–34.
1957   Hickman, W. H.   "The Role of the Liberal Arts in Education,"
Jour. Ed. no. 1, 33–38.
1958   Cragg, C.   "And Truly Teach: Liberal Education and Society,"
Queen's Q. LXV, 277–90.
Frye, N.   "Humanities in a New World" in *3 Lectures* (Toronto:
U. of T. Press), 1–15.
Lacroix, B.   « Sur l'enseignement des humanités », *Culture* XIX,
433–36.
1959   Dobson, W. A. C. H., G. M. Wickens, and N. Keyfitz.   "Near and
Far Eastern Studies; the Obligations of Canadian Universities: A
Symposium," *N.C.C.U.C. Proc.*, 54–76.
Frye, N.   *By Liberal Things.* Address on his Installation as Principal
of Victoria College, University of Toronto. Toronto: Clarke, Irwin.
Pp. 23.
Genest, J.   « L'Humanisme gréco-latin et la préparation des
maîtres », *Coll. et Fam.* XVI, 27–35.
Penfield, W.   "The Liberal Arts in Canada," *Dalhousie Rev.*
XXXVIII, 497–507.

Smith, M. B. "Status and Scholarship in the Humanities," *Dalhousie Rev.* XXXIX, 370–77.

Thomson, W. "Speaking across the Barriers: Humane Studies in a Scientific Environment," *Queen's Q.* LXV, 601–15.

1960 Katsh, A. I. "Current Trends in the Study of Hebrew in Colleges and Universities," *Mod. Lang. Jour.* XLIV, 64–68.

MacDonald, D. K. C., P. R. Gendron, and F. M. Salter. "The Humanities and Modern Science, Two Cultures or One? A Symposium," *N.C.C.U.C. Proc.*, 39–65.

Pirlot, P. « L'Allergie culturelle : sciences-humanités », *Rev. Univ. Laval* XV, 299–315.

Ross, M. G. "Liberal Education for a Free Society" in *The Empire Club of Canada, Addresses 1959–1960* (Toronto: Best), 196–205.

1961 Groulx, L. « Religion et humanisme », *Cah. Acad. Can.-Fr.* VI, 21–33.

Robert, G. « Initiation nécessaire aux arts et littératures du XXᵉ siècle », *Rev. Dom.* LXVII, 286–94.

Stone, J. S. "Humanities and Social Science for Canadian Engineering Students," *Queen's Q.* LXVIII, 402–10.

Tremblay, A. « Projet de réforme de l'enseignement des humanités à l'Université Laval » in G. Stanley and G. Sylvestre, eds., *Canadian Universities Today* (Toronto: U. of T. Press), 67–79.

Whalley, G. "The Humanities and Science: Two Cultures or One?" *Queen's Q.* LXVIII, 237–48.

1962 Gilbert, J. « Les Humanités gréco-latines », *Maintenant*, 259–60.

Grenier, P. « Pour un humanisme authentique », *Act. Nat.* LI, 415–25.

Leddy, J. F. *The Humanities in an Age of Science.* Charlottetown: St. Dunstan's Univ. Pp. 39.

Ostry, B. *Recherches sur les humanités et les sciences sociales au Canada.* Ottawa : Conseil Canadien de Recherche sur les Humanités et le Conseil Canadien de Recherche en Sciences Sociales. Pp. 66./*Research in the Humanities and in the Social Sciences in Canada.* Ottawa: Humanities Research Council of Canada and the Social Science Research Council of Canada. Pp. 58.

Robillard, H.-M. « Les Humanités gréco-latines », *Maintenant*, 107–108.

Underhill, F. H. "The Liberal Arts and Public Affairs," *C.A.U.T. Bull.* X, no. 3, 111–25.

University of Toronto, Department of East Asiatic Studies. *Asian and African Studies at the University of Toronto.* Toronto. Pp. 16.

Williams, E. E. *Resources of Canadian University Libraries for Research in the Humanities and Social Sciences.* Ottawa: *N.C.C.U.C.* Pp. 87.

1963 Corbett, E. A. "Atkinson College," *Continuous Learning* II, 22–25.

Gagnon, N. « L'Idéologie humaniste dans l'enseignement secondaire' », *Recherches Sociographiques* IV, 167–200.

Gibson, F. W. "University and the Student in a Changing Society," *Queen's Q.* LXX, 273–79.

Roy, P.-E. *Les Intellectuels dans la cité.* Montréal : Fides. Pp. 85.

1964 Jackson, B. W. "A Commitment to the Intellect" in W. B. Townley, ed., *The Decisive Years* 1964 (Toronto: Barker Publishing), 29–35.
Priestley, F. E. L. *The Humanities in Canada: A Report Prepared for the Humanities Research Council of Canada.* Toronto: U. of T. Press. Pp. 246.

ARCHAEOLOGY : ARCHÉOLOGIE

1963 Pendergast, J. F. "Canadian Archaeology and History in 1962," *Can. Geog. Jour.* LXVI, 132–39.

ART—MUSIC—DRAMA : ARTS PLASTIQUES—MUSIQUE—THÉÂTRE

1925 Smith, L. "Music in Our Universities," *Can. For.* V (August), 333–35.
1942 Machlin, E. L. "Educational Dramatics in the Maritime Universities in Canada." Unpublished doct. dissertation, Columbia Univ.
1944 Pierce, L. A., ed. *Queen's University Art Foundation . . . 1940–1944.* Toronto: Ryerson. Pp. 24.
1947 Buchanan, D. W. "Towards a National Art School," *Can. Art* IV, 151.
Moss, K. "Art Schools in Canada," *Can. Art* IV, 156, 178–82.
Walter, A., R. Ayre, and H. Voaden. "Music, Fine Arts and Drama in Canadian Higher Education" in W. Kirkconnell and A. S. P. Woodhouse, eds., *The Humanities in Canada* (Ottawa: Humanities Research Council of Canada), 217–36.
1951 Fenwick, G. R. *The Function of Music in Education: Incorporating a History of School Music in Ontario.* Toronto: Gage. Pp. 89.
1954 McGill University, Festival of the Conservatorium of Music 1904–1954. *50th Anniversary Festival, Souvenir Programme.* Montreal: McGill Univ. Pp. 15.
1956 Adaskin, H. "Music and the University," *Can. Music Jour.* I, no. 1, 30–36.
1957 Bornstein, E. "Serigraphy—Why a New University Course Attracts Artists in Saskatchewan," *Can. Art* XIV, 98–100.
"University Students Form an Alliance with Creative Artists in Canada," *Can. Art* XIV, 120–22.
1958 Benson, N. A. "Edward Johnson," *Can. Music Jour.* II, no. 3, 28–34.
Churchley, F. E. "The Piano in Canadian Music Education." Unpublished doct. dissertation, Columbia Univ.
McCullough, N. "The Norman Mackenzie Art Gallery and the School of Art, Regina College," *Can. Art* XV, 224–25.
MacMillan, E. "Music in Canadian Universities," *Can. Music Jour.* II, no. 3, 3–11.
1959 St.-Robert-Marie. « Pourquoi un cours d'initiation à la musique dans nos collèges », *Ens. Sec.* XXXVIII, no 3, 16–22.

1960 Gaboury, P. « Notre Enseignement de la musique est-il culturel ? » *Ens. Sec.* XL, no 1, 11–22.

Kallmann, H. *A History of Music in Canada, 1534–1914.* Toronto: U. of T. Press. Pp. 311.

Maranda, P. « L'Académie d'art dramatique », *Ens. Sec.* XXXIX, no 2, 21–24.

1961 *Can. Art* XVIII, no. 5, an issue devoted to the Canadian Conference of the Arts, includes: Frye, N. "Academy without Walls," 296–98; Underhill, F. "That Academy without Walls," 299–300.

Desrosiers, G. « Art dramatique et diction », *Ens. Sec.* XL, no 4, 21–35.

Graham, G. "Music Where the Wind Blows Free," *Can. Music Jour.* VI, no. 3, 12–18.

Lévesque, G.-H. « De l'importance des arts dans un pays culturel », *Rev. Dom.* LXVII, 270–77.

Pacey, D. "Bruno Bobak at U.N.B.," *Can. Art* XVIII, 140–42.

1962 Barbary, M. « Le Théâtre au collège, moyen de formation », *Ens. Sec.* XLI, no 2, 116–22.

Gaboury, P. « La Musique, instrument d'analyse littéraire », *Ens. Sec.* XLI, no 2, 95–104.

Goulding, W. "The University as an Interpretative Patron," *Can. Art* XIX, 218–21.

Musée des Beaux Arts, Montréal. *Mémoire adressé à la Commission Royale d'Enquête sur l'Enseignement.* Montréal : Le Musée. Pp. 16./Museum of Fine Arts, Montreal. *Brief to the Royal Commission of Inquiry on Education.* Montreal: The Museum. Pp. 16.

1963 Adaskin, J. *et al.* "A Tribute to Sir Ernest MacMillan," *Music across Canada* I, no. 6, 16–39.

Bouchard, A. « Réflexions sur l'enseignement de la musique », *Ens. Sec.* XLII, no 4, 23–26.

Groome, L. J. "Art Education Today for Tomorrow," *Can. Ed. Research Digest* III, 304–15.

Sœur Marie-du-Crucifix. « L'Etudiant-musicien au cours secondaire et collégial », *Ens. Sec.* XLII, no 5, 44–46.

1964 Canadian Cultural Information Centre. *Facilities for Study in the Arts in Canada.* Ottawa: The Centre. Pp. 49.

CLASSICS (GREEK AND LATIN) : LANGUES ANCIENNES (LE GREC ET LE LATIN)

1930 Hutton, M. "The Classics" in *The Sisters Jest and Earnest* (Toronto: Musson), 276–83.

1959 Mère Marie-du-Perpétuel-Secours. « Le Grec au cours secondaire », *Ens. Sec.* XXXVIII, no 3, 27–30.

1960 Leblond, W. « Non le grec dit 'classique' n'est pas mort ! Car il s'entend encore », *Rev. Univ. Laval* XV, 20–35.

Mère Sainte-Suzanne. « Ce Pauvre Grec », *Ens. Sec.* XXXIX, no 4, 32–36.

1961 Dain, A. « Humanités latines et grecques », *Cah. Acad. Can.-Fr.* VI, 81–98.
1962 Lallier, H. « Pour un recouveau des études latines », *Ens. Sec.* XLI, no 1, 7–13.
1963 Ferland, M. « Que vaut notre enseignement du latin », *Ens. Sec.* XLII, no 4, 19–22.
1964 Sissons, C. B. "Forty Years of University Teaching" in *Nil Alienum: The Memoirs of C. B. Sissons* (Toronto: U. of T. Press), 117–42.

ENGLISH : ANGLAIS

1935 Wilson, H. T. "The Teaching of English in French-Canada." Unpublished M.A. thesis, Boston Univ.
1954 MacGregor, S. E. "Dr. V. B. Rhodenizer: A Bibliographical and Critical Sketch." Unpublished M.A. thesis, Acadia Univ.
1958 Elder, A. T. "The Teaching of English to Science Students of the University of Alberta," *Canadian Conference of Pharmaceutical Faculties*, XI, 98–102.
      Frye, N. "The Study of English in Canada," *Dalhousie Rev.* XXXVIII, 1–7.
1960 Whalley, G. "English at School," *Jour. Ed.* no. 4, 63–73.
1961 Michayluk, J. O. "Prediction of Freshman Marks in English." Unpublished M.A. thesis, Univ. of Saskatchewan.
1962 Campbell, M. *et al.* "Report of the English Study Committee," in N. Frye, ed., *Design for Learning* (Toronto: U. of T. Press), 19–78.
      Marion, S. *Innovations dans l'enseignement de la langue seconde au Canada.* Ottawa : Conférence Canadienne sur l'éducation. Pp. 51.
1963 De Bruyn, J. "Maintenance of Teaching Standards in Freshman English," *Jour. Ed.* no. 8, 77–81.

FRENCH : FRANÇAIS

1919 Squair, J. "French in the Educational System of Ontario," *University of Toronto Monthly* XIX, 291–96.
1959 Graham, V. E. "How Can We Teach French?" *Can. Ed.* XIV, no. 3, 3–11.
1960 d'Anjou, J. « Pour mieux enseigner le français », *Relations* XX, 325.
      Gamache, G.-H. « Le Roman en belles-lettres », *Ens. Sec.* XXXIX, no 2, 13–19.
      Graham, V. E. "Improving the Teaching of French," *Can. Mod. Lang. Rev.* XVI, 11–20.
      Klinck, G. « L'Enseignement du français dans nos écoles de langue anglaise », *Rev. Univ. Laval* XV, 43–55.
      Lavergne, C. « La Classe de français », *Ens. Sec.* XXXIX, no 5, 19–23.

Surprenant, A. « Essai sur l'enseignement du français », *Coll. et Fam.* XVII, no 3, 151–59.
1961 Association Canadienne des Educateurs de Langue Française. *Le Parler français : travaux de XIIIe congrès de..., Rimouski, août 1960.* Québec : Editions de l'ACELF. Pp. 197.
Joliat, E. "Scylla or Charybdis," *Can. Mod. Lang. Rev.* XVII, 15–23.

HISTORY : HISTOIRE

1895 Wrong, G. M. *Historical Study in the University and the Place of Medieval History.* Toronto. Pp. 19.
1924 McArthur, D. A. "The Teaching of Canadian History," *Ontario Historical Society Papers & Records* XXI, 206–209.
1959 McConica, J. K. "Kingsford and Whiggery in Canadian History," *Can. Hist. Rev.* XL, 108–20.
Wade, M. "The Place of Canadian Studies in American Universities," *Queen's Q.* LXVI, 377–83.
Winks, R. W. "Thirty Years After: Canadian History in the Universities of the United States," *Can. Hist. Rev.* XL, 38–50.
1960 Morton, W. L. "The Relevance of Canadian History," *Can. Hist. Assoc., Annual Rept.,* 63–76.
1961 Ferguson, W. K. "Presidential Address," *Can. Hist. Assoc., Annual Rept.,* 1–12.
Lavallée, J.-G. « L'Enseignement de l'histoire », *Rev. Univ. Sherbrooke* I, 195–202.
Trudel, M. « L'Histoire », *Cah. Acad. Can.-Fr.* VI, 113–20.
1962 Dray, W. H., D. J. McDougall, and R. H. McNeal. "The Philosophy of History and the Historian," *Can. Hist. Assoc., Annual Rept.,* 82–100.
Preston, R. A. "Presidential Address to the Canadian Historical Association," *Can. Hist. Assoc., Annual Rept.,* 1–19.
Saunders, R. M. "History Pure and Applied," *Can. Hist. Rev.* XLIII, 315–27.
Savard, P. « Les Débuts et l'enseignement de l'histoire et de la géographie au Petit Séminaire de Québec (1765–1830) », *Rev. Hist.* XV, 508–25; XVI, 43–62, 188–212.
Stevenson, H. A. "James H. Coyne: An Early Contribution to Canadian Historical Scholarship," *Ont. Hist.* LIV, 25–42.
1963 Hertzman, L. "The Sad Demise of History: Social Studies in the Alberta Schools," *Dalhousie Rev.* XLIII, 512–21.

MODERN LANGUAGES (OTHER THAN ENGLISH AND FRENCH) : LANGUES MODERNES (À L'EXCEPTION DE L'ANGLAIS ET DU FRANÇAIS)

1936 Needler, G. H. *The Secondary School and University.* Toronto: Ontario Educational Association. Pp. 7.
1947 Parker, J. H. "A Great Hispanist: Milton A. Buchanan," *Bulletin of Spanish Studies* [U.K.] XXIV, 182–84.

1953   Goggio, E. "Modern Language Study: The Challenge of Today," *Ontario Secondary School Teachers' Federation Bulletin* XXXIII, 127, 128, 258.

1954   Goggio, E. "The Status of Italian in the University of Toronto," *Italica* [U.S.] XXXI, 106–108.

      St. Clair-Sobell, J. "Slavonic Studies in Canadian Universities," *External Affairs* VI, 365–66.

1955   Smith, W. C. *The Place of Oriental Studies in a University.* Toronto: American Oriental Society. Pp. 12.

1956   Parker, J. H. "Cien años de estudios hispánicos en la Universidad de Toronto, Canadá," *Acta Salmanticensia, Filosofía y Letras* [University of Salamanca, Spain] X, 23–31.

1958   Rose, W. J. "Slavonic Studies in the University of British Columbia," *Slavonic and East European Review* [U.K.] XXXVII, 246–53.

1959   Nock, F. J. "Foreign Languages as Graduate Study Requirement," *Mod. Lang. Jour.* XLIII, 129–34.

      Trace, A. S. Jr. "The New Look in Foreign Language Instruction: Threat or Promise?" *Mod. Lang. Jour.* XLIII, 82–87.

      Zolobka, V. "The Semi-Centenary of Slavics in the Canadian Learned Institutions, 1900–1950." Unpublished M.A. thesis, Univ. of Ottawa.

1960   Allen, E. D. "The Effects of the Language Laboratory on the Development of Skill in a Foreign Language," *Mod. Lang. Jour.* XLIV, 355–59.

      Lloyd, D. "A Modern Approach to Modern Language Teaching," *Can. Mod. Lang. Rev.* XVI, 12–18.

      Mathieu, G. "A Brief Guide to Sound Labmanship," *Mod. Lang. Jour.* XLIV, 123–27.

      Stock, M. "Modern Language Teaching in Upper Canada a Century Ago," *Can. Mod. Lang. Rev.* XVI, 5–9.

      Strakhovsky, L. I. "The Department of Slavic Studies at the University of Toronto" (in Russian), *Sovremennik* I, 45–47.

      Winkelman, J. "Training College Language Teachers," *Mod. Lang. Jour.* XLIV, 210–17.

1961   Cioffari, V. "What Can We Expect from the Language Laboratory?" *Mod. Lang. Jour.* XLV, 3–10.

      Fairley, B. "German Literature in Universities," *German Canadian Business Review* VII, no. 2, 1–2.

      Gelinas, R. "The Language Laboratory at Collège de l'Assomption, l'Assomption, Québec," *Ont. Jour. Ed. Research* IV, 51–57.

      Steinhauer, D. "The Forward Look in Modern Language Instruction," *Can. Mod. Lang. Rev.* XVII, 23–29.

      Zyla, W. T. *Contribution to the History of Ukrainian and Other Slavic Studies in Canada: Department of Slavic Studies, Univ. of Manitoba, 1949–1959.* Winnipeg: Ukrainian Free Academy of Sciences. Pp. 96.

1962   Adams, C. J. "The Institute of Islamic Studies," *Can. Geog. Jour.* LXV, 34–36.

University of Toronto, Department of East Asiatic Studies. *Asian and African Studies at the University of Toronto*. Toronto. Pp. 16.

1963 Canadian Teachers' Federation. *Seminar on Teaching Modern Languages*. Ottawa: The Federation. Pp. 200.

Goggio, E. "In Memoriam: James Eustace Shaw (1876–1962)," *Italica* [U.S.] XL, 1–6.

Hayne, D. M., G. Shortliffe, S. Baillargeon, et J. Brault. « L'Enseignement de la littérature canadienne-française au Canada », *Culture* XXIV, 325–42.

1964 Gill, C., ed. *International Studies in Canadian Universities/L'Etude des relations internationales et de certaines civilisations étrangères au Canada*. Ottawa: Canadian Universities Foundation/Fondation des Universités Canadiennes. Pp. 79.

Hamlin, D. L. B. *International Studies in Canadian Universities*. Ottawa: Canadian Universities Foundation. Pp. 120. Includes: "Russian and East European Studies," 24–35; "Asian Studies," 36–50; "African Studies," 52–57; "Latin American Studies," 58–64.

Lalande, G. *L'Etude des relations internationales et de certaines civilisations étrangères au Canada*. Ottawa : Fondation des Universités Canadiennes. Pp. 100. Includes : « L'Etude des civilisations afro-asiatiques, ibero-américaines et slaves », 39–87.

Oyler, J. E. "Language Study in Canada," *Can. Mod. Lang. Rev.* XX, no. 2, 25–32.

PHILOSOPHY : PHILOSOPHIE

1819 McCulloch, T. *The Nature and Uses of a Liberal Education Illustrated*. Halifax. Pp. 24. [Only known copy in Nova Scotia Public Archives.]

1877 Murray, J. C. *The Study of Political Philosophy: The Annual University Lecture in McGill College*. Montreal. Pp. 18.

1891 Hume, J. G. *The Value of the Study of Ethics: An Inaugural Lecture*. Toronto. Pp. 24.

1941 De Grandpré, M. « L'Organisation des études philosophiques dans l'enseignement secondaire », *Carnets Viatoriens* VI, no 1, 28–48 et no 2, 90–105.

Hill, F. W. "Philosophy at the University of British Columbia," *Culture* II, 494–96.

1945 Douglas, A. V. "Astronomy, Physics, and Philosophy," *R. Astron. Soc. Jour.* XXXIX, 73–88.

1961 Wojciechowski, J. A. "Philosophy in the Science Curriculum," *Culture* XXII, 55–62.

1962 Langois, J. « Le Rôle de la philosophie dans la culture canadienne », *Dialogue* I, 117–28.

1963 Charette, L. « En marge d'une enquête sur l'enseignement de la philosophie », *Rev. Univ. Sherbrooke* III, 233–42.

Racette, J. « Faire évoluer notre enseignement de la philosophie », *Coll. et Fam.* XX, no 1, 1–15.

RELIGIOUS KNOWLEDGE : RELIGION

1944 Glazier, K. M. "The Place of Religion in the History of the Non-Catholic Universities of Canada." Unpublished doct. dissertation, Yale Univ.
1951 Glazier, K. M. "Religion and Morals" in G. B. Jeffery, ed., *The Year Book of Education* (London: Evans Brothers Limited), 376–85.
1959 Conway, J. S. "The Universities and Religious Studies," *Can. Jour. Theol.* V, 269–73.
1960 Frère Louis-Raoul. « Valeur de notre enseignement religieux », *Ens. Sec.* XL, no 2, 5–20.
1961 Groulx, L. « Religion et humanisme », *Cah. Acad. Can.-Fr.* VI, 21–33.
1962 Owen, D. R. G. "The Presuppositions of the University," *Can. Jour. Theol.* VIII, 137–46.

D. SOCIAL SCIENCES : SCIENCES SOCIALES

GENERAL : GÉNÉRALITÉS

1947 Cassidy, H. W. "The Social Science Foundations of Education for Social Work," *Soc. Worker* XV, no. 5, 1–14.
1958 Garigue, P. « La Faculté des sciences sociales de l'Université de Montréal », *Culture* XIX, 391–98.
      Garigue, P. *Les Sciences sociales dans le monde contemporain.* Montréal : Université de Montréal, Faculté des Sciences Sociales. Pp. 23.
1959 Corbett, D. "The Social Sciences in Canada," *Queen's Q.* LXVI, 56–73.
      Falardeau, J.-C. « Lettre à mes étudiants à l'occasion des 20 ans de la faculté des sciences sociales de Québec », *Cité Libre* X, no 23, 4–14.
      Hughes, E. C. "The Dual Mandate of Social Science: Remarks on the Academic Division of Labour," *Can. Jour. Econ. Pol. Sci.* XXV, 401–10.
      Pouliot, R. « L'Orientation de la faculté des sciences sociales », *Act. Univ.* XXVI, 15–18.
1961 Garigue, P. « Remarques sur une politique des sciences sociales », *Revue Française de Sociologie* II, 3–13.
      Stone, J. S. "Humanities and Social Sciences for Canadian Engineering Students," *Queen's Q.* LXVIII, 402–10.
1962 Macpherson, C. B. *et al.* "Report of the Social Sciences Study Committee" in N. Frye, ed., *Design for Learning* (Toronto: U. of T. Press), 79–117.
      Ostry, B. *Recherches sur les humanités et les sciences sociales au Canada.* Ottawa : Conseil Canadien de Recherche sur les Hu-

manités et le Conseil Canadien de Recherche en Sciences Sociales. Pp. 66./*Research in the Humanities and in the Social Sciences in Canada.* Ottawa: Humanities Research Council of Canada and the Social Science Research Council of Canada. Pp. 58.

Williams, E. E. *Resources of Canadian University Libraries for Research in the Humanities and Social Sciences.* Ottawa: National Conference of Canadian Universities. Pp. 87./*Ressources des bibliothèques des universités canadiennes pour la recherche en humanités et en sciences sociales.* Ottawa : Conférence Nationale des Universités et Collèges Canadiennes. Pp. 93.

1963 Downey, L. W. and F. Enns, eds. *The Social Sciences and Educational Administration.* Edmonton: Univ. of Alberta, Division of Educational Administration. Pp. 109.

ANTHROPOLOGY : ANTHROPOLOGIE

1959 Champagne, J.-E. "The Canadian Research Center for Anthropology," *Anthropologica* I, 3.

ECONOMICS AND POLITICAL SCIENCE : ÉCONOMIQUE ET POLITIQUE

1877 Murray, J. C. *The Study of Political Philosophy: The Annual University Lecture in McGill College.* Montreal. Pp. 18.

1892 Hume, J. G. *Political Economy and Ethics.* Toronto. Pp. 40.

1923 Mackintosh, W. A. "The Psychologist and Economics," *Queen's Q.* XXX, 297–305.

1952 Hodgetts, J. E. "Dives and Lazarus: Three Reports on the Teaching of Political Science," *Can. Jour. Econ. Pol. Sci.* XVIII, 88–92.

1959 Easterbrook, W. "Recent Contributions to Economic History: Canada," *Journal of Economic History* [U.S.] XIX, 76–102.

Gilson, J. C. "Economics in the Agricultural Curriculum," *Can. Jour. Agric. Econ.* VII, 1–12.

Wright, P. A. "Survey of Current Economics Courses in Canadian Agricultural Colleges," *Can. Jour. Agric. Econ.* VII, 12–16.

1960 Taylor, K. W. "Economic Scholarship in Canada," *Can. Jour. Econ. Pol. Sci.* XXVI, 6–18.

1961 Angers, F.-A. « La Science économique et les affaires », *Act. Econ.* XXXVII, 219–37.

Goodwin, C. D. W. *Canadian Economic Thought: The Political Economy of a Developing Nation, 1814–1914.* Durham, N.C.: Duke Univ. Press. Pp. 214.

1963 Association Canadienne des Educateurs de Langue Française. *La Formation économique en éducation ; quinzième congrès.* Québec : Editions de l'ACELF. Pp. 295.

Corry, J. A. *The Changing Conditions of Politics.* Toronto: U. of T. Press. Pp. 59.

Near, H. I. "The Educational Theories of Stephen Leacock." Unpublished doct. dissertation, George Peabody College for Teachers.

1964 Gill, C., ed. *International Studies in Canadian Universities/L'Etude des relations internationales et de certaines civilisations étrangères au Canada.* Ottawa: Canadian Universities Foundation/Fondation des Universités Canadiennes. Pp. 79.

Hamlin, D. L. B. *International Studies in Canadian Universities.* Ottawa: Canadian Universities Foundation. Pp. 120.

Lalande, G. *L'Etude des relations internationales et de certaines civilisations étrangères au Canada.* Ottawa: Fondation des Universités Canadiennes. Pp. 100.

GEOGRAPHY : GÉOGRAPHIE

1958 Taylor, T. G. *Journeyman Taylor: The Education of a Scientist.* London: R. Hale. Pp. 352.

1959 Beauregard, L. « La Géographie dans les écoles normales et autres écoles spécialisées du Québec », *Cah. Géog.* III, 115–18.

Hamelin, L.-E. « Raoul Blanchard » dans *Mélanges géographiques canadiens offerts à Raoul Blanchard* (Québec : Presses Univ. Laval), 13–26.

Lloyd, T. "The Geographer as Citizen," *Can. Geog.* III, no. 13, 1–13.

Robinson, J. L. "Geography at the University of British Columbia," *Can. Geog.* XIV, 46–47.

Wright, E. C. "Canadians and Geography," *Food for Thought* XX, 108–11.

1960 Genest, J. « Enseignement de la géographie au collège », *Coll. et Fam.* XVII, 196–207.

«Le Laboratoire de géographie de l'Université de Montréal », *Bull. ACFAS* II, no 5, 1–3.

1961 Bone, R. M. "The Opinion of a Canadian Scientist on Geography in Canada and the U.S.S.R.," *Can. Geog.* V, 48–52.

Grenier, F. « La Géographie au Canada français », *Cah. Acad. Can.-Fr.* VI, 121–31.

1962 Savard, P. « Les Débuts de l'enseignement de l'histoire et de la géographie au Petit Séminaire de Québec (1765–1830) », *Rev. Hist.* XV, 508–25; XVI, 43–62, 188–212.

1963 Camsell, C. "What Geography Means to Canada," *Can. Geog. Jour.* LXV, 110–11.

Tomkins, G. S. and F. C. Hardwick. "Current Trends in School Geography with Special Reference to the Professional Geographer," *Canadian Association of Geographers, B.C. Division, Occasional Papers No. 4,* 89–103.

1964 Lloyd, T. "McGill Geography Summer School," *Ed. Record Prov. Quebec* LXXX, 8–10.

PSYCHOLOGY : PSYCHOLOGIE

1897 Hume, J. G. *The Practical Value of Psychology to the Teacher: Address to Ontario Teachers' Association, Toronto, 1897.* Toronto. Pp. 8.

1956 Newbigging, P. L. "A Note on Psychology in McMaster University," *Can. Psychologist* V, 76–77.

1960 Beach, N. D. and F. H. Page. "Psychology at Dalhousie," *Can. Psychologist* Ia, 9–14.

Bindra, D. "The Miami Conference on Graduate Education in Psychology," *Can. Psychologist* Ia, 2–8.

Dorken, H., C. B. Walker, and F. R. Wake. "A Fifteen Year Review of Canadian Trained Psychologists," *Can. Psychologist* Ia, 123–30.

Hoyt, R. "Financial Assistance Available in Canada for Students in Psychology," *Can. Psychologist* Ia, 15–20.

Macdonald, J. "The Teaching of Educational Psychology: An Open Letter to Canadian Psychologists," *Can. Psychologist* Ia, 22–23.

Newbigging, P. L. "Psychology at McMaster," *Can. Psychologist* Ia, 106–10.

Payne, R. W. "Professional Training in Psychology," *Can. Psychologist* Ia, 92–96.

1961 Bernhardt, K. S., ed. *Training for Research in Psychology.* Toronto: U. of T. Press. Pp. 130.

McMurray, G. A. "Psychology at Saskatchewan," *Can. Psychologist* IIa, 45–49.

1963 *L'École de Psychologie et d'Education de l'Université d'Ottawa.* Ottawa : Revue de l'Univ. d'Ottawa. Pp. 6.

Ewing, R. M. "Some Thought on the Education and Training of Clinical Psychologists," *Can. Psychologist* IVa, 55–59.

Mooney, C. M. "Clinical Psychology Training in Canada," *Can. Psychologist* IVa, 74–86.

Ruel, P. H. « La Psychologie scolaire au service de l'éducation », *Rev. Univ. Sherbrooke* IV, 13–28.

Wright, M. J. "Psychology at Western," *Can. Psychologist* IVa, 15–18.

1964 Barrett, H. O. "Professional Training for Psychologists in Education," *Can. Psychologist* Va, 93–100.

Grygier, T. "The Teaching of Criminology as Part of the Curriculum of a Department of Psychology," *Can. Psychologist* Va, 35–40.

Hout, R. "Financial Assistance Available in Canada for Students in Psychology," *Can. Psychologist* Va, 53–63.

SOCIOLOGY : SOCIOLOGIE

1905 Gérin, L. *La Vulgarisation de la science sociale chez les Canadiens français.* Ottawa. Pp. 87.

1951 Falardeau, J.-C. « Les Recherches de sociologie religieuse au Canada », *Lumen Vitae* [Bruxelles] VI, 119–32.

1958 Elkin, F. "Canada" in J. S. Roucek, ed., *Contemporary Sociology* (New York: Philosophical Library), 1101–23.

1959 Angell, R. C. "The Moral Dimension in Sociological Theory and Research," *Can. Jour. Econ. Pol. Sci.* XXV, 287–99.

1960 Doyon, R. « Le Centre de recherche en sociologie religieuse », *Vieil Esch.* XII, no 2, 20–22.

1961 Badgley, R. F. "Sociology in the Medical Curriculum," *Jour. Can. Med. Assoc.* LXXXIV, 705–709.

Doyon, R. « Le Centre de recherches en sociologie religieuse », *Sem. Rel. Québec* LXXIII, no 27, 428–32.

Robertson, A. "A Commentary on Sociology in the Medical School," *Can. Med. Assoc. Jour.* LXXXIV, 703–704.

1964 Hall, O. "Carl A. Dawson, 1887–1964," *Canadian Review of Sociology and Anthropology* I, 109–11.

E. MATHEMATICS AND SCIENCES :
MATHEMATIQUES ET SCIENCES

GENERAL : GÉNÉRALITÉS

1870 Dawson, J. W. *Science Education Abroad: Being the Annual University Lecture of the Session 1870–71*. Montreal. Pp. 15.

1948 Burke, C. E. *Science Teaching and Research in the Canadian Democracy*. Hamilton: McMaster Univ. Press. Pp. 20.

1951 Pouliot, A. « La Faculté des sciences », *Rev. Univ. Laval* VI, 378–82.

1957 Earl, R.O. "Education in Science," *Queen's Q.* LXIV, no. 12, 216–28.

1958 Priestley, F. E. L. "Science and the Poet," *Dalhousie Rev.* XXXVIII, 141–54.

1959 Gaudet, M. « Il mesure 25.0 cm ± 1 mm », *Ens. Sec.* XXXVIII, no 4, 21–28.

Genest, J. « La Place des sciences dans le cours classique », *Coll. et Fam.* XVI, 76–86.

Graham, R. P. *et al.* "Failures in First Year University Science," *Chem. Can.* XII, no. 12, 27–30.

Steacie, E. W. R. "Science and Education," *Physics in Canada* XV, 20–26.

Thomson, W. "Speaking across the Barriers: Humane Studies in a Scientific Environment," *Queen's Q.* LXV, 601–15.

1960 Lamontagne, R. « La Contribution scientifique de la Galissonière au Canada », *Rev. Hist.* XIII, 509–24.

Oullet, C. *et al. Science and Society: Papers Delivered at the Mount Allison 1960 Summer Institute*. Sackville: Mount Allison University. Pp. 61.

Pirlot, P. « L'Allergie culturelle sciences–humanités », *Rev. Univ. Laval* XV, 299–315.

1961 Angers, P. « La Place des arts et des sciences dans l'université », *Relations* XXI, 19–21.

De Broglie, L. « Le Rôle de la culture scientifique dans la formation des hommes d'aujourd'hui », *Cah. Acad. Can.-Fr.* VI, 7–19.

Hayes, F. R. "The Development of Science in Canada," *Dalhousie Rev.* XLI, 293–302.

Leddy, J. F. "New Dimensions in the Arts and Science Curriculum," *Improving College and University Teaching* [U.S.] IX, 16–18.

Whalley, G. "The Humanities and Science: Two Cultures or One?" *Queen's Q.* LXVIII, 237–48.

Wojciechowski, J. A. "Philosophy in the Science Curriculum," *Culture* XXII, 55–62.

1962 Delmas, G. « L'Enseignement des sciences au Canada français », *Cité Libre* XIII, no 43, 14–19.

Mackey, W. J. "Science: Universities" in *Canadian Annual Review for 1962* (Toronto: U. of T. Press), 334–38.

Sullivan, C. *et al.* "Report of the Science Study Committee" in N. Frye, ed., *Design for Learning* (Toronto: U. of T. Press), 119–48.

1963 Aubin, R. « Le Professeur des sciences expérimentales dans les classes pré-universitaires : sa formation, sa méthodologie », *Rev. Univ. Laval* XVII, 600–10.

Bonenfant, F. *et al. Cri d'alarme... la civilisation scientifique et les Canadiens français.* Québec : Presses Univ. Laval. Pp. 142.

Thompson, W. P. *Graduate Education in Sciences in Canadian Universities.* Toronto: U. of T. Press. Pp. 112.

ASTRONOMY : ASTRONOMIE

1945 Douglas, A. V. "Astronomy, Physics, and Philosophy," *R. Astron. Soc. Jour.* XXXIX, 73–88.

1958 Douglas, A. V. "Astronomy at Queen's University," *R. Astron. Soc. Jour.* LII, no. 2, 82–86.

BIOLOGY : BIOLOGIE

1927 Vallée, A. *Un Biologiste canadien, Michel Sarazin (1659–1739) : sa vie, ses travaux et son temps.* Québec : Proulx. Pp. 291.

1961 Smith, E. C. *Department of Biology, Acadia University, 1910–1960.* Kentville: Kentville Publ. Co. Pp. 44.

CHEMISTRY : CHIMIE

1937 Lortie, L. « Notes sur le cours abrégé de leçons de chimie de J.-B. Meilleur », *ACFAS* III, 237–65.

Lortie, L. *Le Traité de chimie de J.-B. Meilleur.* Publication No 1 du Laboratoire de Chimie de l'Université de Montréal. Montréal : Univ. de Montréal. Pp. 29.

1945 Lortie, L. "Early Canadian Chemistry," *Can. Chem. & Process Ind.* XXIX, 312–15.

1946 Basterfield, S. "The Department of Chemistry, University of Saskatchewan," *Can. Chem. & Process Ind.* XXX, 47–48.

1947 Graham, R. P. and L. Cragg. "Department of Chemistry at McMaster University," *Can. Chem. & Process Ind.* XXXI, 822–24.

1948 Graham, R. P. "The Genealogy of a Chemistry Department," *Journal of Chemical Education* [U.S.] XXV, 632–34.

1957 Dorrance, R. L. "The Department of Chemistry, Queen's University, Kingston, Ontario," *Journal of the Royal Institute of Chemistry* [U.K.] LXXXI, 560–66.

1959 Foran, M. R. "Chemical Education in the Atlantic Provinces," *Chem. Can.* XI, no. 3, 39–42.

Graham, R. P. "Where do Chemistry Graduates Go?" *Chem. Can.* XI, no. 2, 34–37.

Hazelton, J. W. "Organic Chemistry as a First Course in Chemistry," *Chem. Can.* XI, no. 4, 58–60.

Johnson, A. I. "A Survey of Graduate Study in Chemistry and Chemical Engineering in Canada," *Chem. Can.* XI, no. 12, 38–41.

Laitinen, H. A. "Training in Instrumental Analysis and Instrumentation," *Chem. Can.* XI, no. 12, 32–34.

Lorriman, F. R. "The Department of Chemistry, University of Toronto," *Chem. Can.* XI, no. 10, 38–40.

"Many Problems, Some Solutions in First Year Chemistry Courses," *Chem. Can.* XI, no. 10, 60, 62, 64.

Martin, E.-A. « De l'Enseignement de la chimie organique pharmaceutique », *Rev. Pharm.* X, 147–48.

1960 Campbell, W. M. *et al.* "Chemical Education," *Chem. Can.* XII, no. 8, 39–51.

Holmes, J. M. "The Modern Look—Carleton University," *Chem. Can.* XII, no. 5, 39–42.

Ingram, W. A. *et al.* "Integrating High School Chemistry with University Chemistry," *Chem. Can.* XII, no. 12, 30–35.

Laidler, K. J. "Some Aims of Chemical Education," *Chem. Can.* II, no. 2, 46–52.

"The Old and the New at Ottawa University," *Chem. Can.* XII, no. 4, 36–38.

1961 Davis, S. G. *et al.* "New Chemistry Facilities at University of Alberta, Edmonton," *Chem. Can.* XIII, no. 12, 40–42.

Hodgson, G. W. "Student-Scientist Workshop," *Chem. Can.* XIII, no. 5, 25–28.

"Odds on a Research Career in Canada," *Can. Chem. & Process Ind.* XLV, 97–99.

Streight, H. R. L. "What the Chemical Industry Expects from Graduate Chemists and Chemical Engineers," *Chem. Can.* XIII, no. 10, 44–50.

1962 Graham, R. P. "A Spotlight on Some Chemistry Graduates," *Chem. Can.* XIV, no. 5, 26–31.
1963 Chemical Institute of Canada. "The Lone Voice Crying Nationally," *Chem. Can.* XV (no. 12), 12, 14, 16.
Harris, W. E. "The Graduate Chemistry Program in Canadian Universities," *Chem. Can.* XV, no. 1, 42–44.
Le Roy, D. J. "Lash Miller and a History of Chemistry at the University of Toronto." Toronto: Department of Chemistry, Univ. of Toronto. Typescript. Pp. 14.

GEOLOGY : GÉOLOGIE

1900 Ami, H. M. "Sir John William Dawson [a brief biographical sketch]," *American Geologist* [U.S.] XXVI, 1–48.
1940 Donnay, J. D. H. "The New School of Mines in Quebec" in E. Ewart, ed., *University of Toronto Studies, Geological Series No. 44* (Toronto: U. of T. Press), 21–29.
1952 Fenton, C. L. and M. A. Fenton. *Giants of Geology*. New York: Doubleday. Pp. 318.
1963 Harrison, J. M. and E. Hall. "Dinner Address: William Edmond Logan," *Proc. Geol. Assoc. Can.* XV, 33–42.

MATHEMATICS : MATHÉMATIQUES

1960 Boucher, C. « Introduction aux méthodes de la mathématique moderne », *Rev. Univ. Sherbrooke* I, 45–54.
1962 Robinson, F. G. "New Dimensions in Mathematics Teaching," *Tor. Ed. Q.* II, no. 1, 16–19.
1963 Halperm, I. *et al.* "Symposium on the Training in Mathematics Given at the University to Future High School Teachers" in *Proceedings of the Fifth Canadian Mathematical Congress* (Toronto: U. of T. Press), 43–74.
Pillow, A. F. "The Teaching of Applied Mathematics in Canada" in *Proceedings of the Fifth Canadian Mathematical Congress* (Toronto: U. of T. Press), 88–93.
1964 "Report on Mathematical Instruction in Canadian Universities," *Can. Math. Bull.* VII, 173–76.

PHYSICS : PHYSIQUE

1945 Douglas, A. V. "Astronomy, Physics, and Philosophy," *R. Astron. Soc. Jour.* XXXIX, 78–88.
1959 Brown, J. B. "Physics at the University of British Columbia," *Jour. Éd.*, no. 3, 38–43.
Currie, B. W. "Some Problems of Physics Teaching and Research in the Universities," *Physics in Canada* XV, no. 3, 8–16.

Stokes, H. W.   "McMaster's Swimmingpool Reactor," *Can. Chem. & Process Ind.* XLIII, 104–10.

1960   Kerwin, L.   "Atomic Physics for General Science and Engineering Students," *Physics in Canada* XVI, no. 4, 21–26.

Myers, B. R.   "The Early Physics Courses in the Undergraduate Engineering Curriculum," *Physics in Canada* XVI, no. 4, 14–20.

1962   Bélanger, Y.   "Physical Education in Quebec," *Can. Ed. Research Digest* II, 29–36.

Duckworth, H. E.   "Careers in Canadian Physics," in W. B. Townley, ed., *The Decisive Years* (Toronto: Barker Publishing Co.), 65–67.

Geoffrion, C.   "Graduate Training as the Universities See It," *Physics in Canada* XVIII, no. 5, 5–13.

Livesay, D. L.   "A New Way to Teach Physics," *C.I.L. Oval* XXXI, 14–16.

Marshall, J. S.   "Meteorology at McGill," *Physics in Canada* XVIII, no. 2, 9–16.

Moorcroft, O. R., D. N. Southam, and E. C. Turgeon.   "Employment for Physics Graduates," *Physics in Canada* XVIII, no. 1, 21–23.

Welsh, H. L.   "Graduate Studies in Physics: Aims and Procedures," *Physics in Canada* XVIII, no. 5, 13–18.

1963   Elliott, L. G.   "Graduate Training of Physicists for Research Centers in Canada," *Physics in Canada* XIX, no. 2, 5–9.

Hall, G.   « L'Enseignement de la physique élémentaire au Canada français », *Physics in Canada* XIX, no 5, 27–32.

Whitehead, J. R.   "The Task as Non-Academic Employers See It," *Physics in Canada* XIX, no. 2, 10–17.

F. PROFESSIONAL EDUCATION :
ENSEIGNEMENT PROFESSIONNEL

AGRICULTURE : AGRONOMIE

1859   Paquin, J. M.   *Questions générales sur l'agriculture, à l'usage des écoles.* Montréal. Pp. 22.

1862   Langevin, J.   *Réponses aux programmes de pédagogie et d'agriculture pour les diplômes d'école élémentaire et d'école modèle.* Québec. Pp. 31.

1898   Casgrain, P. B.   *La Vie de Joseph-François Perrault, surnommé de père de l'éducation du peuple canadien.* Québec. Pp. 176.

1909   Greig, R. B.   *Agricultural Education and Research in Canada.* Aberdeen. Pp. 26.

1935   Dunlop, W. J.   "The Agriculturalists' Varsity," *Sch. Prog.* III, no. 6, 11–13.

1947   Wiggin, G. A.   "Agricultural Adult Education Programs in Saskatchewan." Unpublished doct. dissertation, Univ. of Maryland.

1951 MacGregor, H. A. "A Proposal for Canadian Federal-Provincial Participation in Vocational Agriculture." Unpublished doct. dissertation, Oregon State College.

1953 Stewart, A. "Economics in the Curricula of Agricultural Colleges in Canada," *American Economic Review* XLIII, 315–25.

1956 University of Manitoba, Faculty of Agriculture and Home Economics. *Golden Jubilee 1906–1956: A Record of the Years.* Winnipeg: Univ. of Manitoba. Pp. 88.

1959 Baker, H. R. "An Opinion Survey of Agricultural Extension Work in Ontario." Unpublished doct. dissertation, Cornell Univ.

« L'Ecole Supérieure d'Agriculture de Ste-Anne-de-la-Pocatière, 1859–1959 », *La Bonne Terre* XXV, no 4, 1–52.

Gilson, J. C. "Economics in the Agricultural Curriculum," *Can. Jour. Agric. Econ.* VII, no. 2, 1–11.

Glen, R. "Education for Agriculture–Whose Responsibility?" *Agricultural Institute Review* XIV, 20–30.

Gray, H., ed. "Canada's Agricultural Students," *Agricultural Institute Review* XIV, 46–47.

Kirk, L. E. "Recollections and Reminiscences–Early Years in the College of Agriculture," *Sask. Hist.* XII, 23–30.

Lesperance, R. « Echos du Congrès 1959 de la Corporation des Agronomes de la Province de Québec : II, L'Enseignement agronomique », *Agr.* XVI, 163–67.

McLean, D. M. "Agricultural Enrolment," *Agricultural Institute Review* XIV, 23–26.

Mercier, E. « Les Agronomes peuvent-ils renier le défi ? – l'enseignement agronomique et la recherche agricole », *Agr.* XVI, 146–50.

Turner, A. R. "W. R. Motherwell and Agricultural Education, 1905–18," *Sask. Hist.* XII, 81–96.

Weir, J. R. "The Adequacy of Agricultural Education Today," *Agricultural Institute Review* XIV, 16–20.

Wright, P. A. "Survey of Current Economics Courses in Canadian Agricultural Colleges," *Can. Jour. Agric. Econ.* VII, 12–16.

1960 Deschamps, A. "Agricultural Extension," *Food for Thought* XXI, 73–76.

Glen, R. « L'Education agricole : à qui en incombe la responsibilité ? » *Agr.* XVII, 58–60, 86–88.

1961 Comité d'Etude sur l'Enseignement Agricole et Agronomique. *Rapport...* Québec : Imprimeur de la Reine. Pp. 267.

Corporation des Agronomes. « Mémoire de la Corporation des Agronomes au Comité d'Etude sur l'Enseignement Agricole et Agronomique », *Agr.* XVIII, 32–43.

Eagles, B. A. "Agricultural Extension at U.B.C. Past and Present" in Seminar on Agricultural Extension in British Columbia, *Proceedings* (Vancouver: Univ. of British Columbia), 9–23.

1962 Des Hazards, P. « La Nouvelle faculté d'agriculture », *Vieil Esch.* XIV, no 4, 18–20.

1963 Jasmin, J.-J. « L'Ingérance du gouvernement fédéral dans le domaine de l'enseignement technique et professionnel », *Agr.* XX, 139–41.

McCalla, A. G. *Agriculture, Education and the Canadian Dilemma.* Edmonton: Alberta Institute of Agrologists, Agricultural Institute of Canada. Pp. 11.

Magnan, J.-C. *Silhouettes.* Montréal : Fides. Pp. 248.

ARCHITECTURE AND TOWN PLANNING : ARCHITECTURE ET URBANISME

1947 "The Architecture Schools—U.B.C., Manitoba, Toronto, Ecole des Beaux Arts de Montréal, McGill," *R. Arch. Inst. Can. Jour.* XXIV, 144–62.

1950 Lasserre, J. "Architecture Education in British Columbia," *R. Arch. Inst. Can. Jour.* XXVII, 318–19.

Reed, T. A. "Toronto's Early Architects," *R. Arch. Inst. Can. Jour.* XXVII, 46–51.

1954 American Institute of Architects, Commission for the Survey of Education and Registration. *The Architect at Mid-Century.* New York: Reinhold. 2 vols.

1959 "School of Architecture, University of Manitoba," *R. Arch. Inst. Can. Jour.* XXXVI, 64–87.

1961 McGill University, Students of School of Architecture. "Time for Stock-taking," *R. Arch. Inst. Can. Jour.* XXXVIII, 39–52.

1962 Halford, W. "Architectural Education," *R. Arch. Inst. Can. Jour.* XXXIV, 50–55.

Howarth, T. *A History of the College Fellows.* Ottawa: Royal Architectural Institute of Canada. Pp. 28.

Morris, R. S. "Professionalism and Education: A Review of Essential Balances," *R. Arch. Inst. Can. Jour.* XXXIX, 53–56.

Youtz, P. N. "Architectural Education for a Scientific Age," *R. Arch. Inst. Can. Jour.* XXXIX, 57–60.

1963 Howarth, T. "School of Architecture, University of Toronto," *R. Arch. Inst. Can. Jour.* XL, 56–68.

1964 Kaminker, B. "The Practical Training of Architects: Summary of the Report," *R. Arch. Inst. Can. Jour.* XLI, 37–38.

Willis, J. *Education for Town Planning.* (Supplement to *Plan Canada*, April, 1964.) Toronto: Town Planning Institute of Canada. Pp. 41.

BUSINESS ADMINISTRATION AND PUBLIC AFFAIRS : COMMERCE, FINANCE ET ADMINISTRATION

1930 Fox, W. S. "The University and Training for Business," *Canadian Club of Toronto Addresses* XXVIII, 143–53.

1933 Laureys, H. "Education for Commerce," *Sch. Prog.* II, no. 2, 7–8, 19.

1943 Weeks, H. L. "Organization, Administration, and Supervision of

Business Education in British Columbia." Unpublished doct. dissertation, Harvard Univ.

1954 Hennessey, S. G. "Formal Education and Internal Auditing," *Can. Chart. Acc.* LXIV, 305–309.

Isnor, B. "Education: What It Means to a Businessman," *Can. Chart. Acc.* LXIV, 72–76.

MacFarlane, R. O. "Specialized Education for Public Administration," *Proceedings, Institute of Public Administration, Canada 1954,* 301–307.

1955 Chambers, G. A. "The Present Educational Curriculum of the B.C. Institute," *Can. Chart. Acc.* LXVI, 360–64.

1954 MacFarlane, R. O. "Executive Development," *Proceedings, Institute of Public Administration, Canada 1956,* 59–65. Also *Bus. Q.* XXI, 335–43.

1957 King, C. L. "Attracting Students to the Profession," *Can. Chart. Acc.* LXX, 23–32.

1958 Juvet, C. S. "Public Service Training in Canada under the Colombo Plan." Unpublished M.A. thesis, Carleton Univ.

Wright, P. "Chartered Accounting as a Profession," *Can. Chart. Acc.* LXXIII, 529–32.

1959 Allen, P. « Les Carrières des affaires réclament l'élite des jeunes Canadiens français d'aujourd'hui », *Act. Nat.* XLVIII, 263–71.

Bedard, R. J. "Business Training for Professional Engineers," *Eng. Jour.* XLII, 75–80.

Gassard, H. L. "Opportunities for Commerce Graduates in the Investment Field," *Comm. Jour.*, 65–71.

Macpherson, L. G. "More Professional Education," *Can. Chart. Acc.* LXXV, 508–14.

1960 Dumoulin, J. « Introduction à l'étude de la responsabilité administrative », *Rev. Univ. Ottawa* XXX, 40–47.

Graham, J. F. "Business Education under Fire," *Bus. Q.* XXV, 216–20.

Hecht, M. "What Luck for McGill's 1949 Commerce Grads?" *Executive* II, no. 3, 30–32.

Turner, C. L. "Canadian and U.S. Standards of Accountancy Education," *Can. Chart. Acc.* LXXVII, 117–23.

Université de Montréal, Ecole des Hautes Etudes Commerciales. *Contribution des professeurs de l'Ecole des Hautes Etudes Commerciales de Montréal à la vie intellectuelle du Canada... ; catalogue des principaux écrits, octobre 1960.* Montréal : L'Ecole. Pp. 135.

1961 Bisson, A. « L'Evolution de l'enseignement dans nos écoles universitaires de sciences commerciales », *Culture* XXII, 93–99.

Canada, Department of Trade and Commerce. *Management Education: A Survey of Canadian University Courses Available to Business and Supervisors.* Ottawa: Queen's Printer. Pp. 28.

Carmichael, O. C. "The Strategic Role of Graduate Education," *The Educational Forum* XXVI, 5–14.

"Education for Accounting," *Can. Chart. Acc.* LXXVIII, 459–62.

Hand, R. J. "The Case for Graduate Education in Business," *Queen's Q.* XLVIII, 473–81.

King, C. L. "Training for a Career in Accountancy," *Can. Chart. Acc.* LXXIX, 59–65.

Kirby, A. J. "Training: Responsibility of Schools or Industry?" *Plant Admin. Eng.* XXI, no. 1, 44–46, 76.

Main, O. W. "The Role of the University in Business Education," *Comm. Jour.*, 63–68.

Paré, R. « Le Canada français et la vie des affaires », *Act. Nat.* L, 630–42.

Twaits, W. O. "The Need for the Commerce Mind," *Comm. Jour.*, 119–24.

1962 Baiden, R. M. "Is Business a Profession?" *Saturday Night* LXXVII (February 17, 1962), 30–31.

Beere, R. H. "Some Aspects of Business Education in Canada with Particular Reference to Alberta." Unpublished M.A. thesis, Univ. of Alberta.

Isbister, F. "Business Education in Quebec," *Rev. Univ. Sherbrooke* II, 149–54.

McCaffrey, G. "Canada's Newest Universities Need Executives to Start," *Executive* IV, no. 11, 42–47.

MacCullough, A. "University Executive Programs: Their Role and Future," *Bus. Q.* XXVII, no. 2, 55–60.

Main, O. W. "Higher Education for Business," *Can. Chart. Acc.* LXXXI, 50–55.

1963 Bisson, A. et M. Lemay. « Le Centre de recherche de la faculté de commerce », *Vieil Esch.* XV, no 4, 4–7.

Reesor, L. J. "The Examination as a Test of Competence," *Can. Chart. Acc.* LXXXII, 286–89.

1964 Byrd, K. F. "The University's Contribution to the Education of C.A.s," *Can. Chart. Acc.* LXXXIV, 41–47.

DENTISTRY : ART DENTAIRE

1896 "The Dental Profession and Bishop's College," *Canada Medical Record* XXIV, 241–45.

1898 Woodbury, F. "Education of the Dental Surgeon," *Dominion Dental Journal* X, 381–84.

1903 Pearson, C. E. "Report of Dental Education in Ontario, Canada," *Dominion Dental Journal* XV, 304–309.

1914 Woodbury, F. "The Education of the Dentist," *Dominion Dental Journal* XXVI, 120–26.

1918 Conboy, F. J. "Medical and Dental Education in Ontario," *Oral Health* VIII, 185–87.

1924 Gies, W. J. "The Dental Educational Problem," *Oral Health* XIV, 91–106.

1925 Gies, W. J. "Report on Dental Education in America," *Dominion Dental Journal* XXXVII, 156–63.

1930 Garvin, M. H. "Dental Education in Canada," *Oral Health* XX, 513–26.

1941 Walsh, A. L. "Dental Education in Canada during Wartime," *Jour. Can. Dent. Assoc.* VII, 285–92.

1945 De Montigny, G. « La Faculté de chirurgie dentaire », *Act. Univ.* XI, 66–69.

1946 Mason, A. D. "Facilities for Training in Dentistry for Children at the Faculty of Dentistry, University of Toronto," *Ontario Dental Association Journal* XXI, 54–56.

1947 "The Status of Foreign Dentists in Canada," *Oral Health* XXXVII, 387–90.

1948 Ellis, R. G. "Report to the Dental Profession on Dental Education," *Ontario Dental Association Journal* XXIII, 49–55.

1949 Ellis, R. G. "Dental Education and the Profession," *Jour. Can. Dent. Assoc.* XV, 3–7.

1950 Ellis, R. G. and T. Cowling. "University of Toronto (Faculty of Dentistry)," *Dental Record* [U.K.] LXX, 114–22.

1952 Mitton, G. T. "Functions of a Department of Dental Health in the Dental School," *Jour. Can. Dent. Assoc.* XVIII, 528–36.

Williams, C. H. M. and A. W. S. Wood. "The Present Status of Dental Research in Canada," *Jour. Can. Dent. Assoc.* XXII, 712–15.

1956 De Montigny, G. « L'Enseignement dentaire », *Jour. Can. Dent. Assoc.* XXII, 439–42.

Ellis, R. G. "A Review of Dental Education Suggests a Fertile Field for Research," *Australian Dental Journal* I, 8–11.

Macdonald, J. B. *A Prospectus on Dental Education for the University of British Columbia.* Vancouver: Univ. of British Columbia. Pp. 105.

1957 Macdonald, J. B. "Role of Basic Sciences in Dental Education," *Journal of Dental Education* [U.S.] XXI, 17–21.

Mather, J. M. "Changing Picture of Professional Education," *Jour. Can. Dent. Assoc.* XXIII, 453–58.

Timmons, G. D. "Dental Education and the Dental Manpower Shortage," *Jour. Can. Dent. Assoc.* XXIII, 503–509.

1958 Tulley, W. J. "Report on a Visit to the United States and Canada," *Transactions of British Society for the Study of Orthodontics,* 166–74.

"Fifty Years of Dental Education Commemorated by Dalhousie Faculty Opening," *Jour. Can. Dent. Assoc.* XXIV, 659–65.

1959 Ellis, R. G. "Will Today's Plans Satisfy Tomorrow's Needs?" *Journal of Ontario Dental Association* XXXVI, 4–9.

1961 Hollinshead, B. S. *The Survey of Dentistry: The Final Report of the Commission on the Survey of Dentistry in the United States.* Washington: American Council on Education. Pp. 603.

Dunn, W. J. "The Organization and Conduct of an Evening Course for Dental Assistants," *Jour. Can. Dent. Assoc.* XXVII, 491–503.

1962 Farquharson, R. F. *et al.* "Medical and Dental Education in Canadian Universities" in D. Dunton and D. Patterson, eds., *Canada's Universities in a New Age* (Ottawa: N.C.C.U.C.), 61–83.

Nikiforuk, G.   "The Division of Dental Research, University of Toronto," *Jour. Can. Dent. Assoc.* XXVIII, 709–18.

Williams, D. C.   "New Developments in Education," *Jour. Can. Dent. Assoc.* XXVIII, 18–20.

1963   Warnberg, A. S. et M. M. Dines.   « Evolution actuelle de l'enseignement de la périodontie », *Jour. Can. Dent. Assoc.* XXIX, 353–59.

1964   Anderson, P. G.   "Practical Applications in Accelerated Preclinical and Clinical Teaching," *Journal of Dental Education* [U.K.] XXVIII, 130–34.

Grainger, R. M.   "Dental Research at the University of Toronto," *Ontario Dental Association Journal* XLI, 23–24.

Royal Commission on Health Services.   *Report of.* . . . Ottawa: Queen's Printer. 2 vols.

ENGINEERING : GÉNIE

1919   Roy, P.-G.   « Un Hydrographe du roi à Québec, Jean-Baptiste-Louis Franquelin », *Mém. S.R.C.* Sect. I, 47–59.

1941   Université Laval.   *L'Inauguration de l'Ecole des Mines de l'Université Laval.* Québec : Univ. Laval. Pp. 73.

1949   Nelson, L. D.   "The Prediction of Achievement in First Year Engineering." Unpublished M.A. thesis, Univ. of Alberta.

1954   Plewes, A. C.   "The Technical Training of the Canadian Chemical Engineer," *Chem. Can.* XII, 39–42.

Stirling, J. B.   *The First Hundred Years.* Fredericton: Univ. of New Brunswick. Pp. 13.

1958   Conn, H. G.   "Engineering Education in Canada," *Eng. Jour.* XLI, no. 12, 38–42.

Porter, A.   "The Balance between Theory and Practice in Engineering Education" in *Canadian Convention Record 1958* (Toronto: Canadian Sections of the Institute of Radio Engineers), 187–90.

1959   Batke, T. L.   "Engineering Education at Waterloo," *Chem. Can.* XI (August), 43–46.

Beaulieu, P.   "What Happens to Applicants for National Research Council Scholarships in Science and Engineering," *Eng. Jour.* XLII, no. 3, 71–80.

Church, J. A. H.   "Education for Surveyors," *Can. Surveyor* XIV, 361–62.

Christopherson, D. G.   "Engineering as Liberal Education," *Can. Consulting Eng.* I, no. 1, 49–50, 78.

"Ecole Polytechnique—New Engineering Building," *Eng. Jour.* XLII, no. 6, 43–52.

Jones, L. E.   "Computers and the Engineering Student," *Can. Consulting Eng.* I, no. 3, 52–55.

"New Engineers—the Story Three Years Later," *Can. Consulting Eng.* I, no. 5, 34–37.

1960   Bereskin, A. I.   "A Forecast of Saskatchewan Government Need for Surveyors and Some Aspects of Their Training," *Can. Surveyor* XV, 27–31.

Boston, R. E. "The Training of Engineering Technicians," *Jour. Ed.*, no. 4, 79–84.

Campling, C. H. R. "Accreditation for Canadian Engineering Curricula?" *Eng. Jour.* XLIII, no. 3, 87–92.

de Jong, S. H. "The Present Status of Surveying Education in Canada," *Can. Surveyor* XV, 54–60.

Howlett, L. E. "The Crisis in Survey Education," *Can. Surveyor* XV, 67–74.

"Interim Report of Education Subcommittee: Draft Proposal of University Degree Course in Surveying," *Can. Surveyor* XV, 23–25.

Kerwin, L. "Atomic Physics for General Science and Engineering Students," *Physics in Canada* XVI, no. 4, 21–26.

Konecny, G. "The New Bachelor of Surveying Engineering Curriculum at the University of New Brunswick," *Can. Surveyor* XV, 135–37.

Myers, B. R. "The Early Physics Courses in the Undergraduate Engineering Curriculum," *Physics in Canada* XVI, no. 4, 14–20.

Plewes, A. C. "Chemical Engineering Training at Queen's," *Chem. Can.* XII (September), 88–92.

Porter, A. "Keynote Address: Technometrics and Education" in *Proceedings of the Second Conference of the Computing and Data Processing Society of Canada, June 1960* (Toronto: U. of T. Press), 1–12.

Roberts, W. F. "Need for Trained Surveyors as Seen by the Association of New Brunswick Land Surveyors," *Can. Surveyor* XV, 18–20.

Rousseau, L. Z. "Survey Education at Laval University," *Can. Surveyor* XV, 61–67.

"The Universities' Views on Survey Education," *Can. Surveyor* XV, 74–85.

Van Steenburgh, W. E. "The Changing Aspects of Survey Training for Surveys and Mapping by the Federal Government," *Can. Surveyor* XV, 15–17.

1961 "Are Europeans Better Educated Engineers?" *Can. Consulting Eng.* III, no. 9, 60–63.

Beattie, I. M. "Survey Education Discussed at New Brunswick Meeting," *Can. Surveyor* XV, 357–61.

Dick, G.-M. "Engineering for Tomorrow," *Ing.* XLVII, no. 185, 37–41.

"Engineering at McMaster," *Chem. Can.* XIII (February), 40–42.

Goodings, B. H. "The Engineering Technician—His Present and His Future," *Design Eng.* VII, no. 1, 38–40.

Konecny, G. "The Survey Engineering Course; Thoughts after Completion of the First Term," *Can. Surveyor* XV, 371–75.

Myers, B. R. "Trends in Electrical Engineering Education," *Eng. Jour.* XLIV, no. 2, 65–69.

"No Faculty Can Train Engineer and Technician," *Can. Consulting Eng.* III, no. 6, 38–41.

Porter, A. "Trends in Engineering Training," *Eng. Jour.* XLIV, no. 9, 95–100.

Stone, J. S.   "Humanities and Social Sciences for Canadian Engineering Students," *Queen's Q.* LXVIII, 402–10.

"Time for Change in Engineering Education?" *Can. Consulting Eng.* III, no. 5, 38–41.

1962 Dalla Lana, I. G. and D. L. Flock.   "Chemical and Petroleum Engineering at University of Alberta, Edmonton," *Chem. Can.* XIV (April), 31–32.

"Engineering Education in Canada," *Eng. Jour.* XLV, no. 9, 60–70, 96, 98; XLVI, no. 1, 42–49, 62–66.

Golding, R. C.   "Work-and-Study Graduates Join Industry," *Modern Power and Engineering* LVI, 59–61.

Lash, S. D.   "Civil Engineering Education," *Eng. Jour.* XLV, no. 5, 50–53.

McMullen, W. F.   "Engineering Education—Have We a Problem?" *Eng. Jour.* XLV, no. 1, 52–54.

Myers, D. M.   "Urgent Tasks in Engineering Education," *Eng. Jour.* XLV, no. 6, 102–106.

Porter, A.   *Industrial Engineering in Retrospect and Prospect.* Toronto: Faculty of Applied Science and Engineering, Univ. of Toronto. Pp. 37.

"Success at Waterloo: The Changing Face of Engineering Education," *Can. Consulting Eng.* IV, 61.

Warren, J.   "Industrial Design Education . . . Weighed and Found Wanting," *Design Eng.* VIII, no. 9, 49–51.

1963 "Are University Entrance Standards Too High?" *Can. Consulting Eng.* V, no. 4, 44–48.

Bonenfant, F. *et al.* *Cri d'alarme... la civilisation scientifique et les Canadiens français.* Québec : Presses Univ. Laval. Pp. 142.

Christie, A. G.   *What Does an Engineer Do?* New York: Vantage Press. Pp. 306.

Gaudefroy, H.   « L'Etudiant-ingénieur à Polytechnique », *Ing.* XLIV, no 194, 27–31.

Hughes, P. B.   *The Engineering Report in the Under-Graduate Laboratory.* Toronto: Longmans. Pp. 83.

Mackenzie, C. J.   "The Real Application of Science: A Recent Phenomenon," *Can. Surveyor* XVII, 255–60.

Rensaa, E. M.   "Degrees Don't Make an Engineer," *Can. Consulting Eng.* V, no. 10, 51–53.

1964 Booth, A. D.   "Engineering Research in the University of Saskatchewan," *Saskatchewan Engineer* XVIII, 9–11.

Canada, Department of Labour, Economics and Research Branch. *Drop-out Rates in University Engineering Courses.* Ottawa: Queen's Printer.

Flock, D. L.   "Education for the Petroleum Industry," *Journal of Canadian Petroleum Technology* III, no. 1, 20–23.

Freund, C. J.   "How to Teach Engineering Design," *Design Eng.* X, no. 1, 32–34.

Hiscocks, R. D.   "A Career in Aerospace Sciences and Technology," *Canadian Aeronautics and Space Journal* X, no. 3, 73–82; X, no. 4, 93–102.

Myers, B. R. *North of the Border: A Story Resulting From Two Years in Canada.* New York: Vantage. Pp. 214.

Neville, A. M. "Civil Engineering Education in the University," *Eng. Jour.* XLVII, no. 1, 29–31.

Williamson, D. "Why No Challenge for Canada's Industrial Engineers?" *Plant Admin. Eng.* XXIV, no. 1, 34–36.

FORESTRY : GÉNIE FORESTIER

1903 Loudon, J. "Forestry and the University Question," *University of Toronto Monthly* III, 177–84.

1950 Bureau, R. « Un Pionnier de la science forestière au Canada français [J.-C.-K. LaFlamme] », *Rev. Univ. Laval* V, 175–78.

1954 Duff, G. H. "The Glendon Hall Laboratory and Garden, University of Toronto," *Garden Journal* [U.S.] IV, 175–78.

"The University Forest," *University of Toronto Bulletin* (Autumn), 19–22.

1955 University of New Brunswick, Faculty of Forestry. "Cradle of Foresters," *Timber of Canada* XV, no. 6, 40–42.

1956 Gibson, J. M. "Forestry at the University of New Brunswick," *Timber of Canada* XVII, no. 8, 28–31, 34.

1959 Canadian Institute of Forestry. *Forestry Education in Ontario.* Papers Presented at the Meeting for Guidance Directors, March 12th, 1959. Toronto: Southern Ontario Section, Canadian Institute of Forestry. Pp. 38.

Dosne, J. J. E. "The Forester of Tomorrow," *For. Chron.* XXXV, 104–108.

1960 Canadian Institute of Forestry. *Forestry Education in Canada: Proceedings of the Joint Forestry Convention.* Quebec: Canadian Institute of Forestry. Pp. 134.

Maheux, G. « Un Demi-Siècle en retrospective 1910–1960 »/"Half a Century in Retrospective 1910–1960," *For. et Cons.* XXVI, no 10, 14–15, 17–18.

« Les Points saillants de l'histoire de la foresterie dans la Province de Québec », *For. et Cons.* XXVI, no 10, 21–22.

Rousseau, L. Z. « L'Université Laval et la formation professionnelle de l'arpenteur-géomètre », *For. et Cons.* XXVI, no 10, 34–35.

Sisam, J. W. B. "Developing Technical Education Programs: The Ranger School" in *Proceedings of the Fifth World Forestry Congress* (Seattle: Univ. of Washington), 1210–15.

Université Laval. *Cinquantenaire de l'enseignement des sciences forestières à l'Université Laval, 1910–1960.* Québec : Presses Univ. Laval. Pp. 39.

Université Laval, le Comité au Cinquantenaire. « Cinquantenaire de l'enseignement forestier à Laval, 1910–1960 », *Vieil Esch.* XII, no 2, 24–25.

1961 Rousseau, L. Z. "50 Years of Forestry Teaching at Laval," *Pulp and Paper Magazine of Canada* LXII, 227–30.

Sisam, J. W. B.   *Forestry Education at Toronto*. Toronto: U. of T. Press. Pp. 116.

1962   Allen, G. S.   "The Role of Technical Training in Canadian Forestry," *For. Chron.* XXXVIII, 70–73.

Kér, J. W.   "Canadian Experience with the Five-Year Undergraduate Forestry Curriculum," *For. Chron.* XXXVIII, 63–69.

Smith, A., R. W. Wellword, and L. Valg, eds.   "Canadian Theses in Forestry and Related Subject Fields, 1913–1962," *For. Chron.* XXXVIII, 376–94.

1963   Honer, T. G.   "Mathematics and Mensuration in the Forestry Curriculum," *Proceedings, Society of American Foresters*, 42–45.

Lafond, A.   « La Recherche forestière à l'Université Laval », *Vieil Esch.* XV, no 3, 19–21.

Rousseau, L. Z. *et al.*   *The Preparation of Future Canadian Forest Managers: A Symposium*. Montreal: Woodlands Section No. 2219, Canadian Pulp and Paper Assoc. Pp. 12.

1964   Armson, K.   "Professional Education," *For. Chron.* XL, 18–19.

Dumaine, G.   "Training of Foresters," *For. Chron.* XL, 6–8.

Fensom, K. G.   "Blueprinting Forestry Education Patterns in Canada," *For. Chron.* XL, 12–17.

Place, I. C. M.   "Training and Education in a Technological Age," *For. Chron.* XL, 20–26.

HOUSEHOLD SCIENCE : DIÉTÉTIQUE ET SCIENCES DOMESTIQUES

1937   Ferguson, R. H.   "Home Background of Home Economics Students of the University of Manitoba as an Index to College Training for Family Living." Unpublished M.A. thesis, Iowa State College of Agriculture and Mechanic Arts.

1943   Tessier, A.   *L'Enseignement ménager dans la Province de Québec*. Québec. Pp. 141.

1948   Binnie, R.   "In-Service Education of Home Economics Teachers in the Province of Nova Scotia." Unpublished M.A. thesis, Syracuse Univ.

1950   Chapman, E.   "Mrs. Adelaide Hoodless," *Food for Thought* XI, no. 2, 15–20.

1961   Lortie, L.   "Home Economics: Its Place in the University," *Can. Home Econ. Jour.* XI, no. 3, 11, 31.

1962   Patillo, M. H.   "Home Economics Extension Services for Canadian Women," *Can. Home Econ. Jour.* XII, no. 1, 9–12.

Rowles, E. C.   "Home Economics—A Basic Discipline," *Can. Home Econ. Jour.* XII, no. 2, 43–45.

Stedman, L. A.   "Changing Viewpoints in Home Economics," *Can. Home Econ. Jour.* XII, no. 2, 51–54.

1964   Rowles, E. C.   *Home Economics in Canada: The Early History of Six College Programs: Prologue to Change*. Saskatoon: Univ. of Saskatchewan Bookstore. Pp. 128.

JOURNALISM : JOURNALISME

1902 Gadsby, H. F. "Journalism," *University of Toronto Monthly* III, 74–78.

Macmechan, A. "Journalism: Another View," *University of Toronto Monthly* III, 95–99.

1960 Francœur, J. « Conditions d'influence du journalisme étudiant », *Cah. Act. Cath.* CXCVII, 115–22.

1962 Gariépy, G. *Etudiant et journaliste.* Montréal : Centre de Psychologie et de Pédagogie. Pp. 214.

Girard, J. « Le Journalisme étudiant », *Maintenant,* 60–62.

1963 Schrader, E. M. and E. R. Johnston. *Campus Reporter: A Cub Reporter's Introduction to Newspaper Work.* Ottawa: Canadian University Press. Pp. 152.

LAW : DROIT

1889 Pagnuelo, S. *Lettres sur la réforme judiciaire.* Montréal. Pp. 241.

1898 Walton, F. P. *The Work of a Faculty of Law in a University: Annual McGill University Lecture.* Montreal. Pp. 16.

1926 Riddell, W. R. "The Law Society of Upper Canada in 1822," *Ontario Historical Society Papers and Records* XXIII, 450–61.

1933 Coleman, E. H. "Legal Education," *Man. Bar News* V (January), 1–3, 5–6.

Roy, P.-G. *Les Juges de la Province de Québec.* Québec : Rédempti Paradis. Pp. 588.

1942 Nantel, M. « Les Avocats à Montréal », *Cah. Dix* VII, 185–213.

1945 Nantel, M. « La Communauté des avocats », *Cah. Dix* X, 263–91.

1946 Nantel, M. « Nos Institutions politiques et judiciaires », *Cah. Dix* XI, 191–200.

1948 Bassett, J. "The Function of the University in the Modern World," *U.N.B. Law Sch. Jour.* I, 6–13.

McInerney, K. C. "Notes on the Law School History," *U.N.B. Law Sch. Jour.* I, 14–18.

1949 Nantel, M. « L'Etude du droit et le barreau », *Cah. Dix* XIV, 11–38.

Smith, S. E. "Legal Education and Universities," *Univ. Tor. Law Jour.* VIII, 3–6.

University of British Columbia, Faculty of Law. "Symposium on Legal Education in British Columbia," *U.B.C. Legal Notes* I (April 1949), 4–14, (November 1950), 13–25. The November issue includes the following: Cronkite, F. C. "Pre-Legal Education," 13–16; Wright, C. A. "The University Course in Law," 16–20; MacDonald, V. C. "Professional Aspects of Legal Education," 20–22.

1950 Nantel, M. « Un Demi-siècle de vie judiciaire », *Cah. Dix.* XV, 219–45.

Williams, E. K. "Legal Education in Manitoba: 1913–1950," *Can. Bar Rev.* XXVIII, 759–79, 880–92.

1952 Armstrong, C. H. A. and E. Arthur. *The Honourable Society of Osgoode Hall.* Toronto: Clarke, Irwin. Pp. 62.

Hanson, J. C. "The Association of Canadian Law Teachers," *U.N.B. Law Sch. Jour.* VI, no. 1, 7–9.

Nantel, M. « En marge d'un centenaire », *Cah. Dix* XVII, 233–44.

1953 Chitty, R. M. W. "Legal Education," *Chitty's Law Jour.* III, 89–94.

1954 Buchwald, H. "The Manitoba Law School: Forty Years," *Man. Bar News* XXVI (October), 77–82.

Tallin, G. P. R. "Legal Education in Manitoba," *Man. Bar News* XXVI (June), 44–50.

1955 McAllister, G. A. "Some Phases of Legal Education in New Brunswick," *U.N.B. Law Sch. Jour.* VIII (May), 33–50.

1956 Read, H. E. (chairman). "Report of Special Committee on Educational Standards," *Chitty's Law Jour.* VI, 223–26, 231–32.

Schmitt, G. R. "Legal Education," *Sask. Bar Rev.* XXI, no. 2, 19–30.

1957 Abel, A. S. "Introduction to Legal Writing," *Univ. Tor. Law Jour.* XII, 81–86.

Caron, G. "The Faculty of Law of the University of Ottawa," *Univ. Tor. Jour.* XII, 292–95.

Corry, J. A. "The Queen's University Faculty of Law," *Univ. Tor. Law Jour.* XII, 290–92.

Goldenberg, J. M. "Advice to Law Students," *Chitty's Law Jour.* VII, 145–48, 156.

Kilgour, D. G. "Accounting and Trade Regulation," *Univ. Tor. Law Jour.* XII, 86–90.

Leal, H. A. "Osgoode Hall Law School—Today and Tomorrow," *Univ. Tor. Law Jour.* XII, 285–90.

Milner, J. B. "Community Planning Law," *Univ. Tor. Law Jour.* XII, 90–94.

Wright, C. A. "The Outlook for Ontario Legal Education," *Univ. Tor. Law Jour.* XII, 282–85.

1958 Common, E. C. "The Role of the Notary in the Province of Quebec," *Can. Bar Rev.* XXXVI, 333–50.

Pepin, E. «L'Enseignement du droit aérien dans le monde », *McGill Law Jour.* IV, 111–43.

Prevost, Y. « Collaboration nécessaire entre les facultés de droit et les corps professionnels », *Rev. Barr.* XVIII, 449–53.

1959 Bowker, W. F. "Legal Writing at the University of Alberta," *Univ. Tor. Law Jour.* XIII, 85–88.

Conference of the Governing Bodies of the Legal Profession in Canada, Special Committee. "Practical Training in Legal Education," *Can. Bar Jour.* II, 121–31.

Goldenberg, J. M. "Practical Legal Training," *Can. Bar Assoc. Papers,* 204–18.

Milner, J. B. "Fact and Fancy in the Idea of a University Law Faculty," *Univ. Tor. Law Jour.* XIII, 34–44.

Nicholls, G. V. V. "A Course on Legal Research and Writing," *Univ. Tor. Law Jour.* XIII, 88–92.

Read, H. E. "The Programme in Legislation at Dalhousie Law School," *Univ. Tor. Law Jour.* XIII, 81–85.

1960 Bergeron, V. et J.-C.-M. Coutu. « Méthode de recherches juridiques », *Rev. Univ. Ottawa*, XXX, 365–85.

Edwards, J. "Canadian Teaching and Research in Criminology," *Univ. Tor. Law Jour.* XIII, 214–35.

Kilgour, D. G. "A Note on Legal Education in Ontario 125 Years Ago," *Univ. Tor. Law Jour.* XIII, 270–74.

Le Dain, G. "The Practical Training of Law Students in the Province of Quebec," *Can. Bar Jour.* III, 242–47.

Thompson, A. R. "An Introductory Course in Law at the University of Alberta," *Univ. Tor. Law Jour.* XIII, 274–77.

1961 Bonenfant, J.-C. « L'Enseignement du droit romain », *McGill Law Jour.* VII, 213–24.

Castel, J. G. "New Developments at Osgoode Hall Law School: Public International Law and Comparative Law," *Univ. Tor. Law Jour.* XIV, 108–14.

Cohen, M. "Lawyers and Learning: The Professional and Intellectual Traditions," *McGill Law Jour.* VIII, 181–91.

Curtis, G. F. "Trends in Legal Education," *Can. Bar Jour.* IV, 21–29.

Fauteux, G. « Le Barreau et les facultés de droit », *McGill Law Jour.* VII, 203–207.

Gibson, R. D. "Three Experiments," *Can. Bar Jour.* IV, 327–30.

Giffen, P. J. "Social Control and Professional Self-Government: A Study of the Legal Profession in Canada" in S. D. Clark, ed., *Urbanism and the Changing Canadian Society* (Toronto: U. of T. Press), 117–34.

Huberman, D. S. M. "Law Schools Should Teach Estate Planning," *Can. Bar Jour.* IV, 162–79.

Le Dain, G. "Theory and Practice of Legal Education," *McGill Law Jour.* VII, 192–203.

Morton, J. D. "New Developments at Osgoode Hall Law School: The Programme of Studies in Criminal Law," *Univ. Tor. Law Jour.* XIV, 114–15.

Rand, L. C. "The New Faculty of Law at the University of Western Ontario," *Univ. Tor. Law Jour.* XIV, 107–108.

Read, H. E. "The Public Responsibilities of the Academic Law Teacher in Canada," *Can. Bar Rev.* XXXIX, 232–48.

Stein, A. L. "Practical Training for Trial of Civil Cases," *McGill Law Jour.* VII, 207–13.

Willis, J. "Administrative Law in Canada," *Can. Bar Rev.* XXXIX, 251–65.

1962 Beetz, J. « Inauguration de l'Institut de Recherche en Droit Public », *Thémis* XII, 66–68.

Caron, M. «La Formation universitaire des notaires », *Rev. Notariat* LXIV, 11–12, 509–19.

Carrothers, A. W. R. "The Graduate Programme [at U.B.C.]," *U.B.C. Law Rev.* I, 560–62.

Dunlop, B. "A Different Approach to Teaching Evidence," *Univ. Tor. Law Jour.* XIV, 260–62.

Jabour, T. "Law Students Form Association," *Can. Bar Jour.* V, 169–75.

Milner, J. B. "Ontario Legal Education—Some Background Facts," *Can. Bar Jour.* V, 310–21.

Roberts, R. J. "The Bar Admission Course," *Can. Bar Jour.* V, 474–85.

Rosevear, A. B. "McGill's Institute of Air and Space Law," *Univ. Tor. Law Jour.* XIV, 257–60.

Vachon, A. *Histoire du notariat canadien 1621–1960.* Québec : Presses Univ. Laval. Pp. 209.

Wright, C. A. "Law as a University Discipline," *Univ. Tor. Law Jour.* XIV, 253–57.

1963 Azard, P. and T. G. Feeney. "The Canadian and Foreign Law Research Centre at the University of Ottawa," *Univ. Tor. Law Jour.* XV, 186–87.

Lamonte, F. B. "Legal Education in Manitoba," *Man. Bar News* XXXV, 29–33.

Lederman, W. R. "Law Schools and Legal Ethics," *Can. Bar Assoc. Papers,* 28–97.

Patenaude, L. "The Public Law Research Institute at the University of Montreal," *Univ. Tor. Law Jour.* XV, 185–86.

Thompson, A. R. "The Course in Land Titles at the University of Alberta," *Alta. Law Rev.* III, 117–23.

Wright, C. A. "Legal Education: Past and Present" in R. St. J. Macdonald, ed., *Changing Legal Objective* (Toronto: U. of T. Press), 3–16.

LIBRARY SCIENCE : BIBLIOTHÉCONOMIE

1945 Morisset, A. M. *La Bibliothèque de l'Université d'Ottawa, son rôle et ses initiatives.* Montréal : Imprimerie Populaire. Pp. 8.

1948 Snider, W. D. "Extramural Library Service in Libraries and Extension Departments of Canadian Universities." Unpublished M.A. thesis, Columbia Univ.

1952 Campion, A. L. "Education for Special Librarians in the United States and Canada in 1946 and 1952." Unpublished M.A. thesis, Drexel Institute of Technology.

1956 Bassam, B. "Education for Librarianship Today," *Can. Lib. Assoc. Bull.* XII, 139–42.

1957 Carnovsky, L. "Education for Librarianship," *Feliciter* III, 15–22.

1959 Desrochers, E. « Une Législation relative aux bibliothèques », *Relations* XIX, 16–18.

Laplante, R. « Le Livre et ses problèmes », *Culture* XX, 118–30.
Rothstein, S. "Education for Librarianship in the Pacific Northwest," *B.C. Lib. Q.* XXIII, no. 3, 14–16.
Wiedrick, L. *et al.* "A Survey of School Libraries in Canada," *Can. Lib. Assoc. Bull.* XV, 172–97.
1960 Bell, I. F. "Libraries and Librarianship: Canada, 1959/60," *B.C. Lib. Q.* XXIV, no. 2, 5–15.
Canadian Library Association. "Library Education in Canada," *Feliciter* VI, 8–22.
Chemer, A. « La Profession de bibliothécaire et les collèges », *Coll. et Fam.* XVII, 240–45.
Desrochers, E. « Une Ecole professionnelle de bibliothécaires », *Relations* XX, 214–15.
Desrochers, E. "Canadian Library Education and Certification," *American Library Association Bulletin* LIV, 310–12.
Fraser, M. D. E. "Canadian Medical School Libraries and their Collections," *Medical Library Association Bulletin* [U.S.] XLVIII, 149–61.
1961 Bowron, A. W. "Central Processing for Ontario Libraries," *Ont. Lib. Rev.* XLV, 100–104.
Demers, H. « La Bibliothéconomie, une profession ? » *Bull. Bibl.* VII, 115–17.
Denis, L. G. « Ecole de Bibliothéconomie de l'Université de Montréal », *Bull. Bibl.* VII, 78–84.
Desrochers, E. "A Professional School for Librarians," *Feliciter* VI, 31–33.
Desrochers, E. « Bibliographie sommaire sur la profession de bibliothécaire », *Bull. Bibl.* VII, 18–25.
Drolet, A. « Une Bibliothèque de langue française à Québec en 1843 », *Vie Fr.* XV, 229–37.
Gundy, H. P. "A National Library for Canada—A Record and a Promise," *Can. Lib. Assoc. Bull.* XVII, 170–78.
Leduc, J.-R. « Ecole de bibliothécaires de l'Université de Montréal », *Bull. Bibl.* VII, 37–40.
« Réorganisation de l'Ecole de Bibliothécaires à l'Université de Montréal », *Feliciter* VI, 17–18.
Smith, A. M. "Recruiting," *B.C. Lib. Q.* XXIV, no. 4, 13–19.
1962 Association des Bibliothécaires du Québec. A *Brief Submitted to the Royal Commission of Inquiry on Education/Mémoire soumis à la Commission Royale d'Enquête sur l'Enseignement.* Montréal : L'Association. Pp. 91.
Association Canadienne des Bibliothécaires de Langue Française. *Mémoire présenté à la Commission Royale d'Enquête sur l'Enseignement de la Province de Québec, Canada.* Montréal : L'Association. Pp. 35.
Association Canadienne des Bibliothécaires de Langue Française. *La Profession de bibliothécaire.* Montréal : L'Association. Pp. 156. Comprend : Bélisle, G. « Les Ecoles de bibliothécaires :

l'enseignement et la recherche », 62–68; Denis, L. G. « Le Cours sur les bibliothèques de collège dans le programme de l'Ecole de Bibliothéconomie de l'Université de Montréal », 98–102; Allard, G. « Les Collèges affiliés à l'Université de Montréal et les heures de travail personnel 'dérigé' dans les Hautes Classes », 111–14.

Freiser, L. H. "Toronto's New Education Centre Library," *Can. Lib. Assoc. Bull.* XVIII, 157–58.

Kent, C. D. "The Librarian as Educator," *Continuous Learning* I, no. 1, 10–15.

"The School of Librarianship: The University of British Columbia," *Alta. Lib. Assoc. Bull.* IX, no. 2, 16–19.

Taggart, W. R. "The Development of the Library Short Course in British Columbia," *B.C. Lib. Q.* XXV, no. 3, 21–27.

Tanghe, R. *Le Bibliothécariat.* Montréal : Fides. Pp. 117.

Tanghe, R. *L'Ecole de bibliothécaires de l'Université de Montréal 1937–1962.* Montréal : Fides. Pp. 69.

Williams, E. E. *Resources of Canadian University Libraries for Research in the Humanities and Social Sciences.* Ottawa: National Conference of Canadian Universities. Pp. 87./*Ressources des bibliothèques des universités canadiennes pour la recherche en humanités et en sciences sociales.* Ottawa: Conférence Nationale des Universités et Collèges Canadiens. Pp. 93.

1963 Hoeg, E. Z. "Torch—or Caber," *B.C. Lib. Q.* XXVII, no. 2, 18–21.

Peel, B. B. "Library Planning at the University of Alberta," *Can. Lib. Assoc. Bull.* XIX, 359–63.

Rothstein, S. "New School, Old Problem: Admission Policy and Procedure at the University of British Columbia School of Librarianship," *B.C. Lib. Q.* XXVII, no. 1, 3–7.

MEDICINE : MÉDECINE

1853 Hall, A. *An Apology for British and Colonial Medical Degrees or Strictures on the Report of the Special Committee of the Legislative Assembly on the Laws Relative to the Practice of Physic, Surgery and Midwifery in Lower Canada.* Montreal. Pp. 18.

1860 Hall, A. *Introductory Lecture to the Course of Midwifery and the Diseases of Women and Children, Including a Biographical Sketch of the Late A. F. Holmes, M.D., LL.D.* Montreal. Pp. 19.

1882 Howard, R. P. "A Sketch of the Life of the Late Dr. G. W. Campbell, and a Summary of the Early History of the Faculty" in *Semi-Centennial Celebration* (Montreal), 1–24.

1890 Fortier, L. E. *L'Ecole de Médecine.* Montréal. Pp. 16.

Powell, R. W. *The Doctor in Canada—His Whereabouts and the Laws which Govern Him.* Montreal. Pp. 342.

1892 Clark, D. *Notes on Mental Diseases by a Student: Dr. D. Clark, Lecturer.* Toronto. Pp. 96.

Un Etudiant en médecine aux Etats-Unis et dans Ontario. Montréal. Pp. 64.

1893 Macallum, A. B. *Retrospect, Aspect and Prospect in Medical Science: The Inaugural Lecture of the University Medical Faculty for 1893.* Toronto. Pp. 15.

1895 Craik, R. "Sketch of the History of the Faculty of Medicine" in *Annual Report of the Governors, Principal, and Fellows of McGill University for the Year 1894,* 19–28.

1901 Geikie, W. B. "Historical Sketch of Canadian Medical Education," *Canadian Lancet* XXXIV, 225–36.

1906 Gullen, A. S. *A Brief History of the Ontario Medical College for Women.* Toronto. Pp. 11.

1912 Du Sol, J. *Le Dr Hubert LaRue et l'idée canadienne-française.* Québec. Pp. 232.

1913 Clarke, C. K. *A History of the Toronto General Hospital.* Toronto. Pp. 147.

1922 Miller, J. "Colleague Examining: A Plea for its Adoption in Canadian Universities," *Queen's Q.* XXX, 37–41.

1923 Massicotte, E.-Z. « Les Chirurgiens, médecins, etc. de Montréal sous le régime français », *Rapport de l'Archiviste de...* Québec, 122–23, 132–35.

1925 Banting, F. "Medical Research," *Annals of Clinical Medicine* [U.S.] III, 565–72.

1926 Gagner, L.-A. *Droits et devoirs de la médecine et de médecins canadiens-français.* Montréal: Devoir. Pp. 122.

Hattie, W. H. "Modern Trends in Medical Education," *N.S. Med. Bull.* V, no. 10, 5–11.

1928 Gibson, T. "A Short Account of Medical Teaching in Kingston," *Can. Med. Assoc. Jour.* XVIII, 331–34, 446–51.

Wright, A. H. "The Medical Schools of Toronto," *Can. Med. Assoc. Jour.* XVIII, 616–20.

1930 Ferguson, J. *History of the Ontario Medical Association 1880–1930.* Toronto: Murray. Pp. 142.

1931 Gwyn, M. B. "Some Details Connected with the Evolution of Medical Education in Toronto," *University of Toronto Medical Journal* VIII, 224–29.

Reid, E. G. *The Great Physician: A Short Life of Sir William Osler.* Toronto: Oxford. Pp. 299.

1934 Howell, W. B. *F. J. Shepherd, Surgeon: His Life and Times.* Toronto: Dent. Pp. 251.

MacDermot, H. E. *A Bibliography of Canadian Medical Periodicals, with Annotations.* Montreal: Renouf. Pp. 21.

1935 Rankin, A. C. "The Provincial Medical School—The University of Alberta Faculty of Medicine," *Alta. Med. Bull.* I (July), 7–11.

1936 Gwyn, N. B. "A Chapter from the Life of John Rolph," *Academy of Medicine Bulletin* IX, 137–44.

1938 MacDermot, H. E. *Sir Thomas Raddick—His Work in Medicine and Public Life.* Toronto: Macmillan. Pp. 160.

1942 McFall, W. A. "The Life and Times of Dr. Christopher Widmer," *Annals of Medical History* [U.S.] IV, 324–34.

1946 Hall, G. E. "The Aims of Medical Education," *Ont. Med. Rev.* XIII, 64–69.

1950 Douville, R. « Chirurgiens, barbiers-chirurgiens et charlatans de la région trifluvienne sous le régime français », *Cah. Dix* XV, 81–128.

Mathers, A. T. "Some Thoughts on Broadening Medical Education," *N.S. Med. Bull.* XXIX, no. 1, 101–105.

1952 Maheux, A. "Centenary of the Faculty of Medicine of Laval University," *Can. Doctor* XVIII, no. 8, 44–48.

1953 Murphy, A. L. "Medical Education: An Informal Study," *N.S. Med. Bull.* XXXII, no. 1, 72–77.

1954 "Canada's Eleventh Medical School Graduates First Student Doctors," *Can. Doctor* XX, no. 7, 35–39.

Clegg, H., ed. *Proceedings of the First World Conference on Medical Education.* Toronto: Oxford Univ. Press. Pp. 804. Contains the following articles: Weaver, M. M. "Requirements for Entry into Medical School: Selection of Students in Canada," 187–93; Cameron, D. E. "The Teaching of Psychological Medicine," 302–12; Hobbs, G. E. "Present Status of the Teaching of Preventive and Social Medicine in Canada," 592–602.

Creamer, L. "The Faculty of Medicine of the University of Ottawa," *Can. Doctor* XX, no. 11, 28–32.

Malamad, W. "Psychotherapy in Medical Education," *N.S. Med. Bull.* XXXIII, no. 1, 125–33.

Queen's University, Faculty of Medicine. "Queen's Medical Centenary Number," *Can. Med. Assoc. Jour.* LXX, 235–322.

1955 Gundy, H. P. "Growing Pains: The Early History of the Queen's Medical Faculty," *Historic Kingston*, no. 4, 14–25.

1956 Pudymaitis, O. J. "Thoughts and Reflections about Medical Education, Education in General and Synthesis in Medicine," *N.S. Med. Bull.* XXXV, no. 1, 201–209.

1957 Gallie, W. E. "The University of Toronto Medical School—Fifty Years' Growth," *Med. Grad.* III, no. 2, 6–13.

1958 Bruce, H. A. *Varied Operations.* Toronto: Longmans, Green. Pp. 366.

1959 Bélisle, L.-Ph. « Histoire de la radiologie au Canada français », *Union Méd.* LXXXVII, 40–52.

David, P. « L'Institut de Cardiologie de Montréal », *Montréal Méd.* X, no 11, 10–17.

Dufresne, R. « Les Responsabilités d'une faculté de médecine », *Act. Univ.* XXV, 21–22, 25–26.

"Educational Issue," *Can. Med. Assoc. Jour.* LXXX, includes: Thompson, J. S. "Some Factors Shaping the Policies of Faculties of Medicine," 503–35; Scott, J. W. "Undergraduate, Postgraduate and Graduate Medical Education in Canada," 524–25; Macpherson, L. B. *et al.* "Canadian Schools of Medicine," 525–35. [Report on each medical school.]

« L'Enseignement médicale à l'Hôtel-Dieu », *Cah. Hôtel-Dieu* (1958–59), 373–88.

« Les Etudes médicales », *Act. Méd.* XXXV, 99–103.

Gravel, J.-A. « La Chirurgie cardiologie à l'Institut de Québec », *Laval Méd.* XXVIII, 455–67.

Monflette, G. « Mémoire presenté à l'Honorable A. Couturier, M.D. sur la rémunération des internes », *Act. Méd.* XXXVII, 37–46.

Robillard, E. « La Recherche dans l'enseignement universitaire », *Union Méd.* LXXXVIII, 316–19.

Roy, C.-C. « L'Enseignement infirmier à l'Hôtel-Dieu ; Enseignement clinique de base ; L'Enseignement clinique dans le service de Pédiatrie », *Cah. Hôtel-Dieu* (1958–59), 425–49.

Steeves, L. C. "The Dalhousie Post-Graduate Program: An Experience in Continuing Needed Education," *Journal of Medical Education* [U.S.] XXXIV, 236–38.

Wiggins, W. S., G. R. Shepherd, J. Hinman, and A. Tipner. "Medical Education in the United States and Canada," *Journal of the American Medical Association* CLXXI, 1507–75.

1960 Boissonault, C.-M. « Au Temps de Champlain », *Laval Méd.* XXX, 629–32.

Christie, R. V. "Training of a Physician," *McGill Medical Journal* XXIX, 167–72.

Chute, A. L. "Canadian Paediatric Contributions to Medical Progress," *Medical Library Association Bulletin* [U.S.] XLVIII, 37–43.

Drolet, A. « Le Médecin dans le roman canadien-français », *Laval Méd.* XXIX, 220–31.

"Educational Issue," *Can. Med. Assoc. Jour.* LXXXII, includes: Stewart, C. B. "Comments on the Teaching of Preventive Medicine in Canada," 719–23; Robertson, A. "The Place of Social Medicine in the Medical Curriculum," 724–26; Thompson, J. S. "Canadian Medical Education—Its Cost and Personnel," 726–29; Macpherson, L. B. *et al.* "Canadian Schools of Medicine," 529–31. [Report on each of the medical schools.]

Elliott, J. M. "The Early English Surgeons of Quebec," *Laval Méd.* XXX, 78–84.

Feasby, W. R. "The Discovery of Insulin," *Medical Library Association Bulletin* [U.S.] XLVIII, 11–20.

Ferguson, J. K. W. "Canadian Milestones in Medical Research," *Medical Library Association Bulletin* [U.S.] XLVIII, 21–26.

Fraser, M. D. E. "Canadian Medical School Libraries and Their Collections," *Medical Library Association Bulletin* [U.S.] XLVIII, 149–61.

Gibson, R. "Contribution of the Mental Deficiency Institution to the Training of Medical Students," *Can. Med. Assoc. Jour.* LXXXII, 481–84.

Jobin, P. « Le Professeur de carrière », *Laennec Méd.* XI, no 3, 26–29.

Laurin, C. and R. K. Lemieux. "A New Method of Teaching Psychiatry to Medical Students," *Can. Psych. Assoc. Jour.* V, 212–19.

Leblond, S. « Le Docteur Cyrille-Hector-Octave Coté et le mouvement baptiste français au Canada », *Laval Méd.* XIII, 633–42.

le Riche, W. H. "The Character of the Physician in Relation to Social and Economic Consequences of Specialization," *Can. Med. Assoc. Jour.* LXXXIII, 912–14.

Manzi, J. « L'Etudiant et l'hôpital », *Montréal Méd.* XII, no 3, 10–12.

Morin, V. « L'Evolution de la médecine au Canada français », *Cah. Dix* XXV, 65–83.

Robertson, A. "The Role of General Practice in Medical Education," *Can. Med. Assoc. Jour.* LXXXIII, 421–24.

Ross, H. M. "The Manitoba Conference on Education," *Man. Med. Rev.* XL, 457–63.

Severinghaus, A. E. "The Educated Physician," *McGill Medical Journal* XXIX (February), 1–13.

Stewart, C. B. "A Few Thoughts on Medical Education," *Dalhousie Med. Jour.* XIII, no. 1, 7–11.

Tanz, R. D. and R. T. Tanz. "The Honor System in United States and Canadian Medical Schools," *Journal of Medical Education* [U.S.] XXXV, 440–46.

Wiggins, W. S., G. R. Leymaster, A. N. Taylor, and A. Tipner. "Medical Education in the United States and Canada," *Journal of the American Association* CLXXIV, 1423–76.

1961 Badgley, R. F. "Sociology in the Medical Curriculum," *Can. Med. Assoc. Jour.* LXXXIV, 705–709.

Bartlett, L. C. "Study and Examinations," *Can. Assoc. Med. Students & Internes* XX, no. 3, 42–45.

Collip, J. B. "The Place of Research in the Training of Physicians at Both Undergraduate and Postgraduate Levels," *Ont. Med. Rev.* XXVIII, 268–70.

David, P. « Un Institut de Cardiologie : pourquoi ? » *Union Méd.* XC, 56–61.

"Educational Issue," *Can. Med. Assoc. Jour.* LXXXIV, includes: MacFarlane, J. A. "Medical School and Teaching Hospital: Problems of Present and Future Relationships," 683–86; Ettinger, G. H. "The Effects of the 'Farquharson Committee Report' on Canadian Medical Schools," 686–89; Thompson, J. S. "Wanted More and Better Medical Students: The Facts and Figures on Medical Education," 689–91; Williams, D. H. "The New Department of Continuing Medical Education, University of British Columbia: Its Comprehensive Co-operative Purpose," 694–95; Marshall, M. R. "Graduate Medical Training: Its Organization and Administration," 695–97; Stevenson, L. G. "A new Venture at McGill: The Combined Course in Science and Medicine," 697–98; Hastings, J. E. F. "Medical Education—The Challenge of Changing Patterns," 699–702; Williams, D. H. "The Teaching of Dermatology to Undergraduates at the University of British Columbia," 709–20; Macpherson, L. B. *et al.* "Canadian Schools of Medicine," 721–32. [Report on each of the medical schools.]

«L'Enseignement médical à l'Hôtel-Dieu de Québec», *Cah. Hôtel-Dieu* (1960–61), 407–63.

Farquharson, R. F. "Medical Education in Canadian Universities," *Can. Doctor* XXVII, no. 12, 32–37.

Hamilton, J. O. "The Future of Medical Education at the University of Toronto," *Med. Grad.* VIII, no. 1, 2–8.

Harris, R. I. "Fifty Years of Surgery: 1911–1961," *Can. Med. Assoc. Jour.* LXXXIV, 11–20.

Jobin, J.-B. « Evolution de l'enseignement à la faculté de médecine de l'Université Laval », *Laval Méd.* XXXII, 423–32.

Lecours, A. « L'Enseignement à l'hôpital sous l'assurance-hospitalisation en Ontario », *Union Méd.* XC, 515–19.

Macdonald, R. I. "Postgraduate Medical Education," *Ont. Med. Rev.* XXVIII, 274–77.

MacFarlane, J. A. "Medical Education: Prospects and Problems," *Ont. Med. Rev.* XXVIII, 270–74.

MacFarlane, J. A. "Medicine, Law and the University," *Can. Med. Assoc. Jour.* LXXXIV, 35–37.

Mather, J. M. and J. H. Read. "Research and Teaching Opportunities in a University–Centred Child Health Program," *Can. Med. Assoc. Jour.* LXXXV, 131–35.

"More Thoughts on Education in Canada," *Summary of the Shute Institute* (London, Ontario) XIII (December), 42–45.

Patterson, M. A. "The Life and Times of the Hon. John Rolph, M.D. (1793–1870)," *Medical History* [U.K.] V, 15–33.

Penfield, W. "To Cultivate the Groves of Academus," *Can. Med. Assoc. Jour.* LXXXV, 173–75.

Pinsonneault, G. « Progrès et problèmes de la médecine moderne », *Rev. Dom.* LXVII, 96–107.

"Problems in Medical Student Recruitment," *Can. Med. Assoc. Jour.* LXXXIV, 735–36.

Robertson, A. "A Commentary on Sociology in the Medical School," *Can. Med. Assoc. Jour.* LXXXIV, 703–704.

Sawyer, L. and B. Flohil. "Students Find Dollars Prime Qualifier," *Can. Doctor* XXVII, no. 3, 34–37.

Scarlett, E. P. "Fifty Years of Medicine, 1911–1961," *Can. Med. Assoc. Jour.* LXXXIV, 6–11.

Shute, E. V. "Two Types of Medical Education," *Ont. Med. Rev.* XXVIII, 278–80, 315.

Tremblay, V. « Le Docteur Cyrille Dubois, premier médecin de Chicoutimi », *Laval Méd.* XXXI, 183–90.

1962 "Argus." « L'Orientation vers la médecine », *Act. Méd.* XXXVIII, 102–108.

Bartlett, L. C. "Post-Graduate Surgical Education at the University of Manitoba," *Journal of Medical Education* [U.S.] XXXVII, **1021–23.**

David, P. « Au Cœur de la médecine », *Bull. Inf. Cath.* XXXIX, 133–39.

David, P. « La Nécessité de la recherche dans un hôpital d'enseignement », *Union Méd.* XCI, 656–59.

Drolet, A. « La Société canadienne d'histoire de la médecine (1957–1961) », *Laval Méd.* XXXIII, 117–19.

"Educational Issue," *Can. Med. Assoc. Jour.* LXXXVI, includes: Thompson, J. S. "The Facts and Figures of Canadian Medical Education," 605–608; Bocking, D. "Trends in Medical Education," 608–10; Jobin, J.-B. "Development of Instruction at the Faculty of Medicine, Laval University," 621–24; Martin, J. K. and T. R. Nelson. "Curriculum Planning: University of Alberta," 630–33; Williams, D. H. "The Department of Continuing Medical Education, University of British Columbia: A First Report—the Organizational Phase," 639–44; Millar, G. J. "Skip the Health Lesson, Teacher!" 644–47.

« L'Enseignement médical à l'Hôtel-Dieu », *Cah. Hôtel-Dieu* (1962), 337–70.

Farquharson, R. F. *et al.* "Medical and Dental Education in Canadian Universities" in *Canada's Universities in a New Age* (Ottawa: N.C.C.U.C.), 61–83.

Gilbert, J. « La Reconnaissance et l'enseignement de la chiropratique », *Maintenant*, 299–300.

Hunter, R. C. A., J. G. Lohrenz, and A. E. Schwartzman. "A Fifteen-Year Follow-Up Study of Medical Graduates," *Can. Med. Assoc. Jour.* LXXXVII, 865–67.

Jasmin, G. *et al.* « Les Départements de recherche à la faculté de médecine », *Montréal Méd.* XIV, no 2, 7–21.

Kourilsky, R. « Le Rayonnement spirituel du Canada en médecine », *France-Amérique* [France] LI, 151–52.

Langois, M. « La Bibliothèque médicale de l'Hôtel-Dieu de Québec (1600–1900) », *Laval Méd.* XXXIII, 38–42.

Lewis, D. S. *The Royal College of Physicians and Surgeons of Canada, 1930–1960.* Montreal: McGill Univ. Press. Pp. 241.

Stokes, A. B. "The Teacher-Pupil Relationship as the Basis of Psychiatric Education," *Can. Psych. Assoc. Jour.* II, 3–9.

1963 Anderson, D. O., E. Riches, and R. Zickmantel. "Factors Relating to Academic Performance of Medical Students at the University of British Columbia," *Can. Med. Assoc. Jour.* LXXXIX, 881–87.

Caron, W.-M. « La Formation du chirurgien », *Laval Méd.* XXXIV, 1032–37.

Clute, K. F. *The General Practitioner: A Study of Medical Education and Practice in Ontario and Nova Scotia.* Toronto: U. of T. Press. Pp. 566.

Corry, J. A. "Expansion of Higher Education," *Ont. Med. Rev.* XXX, 779–81.

De la Broquerie, F. « L'Enseignement de la pédiatrie à la faculté de médecine de Québec », *Laval Méd.* XXXIV, 870–81.

Detwiller, L. F. "The Teaching Hospital," *Can. Hosp.* XL, 48–54.

Detwiller, L. F. "University of British Columbia Health Science Centre," *Can. Hosp.* XL, 35–38.

Dryer, B. V. "Thinking Men and Thinking Machines in Medicine," *Can. Assoc. Med. Students & Internes* XXII, no. 2, 9–16.

"Educational Issue," *Can. Med. Assoc. Jour.* LXXXVIII, includes: Badgley, R. F. *et al.* "A Prospectus for Canadian Studies in Medical Education," 690–93; Macpherson, L. B. and B. J. Yoell. "The Social Background and Finances of Medical Students at Dalhousie University," 701–704; MacLeod, J. W. "Curriculum in Canadian Medical Education," 705–12; Stewart, C. B. and R. A. Stanley. "The Adequacy of Medical Education for General Practice," 712–20.

Gelinas, J. « Regards sur l'avenir de la profession médicale », *Laval Méd.* XXXIV, 357–64.

Gilbert, J. *L'Education sanitaire.* Montréal : Presses Univ. Montréal. Pp. 141.

Jobin, P. « Notre Enseignement de la médecine, est-il complet ? » *Union Méd.* XCII, 515–17.

Jobin, P. "Osler and Medical Education," *Laval Méd.* XXXIV, 864–69.

Mylks, G. R. W. "Medical Education," *Ont. Med. Rev.* XXX, 717–20.

Penfield, W. *The Second Career.* Boston: Little, Brown. Pp. 189.

Stokes, A. B. "Psychiatric Training for Future Responsibilities," *Can. Psych. Assoc. Jour.* VIII, 138–43.

1964 Botterell, E. H. "Problems of Medical Education in Canada," *Med. Grad.* X, no. 2, 2–4.

Chute, A. L. "Lecture on Medical Education," *Can. Assoc. Med. Students & Internes* XXIII, no. 2, 26–32.

"Educational Issue," *Can. Med. Assoc. Jour.* XC, includes: Law, J. T. "Hospital-Medical School Relationships," 819–23; Armstrong, H. S. "The Medical Faculty and Community," 830–33.

Judek, S. *Medical Manpower in Canada.* Study prepared by the Royal Commission on Health Services. Ottawa: Queen's Printer. Pp. 413.

Kling, S. "The Challenge of Continuing Medical Education," *Alta. Med. Bull.* XXIX, no. 1, 2–9.

MacFarlane, J. A. *et al. Medical Education in Canada.* Study prepared by the Royal Commission on Health Services. Ottawa: Queen's Printer. Pp. 373.

Royal Commission on Health Services. *Report of.* . . . Ottawa: Queen's Printer. 2 vols.

Simon, B. V. *Library Support of Medical Education and Research in Canada: Report of a Survey of the Medical College Libraries of Canada, together with Suggestions for Improving and Extending Medical Library Sources at Local, Regional and National Levels.* Ottawa: Assoc. of Canadian Medical Colleges. Pp. 133.

Weil, R. J. and S. Hirsch. "Psychotherapy and the Basic Training of the Psychiatrist," *Can. Psych. Assoc. Jour.* XIX, 72–77.

Wilson, P. L. "The Place of Internship and Residencies in Medical Education, Parts I and II," *Ont. Med. Rev.* XXXI, 195–202, 275–79, 284.

MILITARY COLLEGES : COLLÈGES MILITAIRES

1948   Chatwin, A. E. "Canadian Armed Forces" in G. B. Jeffery, ed., *The Year Book of Education* (London: Evans Brothers Limited), 164–68.

1955   Jeffels, R. R. "School for Subalterns," *Can. Army Jour.* IX, no. 1, 90–95.

1959   Kerr, J. G. "Address, National Conference of Canadian Universities and Colleges," *N.C.C.U.C. Proc.*, 18–23.

Rowley, R. "The New Staff College Course," *Can. Army Jour.* XIII, no. 3, 42–46.

1960   Lamontagne, L. « Le Collège Militaire Royale au Canada (Kingston) et la formation qu'il dépense », *Mém. S.R.C.* Sect. I, 37–47.

1961   Gunn, W. S. D. "The Army and the Universities," *Can. Army Jour.* XV, no. 1, 72–83.

Jette, J. A. T. M. « Vous êtes lents, messieurs ! » *Canadian Shipping and Marine Engineering News*, XXXII, 78–81, 106.

McCaughey, G. S. "The Canadian Services Colleges," *Professional Public Service* XL, no. 8, 11–15.

1962   McCaughey, G. S. "The Canadian Services Colleges," *Sch. Prog.* XXXI, no. 7, 44–46.

1963   "Military Education" in J. G. Glassco, Chairman, *Royal Commission on Government Organization, Report III* (Ottawa: Queen's Printer), 164–71.

Newson, W. F. M. "Professional Education in the R.C.A.F.," *Can. Army Jour.* XVII, no. 2, 47–55.

Percy, H. R. "Training the Navy's Officers," *Can. Army Jour.* XVII, no. 3, 57–69.

1964   "Kingston and its Universities," *Chem. Can.* XVI, no. 2, 41–44.

NURSING

1913   Clarke, C. K. *A History of the Toronto General Hospital.* Toronto. Pp. 147.

1920   Russell, E. K. "Public Health Field Work for the Undergraduate Nurse," *Can. Nurse* XVI, 462–64.

1922   Clarke, H. "A Study of Dietetic Courses for Pupil Nurses in Class 'A' Hospitals in the United States and Canada." Unpublished M.A. thesis, Ohio State Univ.

1940   Defries, R. D., ed. *The Development of Public Health in Canada: A Review of the History and Organization of Public Health in the Provinces of Canada.* Toronto: Canadian Public Health Association. Pp. 184.

MacDermot, H. E. *History of the School for Nurses of the Montreal General Hospital.* Montreal: The Alumnae Association. Pp. 125.

1943 Munroe, M. D. *The Training School for Nurses, Royal Victoria Hospital, 1894–1943.* Montreal: Alumnae Association. Pp. 92.

1945 Forest, J. "The Preparation of Survey Schedules for the Selection of the Facilities in Three Canadian Provinces for the Organization of a Collegiate Program in Nursing." Unpublished M.A. thesis, Catholic Univ. of America.

1947 LaFlamme, M. J. "A Study of Educational Requirements as Stated in Acts Relating to the Registration of Nurses Passed in the Nine Provinces of Canada from 1910 to 1944." Unpublished M.A. thesis, Catholic Univ. of America.

1950 Canadian Public Health Association. *Report of the Study Committee on Public Health Practice in Canada.* Toronto: The Association. Pp. 78.

1951 Lyons, C. M. "A Proposed Four-Year Curriculum Leading to a Baccalaureate Degree in Nursing in the Catholic Schools of Nursing in Nova Scotia." Unpublished M.A. thesis, Catholic Univ. of America.

Robert, F. C. "A Study of Advanced Programs in Teaching Supervision, and Administration in Nursing Education Offered by Four Canadian Universities." Unpublished M.A. thesis, Catholic Univ. of America.

1952 Lavigne, D. M. "Present Status and Needs of Nurse Instructors in a Selected Group of Canadian Schools of Nursing." Unpublished M.A. thesis, Catholic Univ. of America.

1953 Wekel, M. F. "An Analysis of the R.N. Examinations in the Province of Quebec for a Twelve-Year Period." Unpublished M.A. thesis, Catholic Univ. of America.

1956 Charbonneau, M. L. G. "The History of the School of Public Health Nursing at the University of Montreal, Canada, 1925–1950." Unpublished M.A. thesis, Catholic Univ. of America.

1957 Clancey, I. L. W. and J. Cummings. "Training Psychiatric Nurses —a Re-Education," *Can. Psych. Assoc. Jour.* II, 26–33.

1959 Elliss, J. D. "Evaluating a Supervisory Training Course," *Bus. Q.* XXIV, 105–14.

« L'Ecole des Hospitalières, bref rappel historique », *Cah. Hôtel-Dieu* V, 427–31.

Henriksen, H. L. « Les Soins infirmiers d'hygiène du travail et le programme d'études de l'infirmière », *Revue de l'Hygiène Professionnelle* X, no 2, 89–91.

Kingston, J. « Historique des soins infirmiers d'hygiène du travail au Canada », *Revue de l'Hygiène Professionnelle* X, no 2, 1–8.

Sister Sainte-Louise de Morillac Frenette. "An Integrated Curriculum for Laval University Collegiate School of Nursing," *Cah. Hôtel-Dieu* V, 432–42.

Sœur Ste-Eugénie-de-Rome. « Devons-nous opter pour l'internat ou l'externat dans nos écoles d'infirmières ? » *Bull. Inf. Cath.* XXVI, 69–81, 105–13.

1960   Adams, H. W.   "Health Education—the Basic Structure of Public Health," *Can. Jour. Pub. Health* LI, 446–50.

Bélanger, T.   « L'Officière », *Cah. Nursing* XXXIII, no 9, 7–11.

Duncanson, B.   "The Nightingale School of Nursing, Toronto," *Can. Nurse* LVI, 802–806.

Duvillard, M.   « La Préparation de l'infirmière administratice dans le cadre de l'enseignement infirmier de base », *Cah. Nursing* XXXIII, no 7, 13–18.

Edwards, M. P.   "Public Health Nursing in Saskatchewan," *Can. Nurse* LVI, 413–17.

Grant, A.   "Health Education Training in Canada," *Can. Jour. Pub. Health* LI, 489–92.

Gordon, E. M. and V. M. Huffman.   "Evaluating an Occupational Health Nursing Program by a Work Sampling Study," *Can. Nurse* LV, 314–20.

Harnett, R.   "Public Health Nursing in Newfoundland," *Can. Nurse* LIX, 818–22.

McArthur, H. G.   "A College of Nurses for Ontario?" *Can. Nurse* LVI, 515–18.

McDowell, E. M.   "The Profession and the University," *Can. Nurse* LVI, 129–31.

MacLaggan, K.   "U.N.B.'s School of Nursing," *Can. Nurse* LVI, 424–26.

Mallory, E.   "Whither We are Tending," *Can. Nurse* LVI, 521–38.

Mère Jeanne-Mance.   « Formation professionnelle des religieuses hospitalières », *Cah. Nursing* XXXIII, no 12, 5–10.

Morrison, R. M.   "Providing for Depth of Learning," *Can. Nurse* LVI, 730–34.

Mussallem, H. K.   "Spotlight on Nursing Education," *Can. Nurse* LVI, 900–906.

Rosen, G.   "Reflections on Education for Prevention," *Can. Jour. Pub. Health* LI, 8–14.

Willis, L. D.   "The Scope of Professional Nursing," *Can. Nurse* LVI, 624–32.

1961   Conference Canadienne des Ecoles Catholiques d'Infirmières. *Compte-rendu de l'institut national 3ème 1961 : le nursing vu à travers un prisme.* Ottawa : Association des Hôpitaux Catholiques du Canada. Pp. 145.

Lucow, W. H.   "Test Construction in Nursing Education," *Can. Nurse* LVI, 23–33.

Ross, A.   *Becoming a Nurse.* Toronto: Macmillan. Pp. 420.

Sholtis, L. A. and J. S. Bragdon.   *The Art of Clinical Instruction.* Montreal: Lippincott. Pp. 210.

Sœur Sainte-Marguerite-Marie-Alcoque.   « La Directrice du 'Nursing' : dualité ou unité de fonction ? » *Bull. Inf. Cath.* XXVII, 182–200.

1962   Association des Infirmières Catholiques du Canada.   « Rapport du IIIe Congrès provincial de l'A.I.C.C. », *Bull. Inf. Cath.* XXIX, 1–36.

Broussole, D. « La Formation des infirmières psychiatriques au Canada », *Cah. Nursing* XXXV, no 4, 20–22.

Chittick, R. "One Nurse's Utopia," *Can. Doctor* XXXVIII, 43–47.

Goyer, G. « Problèmes psychologiques du Nursing », *Bull. Inf. Cath.* XXIX, 140–46.

Hart, M. E. "Needs and Resources for Graduate Education in Nursing in Canada." Unpublished doct. dissertation, Columbia Univ.

Hassenplug, L. W. "Nursing Education for a World of Change," *Can. Nurse* LVIII, 802–808.

Hickman, W. H. "Educating for the Future," *Can. Nurse* LVIII, 880–86.

Jourard, S. M. "Integrating Mental Health into the Curriculum," *Can. Nurse* LVIII, 307–13.

Lenicque, P. « Infirmière, vocation ou profession ? » *Bull. Inf. Cath.* XXIX, 236–44.

Paré, S. « Profession et service », *Bull. Inf. Cath.* XXIX, 222–35.

Sewell, M. E. *et al.* "An Overview of In-Service Education," *Can. Nurse* LVIII, 413–30.

Solomon, D. N. "The Professional School in the University," *Can. Nurse* LVIII, 50–56.

1963 Badgley, R. F. "The Tragedy of Nursing Education," *Can. Nurse* LIX, 722–25.

Bertrand, M.-A. « Sciences sociales et Nursing », *Bull. Inf. Cath.* XXX, 57–59.

Duval, D. « Nursing universitaire », *Maintenant* XXIII, 338–39.

Girard, A. « L'Infirmière et les progrès techniques », *Bull. Inf. Cath.* XXX, 12–18.

Long, L. "Changes in Nursing Education in Saskatchewan," *Can. Nurse* LIX, 935–41.

Mailhiot, B. « Nursing catholique et psychologie », *Bull. Inf. Cath.* XXX, 93–106.

Mussallem, H. K. "A Plan for the Development of Nursing Education Programs within the General Educational System of Canada." Unpublished doct. dissertation, Columbia Univ. Teachers College.

Neylan, M. "Psychosocial Aspects of Nursing Education," *Can. Mental Health* XI, no. 6, 16–20.

Nobert, R. *et al.* « Nursing catholique et promotion sociale de l'infirmière », *Bull. Inf. Cath.* XXX, 193–206.

Péloquin, L. « Les Fonctions de la directrice du nursing », *Cah. Nursing* XXXVI, no 11, 5–11.

Pharmaciens de l'Hôpital Saint-François d'Assise, Québec. « L'Enseignement de la pharmacologie au nursing », *Cah. Nursing* XXXVI, no 10, 25–29, no 11, 21–24.

Sœur Saint-Augustin. « Qualification et fonctions de l'infirmière enseignante », *Cah. Nursing* XXXVI, no 5, 18–21.

Sœur Sainte-Louise-de-France. « Est-il préférable que l'enseignement du nursing soit donné par la même personne à l'hôpital et à l'école ? » *Cah. Nursing* XXXVI, no 11, 28–32 ; no 12, 23–27.

Stahl, M. A. "Educational Requirements for Admission to Schools of Nursing in Ontario." Thesis in Toronto: Dept. of Education, Guidance Branch.

Van Massenhove, C. « Devoirs du dialogue de l'infirmière catholique », *Bull. Inf. Cath.* XXX, 243–52.

Wallace, J. O. "U. of Alberta Hospital Organizes a Nursing Reserve," *Can. Hosp.* XL, 78–81.

1964   Burwell, D. M. "Changing Attitudes and Images in Psychiatric Nursing," *Can. Nurse* LX, 122–25.

Royal Commission on Health Services. *Report of.* . . . Ottawa: Queen's Printer, 2 vols.

PHARMACY : PHARMACIE

1953   Lewis, W. H. "Pharmaceutical Education in Ontario 1867–1900." B.Sc.Phm. thesis, Univ. of Toronto.

1954   Smith, S. "The Purpose of Pharmacy Education," *Ont. Coll. Pharm. Bull.* III, no. 4, 47–51.

Wensley, W. R. "Admission Requirements to College of Pharmacy." B.Sc.Phm. thesis, Univ. of Toronto.

1956   McDougall, D. "The History of Pharmacy in Manitoba" in J. A. Jackson, W. L. Morton, and P. Yuzyk, eds., *Historical and Scientific Society of Manitoba, Papers*, Ser. III, no. 11 (Winnipeg: Stovel-Advocate Printers), 18–29.

1957   Coderre, E. *An Outline of the History of Pharmacy in the Province of Quebec from 1617 to 1930.* Toronto: Univ. of Toronto, Faculty of Pharmacy, Canadian Academy of the History of Pharmacy. Pp. 12.

1958   Paterson, G. R. "The Canadian Conference of Pharmaceutical Faculties," *American Journal of Pharmaceutical Education* XXII, 201–208.

Swartz, S. G. "Pharmaceutical Education in Ontario 1900–1950." B.Sc.Phm. thesis, Univ. of Toronto.

1959   Courtois, J.-E. « Principaux Buts de l'enseignement pharmaceutique », *Rev. Pharm.* X, 218–21, 242.

Larose, A.-F. « Dix Ans de progrés à la faculté de pharmacie de Montréal », *Rev. Pharm.* XI, 12–13.

Martin, E.-A. « De l'enseignement de la chimie organique pharmaceutique », *Rev. Pharm.* X, 147–48.

1960   Archambault, A. « La Fonction de la faculté de pharmacie et du pharmacien », *Rev. Pharm.* XII, 38–40.

Hughes, F. N. "The Changing Picture of Canadian Pharmacy," *Medical Library Association Bulletin* [U.S.] XLVIII, 162–67.

Hughes, F. N. "Graduate Study and the Canadian Research Conference," *Ont. Coll. Pharm. Bull.* IX, 3–6.

Larose, R. « La Vie et l'orientation de la faculté doivent préoccuper chaque pharmacien », *Rev. Pharm.* II, 346–48.

1961   Huston, M. J. "Graduate Studies in a Pharmacy College," *Can.*

Pharm. Jour. XCIV, no. 10, 22–24, 47.

Larose, R. « Déontologie en législation pharmaceutique », *Rev. Pharm.* XII, 245–46, 251, 260–61.

1962 Archambault, A. « L'Enseignement pharmaceutique se renouvelle et la recherche scientifique devient une nouvelle source de prestige pour la faculté de pharmacie de l'Université de Montréal », *Rev. Pharm.* XIII, 216–24.

1963 Archambault, A. "Continuing Education for the Practicing Pharmacist," *Can. Pharm. Jour.* XCVI, no. 2, 20, 22, 28.

Archambault, A. « Le Cours actuel forme des pharmaciens capables d'assumer toutes leurs responsabilités », *Pharmacien* XXXVII, no 7, 21–22, 39–40.

Matthews, A. W. *et al. Facilities and Curricula for Pharmacy Education in Canada.* Special Supplement, compiled by the Canadian Pharmaceutical Association in cooperation with the Dean and directors of the Faculties, Schools and College of Pharmacy in Canada. *Can. Pharm. Jour.* XCV, 215–36.

Nairn, J. G. and D. R. Kennedy. "Continuing Education for the Pharmacist," *Can. Pharm. Jour.* XCVI, no. 11, 9, 26–27.

Sister M. Giovannio. "The Role of Religion in Pharmacy under Canada's Ancient Regime," *Culture* XXIV, 13–22, 138–51.

1964 Royal Commission on Health Services. *Report.* . . . Ottawa: Queen's Printer. 2 vols.

PHYSICAL AND HEALTH EDUCATION : EDUCATION PHYSIQUE

1948 Panton, J. "A Survey of Men's Intramural Program in University and Secondary Schools in Manitoba, Saskatchewan, Alberta and British Columbia and a Suggested Plan for Organization in Secondary Schools." Unpublished M.Sc. thesis, Univ. of Washington.

1955 Kennedy, W. F. R. "Health, Physical Education, and Recreation in Canada: A History of Professional Preparation." Unpublished doct. dissertation, Columbia Univ.

Sheedy, A. "Relationship of Health Knowledge and Emotional Stability with Health Practice of Senior High School, College Freshmen, Sophomore and Graduate Students of the University of Ottawa, Ontario." Unpublished M.S. thesis, Univ. of Illinois.

1957 Bray, M. "The History of the Canadian Association for Health, Physical Education and Recreation." Unpublished M.A. thesis, Univ. of Oregon.

Smith, J. W. "Outdoor Education in the College of Physical Education Curriculum," *Journal of Canadian Association for Health, Physical Education and Recreation* XXIV, no. 4, 27–30.

Smith, W. D. "A Study of the Development of the Physical Education Branch, Department of Education, Province of Ontario, Canada." Unpublished doct. dissertation, Univ. of Buffalo.

1958 Errington, J. "An Evaluation of Undergraduate Professional Preparation in Physical Education for Men in Canada." Unpublished doct. dissertation, Indiana Univ.

Meagher, J. W. "A Projected Plan for the Reorganization of the Physical Education Teacher-Training Program in Canada." Unpublished doct. dissertation, Pennsylvania State Univ.

Meagher, J. W. "The Status of Degree Graduates of Four Canadian Schools of Physical Education." Unpublished M.A. thesis, Pennsylvania State Univ.

Pelletier, P. A. "A Summary of Physical Education and Athletic Administration in Canadian Universities and Colleges." Unpublished M.S. thesis, Springfield College.

1959 Anderson, R. O. "Leisure Time Interests and Activities of First Year Women at the University of Alberta." Unpublished M.Ed. thesis, Univ. of Alberta.

Dumais, L. « Laval au premier plan dans le domaine de l'éducation physique », *Vieil Esch.* XI, no 2, 7–10.

Lowenberger, A. G. "The Relationship between Participation in Intramural Athletics and Scholastic Achievement of Male Students at the University of Saskatchewan during the 1959 University Year." Unpublished M.S. thesis, Univ. of Washington.

1960 Paplaushas-Ramunas, A. *L'Education physique dans l'humanisme intégral.* Ottawa : Univ. d'Ottawa. Pp. 113.

Wood, W. E. "The Two-Year Diploma Course at McGill," *Journal of Canadian Association for Health, Physical Education and Recreation* XXVI, no. 5, 16–17.

1961 Badgley, R. F. "An Interdisciplinary Assessment of Health Education," *Food for Thought* XXI, Supplement A, 26–31.

Eriksson, A. "Health Education, University of Alberta," *Journal of the Canadian Association for Health, Physical Education and Recreation* XXVIII, no. 4, 29–32.

Orban, W. A. R. "Research at the University of Saskatchewan," *Journal of the Canadian Association for Health, Physical Education and Recreation* XXVIII, no. 2, 31–34.

Parkes, A. E. M. *The Development of Women's Athletics at the University of Toronto.* Toronto: Women's Athletic Assoc., Univ. of Toronto. Pp. 59.

1962 Bélanger, Y. "Physical Education in Quebec," *Can. Ed. Research Digest* II, 29–36.

Goodwin, L. "An Evaluation of Teacher Education in the Physical Degree Program at the University of Alberta." Unpublished doct. dissertation, Univ. of Washington.

Millar, G. J. "Skip the Health Lesson, Teacher!" *Can. Med. Assoc. Jour.* LXXXVI, 644–47.

Roy, B. « Aptitude physique et éducation physique », *Ens. Sec.* XLI, no 5, 22–27.

1964 Guay, D. « Propos sur l'éducation physique », *Instr. Publ.* VIII, no 4, 338–40.

PHYSICAL AND OCCUPATIONAL THERAPY : THÉRAPEUTIQUE PHYSIQUE ET PROFESSIONNELLE

1923 Stewart, J. H. "Occupational Therapy in Canada," *Archives of Occupation Therapy* [U.S.] II, 381–83.

1927 "Report of the Secretary-Treasurer." (Statements on Dr. Goldwin Howland of the Faculty of Medicine, University of Toronto and the Toronto course in Occupational Therapy.) *Archives of Occupational Therapy* IV, 331, 484.

1928 "Report of the Committee on Teaching Methods," *Archives of Occupational Therapy* VII, 287–300.

1933 Dunlop, W. J. "A Brief History of Occupational Therapy," *Can. Jour. Occup. Therapy* I, 6–10.

1935 LeVesconte, H. P. "Expanding Fields of Occupational Therapy," *Can. Jour. Occup. Therapy* III, 4–12.

1944 "The New School of Physiotherapy," *Can. Physiotherapy Assoc. Jour.* I, 19–20.

1947 LeVesconte, H. P. "University of Toronto," *American Journal of Occupational Therapy* I, 49–51.

1949 "Physiotherapy Course to be Administered by U. of T. Medical Faculty," *Can. Physiotherapy Assoc. Jour.* II, 7.

1950 "Amalgamation of the Courses in Physical and Occupational Therapy at U. of T.," *Can. Physiotherapy Assoc. Jour.* II, 19–21.

Devitt, I. A., E. F. Rowand, and M. K. Schwartz. "The Edmonton Viewpoint," *Can. Jour. Occup. Therapy* XVII, 51–54.

"Post Graduate Course in the Teaching of Physical and Occupational Therapy," *Can. Physiotherapy Assoc. Jour.* II, 21–22.

1953 Whillans, M. G. "Occupational Therapy and Research," *Can. Jour. Occup. Therapy* XX, 87–92.

1954 Krusen, F. H. "Relationships between Occupational Therapy and Physical Medicine and Rehabilitation," *Can. Jour. Occup. Therapy* XXI, 3–9.

LeVesconte, H. P. "Training in Physical and Occupational Therapy," *Proceedings of the First International Congress of the World Federation of Occupational Therapists*, 94–95.

Martin, B. E. "The Third School," *Can. Physiotherapy Assoc. Jour.* VI, 19–20.

Nicholson, H. M. "Changes in Therapy Course at McGill," *Can. Physiotherapy Assoc. Jour.* VI, 7–8.

1955 Bagnall, A. W. *et al.* "A Panel Discussion of Constructive Criticism of Occupational and Physical Therapy," *Can. Jour. Occup. Therapy* XXII, 81–91.

Bradshaw, R. "Impressions of the Post Graduate Teachers Training Course," *Can. Physiotherapy Assoc. Jour.* VII, 17–18.

1957 Azima, H. and E. D. Wittkower. "A Partial Field Survey of Psychiatric Occupational Therapy," *Can. Jour. Occup. Therapy* XXIV, 69–80.

1958 Wittkower, E. D. and A. M. Johnson. "New Developments in and

Perspectives of Psychiatric Occupational Therapy," *Can. Jour. Occup. Therapy* XXV, 5–11.

1960   Driver, M. F. "Report of Special Course in Occupational Therapy," *Can. Jour. Occup. Therapy* XXVII, 129–30.

1961   Fisk, G. H. "Some Guiding Principles in the Education of Physical and Occupational Therapists," *Jour. Can. Med. Assoc.* LXXXV, 1451–53.

Fowler, J. R. *et al.* "The School of Physical & Occupational Therapy, University of Alberta," *Can. Physiotherapy Assoc. Jour.* XIII, 21–24.

Sommer, R. "Professionalism and Occupational Therapy," *Can. Jour. Occup. Therapy* XXVIII, 23–28.

1962   Dunkim, E. N. "Educationally Speaking," *Can. Jour. Occup. Therapy* XXIX, 63–65.

Sister Jean de la Charité. "The Neglected Phase of Rehabilitation," *Can. Jour. Occup. Therapy* XXIX, 83–101.

1963   Carlton, P. "An Approach to Clinical Studies," *Can. Physiotherapy Assoc. Jour.* XV, 208–11.

McLeod, M. "Psychiatric Refresher Course—1963," *Can. Jour. Occup. Therapy* XXX, 153–54.

Vatcher, M. G. "A Backward Glance," *Can. Physiotherapy Assoc. Jour.* XV, 176–78.

1964   Royal Commission on Health Services. *Report.* . . . Ottawa: Queen's Printer. 2 vols.

PUBLIC HEALTH: HYGIENE AND PREVENTIVE MEDICINE : SANTÉ PUBLIQUE :
HYGIÈNE ET MÉDECINE PRÉVENTIVE

1940   Defries, R. D., ed. *The Development of Public Health in Canada: A Review of the History and Organization of Public Health in the Provinces of Canada.* Toronto: Canadian Public Health Association. Pp. 184.

1954   Hobbs, G. E. "Present Status of the Teaching of Preventive and Social Medicine in Canada" in *Proceedings of the First World Conference on Medical Education* (Toronto: Oxford Univ. Press), 592–98.

1957   Defries, R. D. "Postgraduate Teaching in Public Health in the University of Toronto, 1913–1955," *Can. Jour. Pub. Health* XLVIII, 285–94.

1959   le Riche, W. H. and W. B. Stiver. "The Work of Specialists and General Practitioners in Ontario," *Can. Med. Assoc. Jour.* LXXXI, 37–42.

Smillie, W. G. and M. Luginbuhl. "Training of Public Health Personnel in the United States and Canada: A Summary of 10 Years' Advance in Schools of Public Health 1947–1948 to 1957–1958," *American Journal of Public Health* XLIX, 455–62.

1960   American Public Health Association. "Schools of Public Health in the United States and Canada: 1959-1960," *American Journal of Public Health* L, 1770–90.

le Riche, W. H. "The Character of the Physician in Relation to Social and Economic Consequences of Specialization," *Can. Med. Assoc. Jour.* LXXXIII, 912–14.

McLaren, K. S. "Graduate Education in Hospital Administration," *Can. Hosp.* XXXVII, 37–40, 72, 82.

Robertson, A. "The Place of Social Medicine in the Curriculum," *Can. Med. Assoc. Jour.* LXXXII, 724–26.

Stewart, C. B. "Comments on the Teaching of Preventive Medicine in Canada," *Can. Med. Assoc. Jour.* LXXXII, 719–23.

Stuart, E. M. *Practical Studies in Education for Hospital Administration.* Rev. ed. Toronto: U. of T. Press. Pp. 219.

1961 American Public Health Association. *Schools of Public Health in the United States and Canada: 1960–61.* New York: The Association. Pp. 27. (See also *American Journal of Public Health* LI, 1597.)

Hastings, J. E. F. "Medical Education: The Challenge of Changing Patterns," *Can. Med. Assoc. Jour.* LXXXIV, 699–702.

Mather, J. M. and J. H. Read. "Research and Teaching Opportunities in a University-centred Child Health Program," *Can. Med. Assoc. Jour.* LXXXV, 131–34.

McLaren, K. S. "University Graduates in Hospital Administration," *Can. Hosp.* XXXVIII, 54–56, 80.

Rhodes, A. J. "Diplomas or Master's Degrees: Patterns of Postgraduate Education in Public Health," *Can. Jour. Pub. Health* LII, 142–44.

Rhodes, A. J., J. E. F. Hastings, and W. H. le Riche. "Statement to the Royal Commission on Health Services from the School of Hygiene, University of Toronto," *Can. Jour. Pub. Health* LII, 490–94.

Rosen, G. "Evolving Trends in Health Education," *Can. Jour. Pub. Health* LII, 499–506.

University of Toronto, Department of Hospital Administration. *The Program in Hospital Administration, Past, Present, and Future.* Toronto: U. of T. Press. Pp. 311.

1962 American Public Health Association. *Some Aspects of the Schools of Public Health in the United States and Canada: 1961–62.* New York: The Association. Pp. 32. (See also *American Journal of Public Health* LIII, 286–88, 1963.)

Greenhill, S. "Preparing Today's Medical Student for Tomorrow's Society: The Role of a Department of Social Medicine in a Medical School," *Can. Med. Assoc. Jour.* LXXXVI, 611–13.

Hastings, J. E. F. "The Challenge of Changing Times and Nursing Preparation," *Can. Jour. Pub. Health* LIII, 105–108.

le Riche, W. H. "The Curriculum Content of the Toronto Diploma in Public Health: An Opinion Survey of Canadian Public Health Physicians," *Can. Jour. Pub. Health* LIII, 366–70.

le Riche, W. H.   "New and Greener Fields for the Medical Officer of Health," *Can. Jour. Pub. Health* LIII, 463–71.

le Riche, W. H.   "University and Hospital Training of Public Health Physicians in Canada," *Can. Med. Assoc. Jour.* LXXXVII, 1322–25.

Rhodes, A. J.   "Changing Emphasis in Public Health in Canada," *Can. Jour. Pub. Health* LIII, 318–25.

University of Toronto, School of Hygiene.   *Brief . . . Presented [to] the Royal Commission on Health Services.* Toronto: Univ. of Toronto. Pp. 310.

1963   American Public Health Association.   *Schools of Public Health in the United States and Canada, for the Year Ending June 1963.* New York: The Association. Pp. 32.

Association of Schools of Public Health, Committee on Studies.   *International Roles of the Schools of Public Health of North America: A Pilot Study.* Chapel Hill, North Carolina: The Association. Pp. 309.

Badgley, R. F.   "Social Science and Public Health," *Can. Jour. Pub. Health* LIV, 147–53.

Best, E. W. R., W. H. le Riche, G. H. Josie, and A. C. McKenzie.   "Highlights of a Survey of Health Units in Canada," *Can. Jour. Pub. Health* LIV, 349–56.

Clute, K. F.   *The General Practitioner: A Study of Medical Education and Practice in Ontario and Nova Scotia.* Toronto: U. of T. Press. Pp. 566.

Gilbert, J.-A.   *L'Education sanitaire.* Montréal : Presses Univ. Montréal. Pp. 141.

Josie, G. H.   "Research Methods in Public Health: An Annotated Bibliography with Special Reference to Canadian Problems and Experience," *Can. Jour. Pub. Health* LIV, 33–42.

Read, J. H.   "Preventive Pediatrics in Medical Education: II, A Method of Teaching Preventive Paediatrics in the Medical School Curriculum," *Can. Med. Assoc. Jour.* LXXXVIII, 727–29.

Rhodes, A. J.   "Graduate Education in Medical Microbiology: A Report on Five Years' Experience with the Course Leading to the Diploma in Bacteriology, University of Toronto," *Can. Med. Assoc. Jour.* LXXXVIII, 735–37.

Rhodes, A. J. and M. C. Cahoon.   "Graduate Preparation in Health Education: A Brief Report on the Philadelphia Conferences, July, 1962," *Health Education* II, 2–8.

1964   Rhodes, A. J.   "Recent Revisions in Basic and Advanced Courses in Public Health Offered at Toronto," *Can. Jour. Pub. Health* LV, 435–44.

Royal Commission on Health Services.   *Report. . . .* Ottawa: Queen's Printer. 2 vols.

SOCIAL WORK : SERVICE SOCIAL

1942   King, D.   "War and the Education of Social Workers," *Soc. Worker* X, no. 2, 2–3, 23.

1944 King, D. "Professional Training for Social Work in Canada." Unpublished M.A. thesis, New York Univ.

1947 Cassidy, H. M. "The Social Science Foundations of Education for Social Work," *Soc. Worker* XV, no. 5, 1–14.

King, D. *et al.* "Trends in Schools of Social Work" [Universities of Toronto, British Columbia, Manitoba, Montreal, Laval, and Maritime School of Social Work], *Soc. Worker* XV, no. 3, 1–18.

1951 Vandry, F. « L'Université Laval et le service social », *Serv. Soc.* I, no 1, 38–39.

1954 Fortier, E. « La Formation en service social et les besoins des services sociaux publics », *Serv. Soc.* IV, no 1, 18–23.

Jean, L. « La Formation pratique des étudiants en service social personnel », *Bien-être* VI, no 3, 4–6.

1955 Guillemette, A. M. « La Formation professionnelle universitaire en service social », *Serv. Soc.* V, no 1, 4–7.

Peck, M. « Formation de la travailleuse sociale médicale », *Rapport du 3ème congrès général de Caritas-Canada, 1955*, 470–71.

1957 Moore, J. J. "Education for Correctional Work," *Soc. Worker* XXVI, no. 1, 20–25.

"News from Schools of Social Work," *Soc. Worker* XXVI, no. 1, 40–45.

Weaver, K. R. "Some Trends and Aspects of Social Work in a Medical Setting," *Soc. Worker* XXVI, no. 1, 26–31.

1958 Abrahamson, A. C. "Curriculum Objective in Field Teaching," *Soc. Worker* XXVI, no. 3, 31–36.

Daniels, P. *et al.* "Student Impressions of Course in Social Administration," *Soc. Worker* XXVI, no. 3, 46–51.

Dorgan, J. "Education for Social Work and the Mental Health Grant," *Soc. Worker* XXVI, no. 2, 48–53.

Paré, S. « Intégration du service social des groupes dans l'enseignement et la pratique du service social », *Serv. Soc.* VIII, no 4, 210–12.

Shapiro, P. C. and J. Hope-Wallace. "The Caseworker, the Welfare Officer, and the Administrator in the Social Services," *Soc. Worker* XXVI, no. 2, 3–20.

Twohey, G. A. "A Survey of the Employment, Interests, Status and Background of 71 Holders of the Master of Social Work Degree from the School of Social Welfare." Unpublished M.A. thesis, Univ. d'Ottawa.

1959 Charpentier, A. « Un Enseignement méconnu », *Relations* XIX, 230–33.

Morgan, J. S. "Social Work Education—Problems and Prospects," *Soc. Worker* XXVII, no. 4, 55–59.

1960 Couillard, C. "Perspectives on Education for Social Work," *Soc. Worker* XXVIII, no. 1, 57–63.

Williamson, E. L. R. "Social Research or Suicide?" *Executive* II, no. 3, 36–41.

1961 Brown, J. L. "Problems of Establishing Criteria for Social Casework Research," *Soc. Worker* XXIX, no. 4, 48–52.

Garigue, P. « Les Problèmes théoriques du service social », *Serv. Soc.* X, 43–62.

Kerry, E. W. "Early Professional Development in Montreal," *Soc. Worker* XXIX, no. 3, 35–42.

Knight, N. "The Case for Maintaining the 'Status Quo,' " *Soc. Worker* XXIX, no. 1, 7–8.

Munns, V. "The Case for Full Professional Education," *Soc. Worker* XXIX, no. 1, 4–6.

Perretz, E. A. "The Principles Involved in the Development of the Social Work Component in Ontario Mental Health Services," *Soc. Worker* XXIX, no. 2, 49–57.

Rupp, M. "Continuing Education for Social Workers—A Family Agency Experiment," *Soc. Worker* XXIX, no. 4, 53–60.

1962   Boissinot, Y. « Le Service social rural », *Serv. Soc.* X, 116–21.

Denault, H. « Les Débuts de l'expérience d'enseignement du service social à l'école de Laval », *Serv. Soc.* X, 102–109.

Denault, H. « L'Insertion du service social dans le milieu canadien-français », *Serv. Soc.* X, 4–29.

Morin, C. « La Méthode d'organisation communautaire dans le milieu canadien-français », *Serv. Soc.* X, 46–63.

Morin, C. « Pour améliorer le climat social », *Bien-être* XIV, 89–93.

Paré, S. « Le Rôle du service social des groupes dans notre milieu », *Serv. Soc.* X, 30–45.

Perretz, E. A. "A Critical Review of Undergraduate Education for Social Work," *Soc. Worker* XXX, no. 4, 5–14.

Vanier, N. « Aperçu historique de l'Ecole de Service Social de l'Université de Montréal », *Serv. Soc.* X, 95–101.

Zay, N. « Assistance publique et service social », *Serv. Soc.* X, 64–85.

1963   Woodsworth, D. M. "An Open Letter to the Profession," *Soc. Worker* XXXI, no. 4, 40–44.

Younge, E. R. "Dorothy King, O.B.E., M.A., Pioneer Social Work Educator," *Soc. Worker* XXXI, no. 2, 33–35.

TEACHER TRAINING : EDUCATION

1881   La Flèche, L. F. *Réponse aux remarques de M. l'Abbé Verreau sur le mémoire appuyant la demande d'une école normale dans la ville des Trois-Rivières.* Trois-Rivières. Pp. 69.

1907   Gosselin, A. H. « L'Abbé Holmes et l'instruction publique », *Mém. S.R.C.*, Sect. I, 127–73.

1908   Dole, H. P. "The Professional Training of Canadian Teachers." Unpublished M.A. thesis, Columbia Univ.

1909   Desrosiers, A. *Les Ecoles normales primaires de la province de Québec et leurs œuvres complémentaires.* Montréal. Pp. 390.

1915   Jones, F. A. "Training of Teachers in the Province of Ontario, Canada." Unpublished M.A. thesis, Univ. of Chicago.

1925   Halnon, W. "A Descriptive Critical and Constructive Study of the

Control Organization and Administration of Training Elementary School Teachers in England, Canada and the United States." Unpublished doct. dissertation, Indiana Univ.

1930 Marshall, M. V. "An Evaluation of the Present Teacher-Training Program in Nova Scotia, with Recommendations for Improvement." Unpublished doct. dissertation, Harvard Univ.

1936 Ault, O. E. *The Training of Special Teachers; or the Relation of Certain Problems to the Training of Teachers in the U.S., Ontario, France, Scotland and Germany.* Ottawa: National Printers Ltd. Pp. 196.

Canadian Teachers' Federation. *Report on the Training of Teachers in Normal Schools and Departments of Education Throughout the Provinces of the Dominion.* Toronto: The Federation. Mimeo. Pp. 35.

Ontario Public and Separate School Inspectors. *The Training of Teachers-in-Service.* Toronto: Clarke, Irwin. Pp. 294.

1937 McIntosh, H. W. "Examination of Normal School Students: A Study in Teacher Selection and Appraisal." Unpublished doct. dissertation, Univ. of Toronto.

1940 Cook, J. T. "Teacher Training in the Province of New Brunswick: An Historical and Analytical Study of the Evolution together with Proposed Measures of Practical Reform." Unpublished doct. dissertation, Harvard Univ.

1941 Sheane, G. K. "The Selection of Prospective Teachers." Unpublished M.A. thesis, Univ. of Alberta.

1946 McDougall, W. D. "Suggestions for the Improvement of Elementary Teacher Education in the Province of Alberta." Unpublished doct. dissertation, Columbia Univ.

Sly, H. F. "A Comparative Study of Teacher Education in the English-speaking Countries, with Special Emphasis upon Canada." Unpublished M.Ed. thesis, Univ. of Saskatchewan.

Staples, R. O. "The Ontario Rural Teacher—Selection, Professional Training and In-Service Guidance." Unpublished doct. dissertation, Univ. of Toronto.

1948 Lorimer, W. C. "The Improvement of Teacher Education in the Normal School of Saskatchewan." Unpublished doct. dissertation, Columbia Univ.

Pettifor, R. E. "Public Opinion Concerning the Selection and Training of Teachers." Unpublished M.Ed. thesis, Univ. of Alberta.

Shipley, C. M. "Proposals for Developing the Curriculum for a Two-Year Program in Nova Scotia's Provincial Normal College." Unpublished doct. dissertation, Columbia Univ.

1949 Canadian Education Association. *Recommendations Concerning the Status of the Teaching Profession.* Toronto: The Association. Pp. 149.

MacLeod, N. B. "A Plan for Teacher Education in Nova Scotia, with Emphasis on In-Service Education." Unpublished doct. dissertation, Columbia Univ.

Singleton, I. D. "Teacher Training and Certification in the North-West Territories from 1885–1905 and in Saskatchewan from 1905–1937." Unpublished M.Ed. thesis, Univ. of Saskatchewan.

Smith, D. "The Dynamic Aspects of Teacher Training." Unpublished M.Ed. thesis, Univ. of Alberta.

1950 Keddy, J. A. "Selection of Candidates for Entrance to Ontario College of Education." Unpublished doct. dissertation, Univ. of Toronto.

Martin, J. I. "Prediction Success of Education Students in Academic Courses and in Teaching." Unpublished M.Ed. thesis, Univ. of Alberta.

Miles, G. W. "The Preparation of Industrial Arts Teachers in the United States and Canada." Unpublished M.A. thesis, Colorado State College of Education.

Sœur Saint-Martin. « Formation des institutrices adaptée aux besoins des temps actuels ». Thèse de Licencié en Pédagogie, Univ. de Montréal.

1951 Constantine, D. E. "The Manitoba Training Program for Trade and Industrial Teachers Compared with Other Provinces and States." Unpublished M.A. thesis, Colorado Agricultural and Mechanical College.

1952 Dupuis, L. J. "A History of Elementary Teacher Training in Ontario." Unpublished M.A. thesis, Univ. of Ottawa.

Lucas, J. R. "The Philosophy of Future School Teachers." Unpublished doct. dissertation, Univ. of Ottawa.

1954 Arvelo, H. P. "A Study of Students' Opinions Regarding Teaching Practices." Unpublished M.Ed. thesis, Univ. of Toronto.

Gray, R. H. A. "Teacher Evaluation." Unpublished M.Ed. thesis, Univ. of Manitoba.

Pippy, G. M. "A History of Secondary School Teacher Training at the Ontario College of Education." Unpublished M.A. thesis, Univ. of Toronto.

1955 McCarthy, J. P. "One Hundred Years of Teacher Education, the Centenary of the Nova Scotia Normal College," *N.S. Journal of Education* V, no. 1, 5–20.

1956 Sister Dunphy, M.A. "A History of Teacher Training in Newfoundland, 1726–1955." Unpublished B.Ed. thesis, Mount St. Vincent College.

Frey, G. J. "A Study of Some of Dr. Neatby's Claims Concerning Instructors in Teacher-Training Schools." Unpublished M.A. thesis, Univ. of Ottawa.

"The New Toronto Teachers' College." *Sch. Prog.* XXV, no. 3, 41–46, 48.

1957 Campbell, P. R. "Speech Education in the English-Speaking Teacher Training Institutions of Canada." Unpublished doct. dissertation, Univ. of Wisconsin.

Cann, M. M. "An Historical Study of the Office of Co-ordinator of Teacher Education in the Canadian Provinces of New Brunswick, Ontario, Saskatchewan, Alberta, and British Columbia. Unpublished doct. dissertation, Univ. of Maryland.

Davis, F. M. "The History of the Growth of the Faculty of Education within the University of Manitoba." Unpublished M.A. thesis, Univ. of Manitoba.

Deane, S. G. "A Survey of the Financial Assistance Available for Graduate Study in the Field of Education at Canadian Universities." Unpublished M.A. thesis, Univ. of Alberta.

McGill University, Institute of Education. A Century of Teacher Education, 1857–1957. Montreal: McGill Univ. Pp. 96.

University of Toronto, Ontario College of Education, Department of Educational Research. A Study of Teacher Training in British Columbia. Toronto: The Department. Pp. 47.

1958   Canadian Teachers' Federation. Trends in Certification Standards, 1939–1957. Ottawa: The Federation, Research Division. Pp. 30.

Carrière, G. Un Grand Educateur : le R. P. René Lamoureux, o.m.i., 1890–1958, fondateur de l'Ecole Normale de l'Université d'Ottawa. Ottawa : Editions de l'Université. Pp. 136.

Friesen, D. "The Differential Aptitude Tests as Predictors in Education I at the University of Manitoba." Unpublished M.A. thesis, Univ. of Manitoba.

Kendrick, A. C. "To Make Recommendations for a Program of Industrial Arts Teacher Education with Special Reference to British Columbia." Unpublished M.A. thesis, Western Washington College of Education.

Lee, M. O. "A Study of the Needs of Students in Relation to the Adequacy of Courses in Social Understandings at the Toronto Teachers' College." Unpublished M.A. thesis, Cornell Univ.

Levirs, F. "Concepts of Supervision," Jour. Ed. no. 2 (March), 69–75.

Meagher, J. W. "A Projected Plan for the Reorganization of Physical Education Teacher-Training Programs in Canada." Unpublished doct. dissertation, Univ. of Pennsylvania.

Plante, L. « Préparation des professeurs-hygiénistes pour les écoles normales françaises du Québec », Jour. Ed. no 2, 63–68.

1959   Beauregard, L. « La Géographie dans les écoles normales et autres écoles spécialisées du Québec », Cah. Géog. V, 115–19.

Cameron, A. A. "Teaching Success of Teachers College Graduates," Proceedings, Conference on Educational Research, 12–18.

Canadian Teachers' Federation. Teacher Influence on Curriculum: A Study of the Part Played by Teachers in Curriculum Revision and Implementation in Ontario, 1948–1958. Ottawa: The Federation, Research Division. Pp. 56.

Dale, E. "Education of Teachers," Alberta Teachers' Association Magazine XXXIX (January), 13–14, 52–54.

"Emergency Training Plan to Prepare University Graduates as High School Teachers," Nova Scotia Education Office Gazette VIII (March), 23–30.

Johnson, F. H. "Why Should Elementary Teachers Hold Degrees?" B.C. Teacher XXXVIII, 397–400.

LaBerge, R. « Le Perfectionnement du professeur », Ens. Sec. XXXVIII, no 5, 33–38.

Royal Commission on Education in Alberta. *Report*. . . . Edmonton: Queen's Printer. Pp. 351.

Vinette, R. *The Preparation of Teachers in French-Speaking Quebec*. Toronto: Gage. Pp. 14.

1960   Brown, A. M. "A Study of Teacher Education and Certification for the Teaching of Music in Canadian Public Schools." Unpublished doct. dissertation, Florida State Univ.

Cheng, C.-S. "The Main Factors that Led to the Establishment of the University of Ottawa Teachers' College." Thèse de doctorat, Univ. d'Ottawa.

Earle, J. A. "The Development of the Teaching Profession in Nova Scotia." Unpublished M.A. thesis, Saint Mary's Univ.

Hall, C. W., ed. *Fifth Annual Conference of the Canadian Association of Professors of Education*. Toronto: Macmillan. Pp. 62.

Heywood, R. H. "An Evaluation of the Training Program for Commerce Teachers at the University of British Columbia College of Education." Unpublished M.A. thesis, Univ. of British Columbia.

Seaman, B. E. "A Study of Academic Underachievement among Education Students at the University of Alberta." Unpublished M.A. thesis, Univ. of Alberta.

1961   Johnson, F. H. "Preparing Teachers for the Elementary Schools of Tomorrow," *Jour. Ed.* no. 6 (December), 139–47.

Mann, G. "Alberta Normal Schools: A Descriptive Survey of their Development 1905–1945." Unpublished M.Ed. thesis, Univ. of Alberta.

Munroe, D. C. "New Horizons in Teacher Education," *Ed. Record Prov. Quebec* LXXVII (April–June), 87–94.

Stein, H. L. "Master's Degrees for Teachers," *B.C. Teacher* XL (April), 352–55.

1962   Canadian Teachers' Federation. *Four Year Bachelor of Education Programmes for Elementary School Teachers in Canada*. Ottawa: The Federation. Pp. 59.

Cottingham, M. E. "An Experiment in Internship in Practice Teaching," *Jour. Ed.* no. 7 (June), 48–55.

De Grandpré, M. « La Préparation des maîtres », *Coll. et Fam.* XIX, 56–63.

Ende, R. S. "The Elementary Teacher Education Program at North Park College." Unpublished doct. dissertation, Univ. of Ottawa.

Goodwin, L. "An Evaluation of Teacher Education in the Physical Degree Program at the University of Alberta." Unpublished doct. dissertation, Univ. of Washington.

Harris, R. S. "On Teaching" in W. B. Townley, ed., *The Decisive Years* (Toronto: Barker Publishing Co.), 21–24.

Lawson, D. "Literature and the Teaching of Educational Philosophy," *Jour. Ed.* no. 7 (June), 61–68.

Ontario, Department of Education. *Report of the Minister's Committee on the Training of Secondary School Teachers*. Toronto: The Department. Pp. 229.

Paton, J. M. *The Role of Teachers' Organizations in Canadian Education.* Toronto: Gage. Pp. 89.

Saucier, P. « Un Instrument de formation de premier ordre ; l'Ecole Normale Supérieure de Montréal », *Maintenant*, 7–8.

Tremblay, J. *Scandale au D.I.P.* [Département de l'Instruction Publique] : *l'affaire Guérin ou le Frère Untel avait raison.* Montréal : Editions du Jour. Pp. 124.

1963 Aalborg, A. O. "History of Teacher Education in Alberta," *Alberta Teachers' Association Magazine* XLIV (November), 26–27, 29–30.

Aubin, R. « Le Professeur des sciences expérimentales dans les classes pré-universitaires : sa formation, sa méthodologie », *Rev. Univ. Laval* XVII, 600–10.

Figur, B. "The History of the Teaching of Educational Philosophy in Canada." Unpublished doct. dissertation, Stanford Univ.

Johns, W. H. "The University's Role in Teacher Education," *N.T.A. Journal* (November), 15–18, 60–63.

Katz, J. "Education and Training of Teachers in Canada" in G. Z. F. Bereday, ed., *The Yearbook of Education* (London: Evans Brothers Limited), 213–27.

Labrie, R. « La Formation du professeur du cours classique », *Ens. Sec.* XLII, no 4, 3–8.

Letarte, L. « Les Etudiants des écoles normales de la province de Québec pour l'année scolaire 1962–63 et les motifs de leur choix de l'enseignement comme carrière ». Thèse de Maîtrise, Univ. Laval.

Londerville, J. J. D. "The History of Curriculum Used in the Education of Elementary School Teachers for the Province of Ontario." Unpublished doct. dissertation, Univ. of Toronto.

Newcombe, E. E. "The Development of Elementary School Teacher Education in Ontario in the Present Century." Unpublished doct. dissertation, Univ. of Toronto.

O'Bready, M. « Nos Ecoles normales », *Rev. Univ. Sherbrooke* III, 145–50.

Ramsmeyer, J. A. "Professional Development of the Teaching Staff," *Can. Ed. Research Digest* III, 194–203.

Sissons, C. K. "Recollections of the Ontario School of Pedagogy, 1894–95," *Douglas Library Notes* XII, no. 3, 4–8.

1964 Bailey, A. W. "The Professional Preparation of Teachers for the Schools of the Province of New Brunswick, 1784 to 1964." Unpublished doct. dissertation, Univ. of Toronto.

THEOLOGY : THÉOLOGIE

1862 Townley, A. *A Letter to the Lord Bishop of Huron: In Personal Vindication: And on the Inexpediency of a New Diocesan College.* Brantford. Pp. 11.

1887 Wood, J. *Memoirs of Henry Wilkes, D.D., LL.D.: His Life and Times.* Montreal. Pp. 280.

1891 Toronto Baptist College. *Memoirs of Daniel Arthur McGregor, Late Principal of Toronto Baptist College*. Toronto. Pp. 145.

1903 Committee of the Executive of the Twentieth Century Fund. *Historic Sketches of the Pioneer Work and the Missionary, Educational and Benevolent Agencies of the Presbyterian Church in Canada*. Toronto. Pp. 128.

1905 Charlton, J. "Queen's University—Presbyterian Theological College" in *Speeches and Addresses Political, Literary and Religious* (Toronto), 291–304.

1921 Congregational College of Canada. *A Short History and a Plea*. Montreal. Pp. 31.

1930 Strerig, J. M. "History of the Missionary Education Movement in the United States and Canada." Unpublished doct. dissertation, New York Univ.

1933 Morris, R. P. "A Study of the Library Facilities of a Group of Representative Protestant Theological Seminaries in the United States and Canada." Unpublished M.A. thesis, Columbia Univ.

1937 Sweet, W. W. "The Rise of Theological Schools in America," *Church History* [U.S.] VI, 260–74.

1938 McKinnon, C. *Reminiscences*. Toronto: Ryerson. Pp. 236.

1943 Université Laval. *Faculté de droit canonique : La Faculté de droit canonique de Laval et les vingt-cinq ans du Code pro-benédiction*. Québec : Univ. Laval. Pp. 17.

1945 Hughes, N. L. "A History of the Development of Ministerial Education in Canada from its Inception until 1925 in Those Churches Which Were Tributary to the United Church in Ontario, Quebec and the Maritime Provinces of Canada." Unpublished doct. dissertation, Univ. of Chicago.

1950 Boon, H. W. "The Development of the Bible College or Institute in the United States and Canada since 1880 and its Relationship to the Field of Theological Education in America." Unpublished doct. dissertation, New York Univ.

Cooper, A. J. "The Development of a Department of Practical Theology at St. Stephen's College, Edmonton, Canada." Unpublished doct. dissertation, Columbia Univ.

Farley, P.-M. « Le Collège Joliette, séminaire diocésain », Société canadienne d'Histoire de l'Eglise Catholique, *Rapport Annuel*, 37–53.

1953 Imayoshi, K. "The History of Okanagan Baptist College, 1907–1915." Unpublished B.D. thesis, McMaster Univ.

O'Grady, W. E. "The Fathers and Higher Education." Unpublished B.D. thesis, Acadia Univ.

1954 Cochran, O. D. "The Development of Theological Education at Acadia University." Unpublished B.D. thesis, Acadia Univ.

1957 Provost, H. « Les Origines éloignées du Séminaire de Québec », *Can. Cath. Hist. Assoc., Annual Rept., 1955–56*, 25–31.

1959 Alla, L. « Le Bienheureux Père Eymard et les séminaristes », *Revue Eucharistique du Clergé* LXII, 248–54.

Grondin, C. « Le Problème des vocations », *Revue Eucharistique du Clergé* LXII, 307–12.

Peake, F. A. "Theological Education in British Columbia," *Can. Jour. Theol.* V, 251–63.

1960 « La Faculté de théologie », *Vieil Esch.* XII, no 1, 7–12.

Robillard, H.-M. « Théologie et culture », *Prêtre* X, 273–86.

1961 Klaver, R. "Why do Seminarians Leave the Seminary?" *Séminaire* XXVI, 203–14.

MacRae, A. W. M. J. "A History of the Evangelical Movement in the Canadas, 1840–1880; With Special Emphasis on Evangelical Principals in Anglican Theological Education." Unpublished M.A. thesis, McGill Univ.

1962 Eddy, E. B. "Henry Wilkes," *United Church of Canada Committee on Archives Bulletin*, 10–21.

Fédération des Collèges Classiques. *Programmes d'études et formation des candidates au sacerdoce.* Document no 18. Montréal : La Fédération. Pp. 133.

Fournier, N. « Pour une meilleure formation des catéchistes », *Vie des Communautés Religieuses* XX, 114–16.

1963 Carrington, P. *The Anglican Church in Canada.* Toronto: Collins. Pp. 320.

Howard, O. *The Montreal Diocesan Theological College: A History from 1873 to 1963.* Montreal: McGill Univ. Press. Pp. 141.

Mathers, D. "Does Theology Belong in a University?" *Queen's Q.* LXX, 264–67.

Vachon, L.-A. *Mémorial.* Québec : Presses Univ. Laval. Pp. 165.

Yelle, G. « Décret d'érection des séminaires », *Séminaire* XXVIII, 175–79.

VETERINARY SCIENCE : MÉDECINE VÉTÉRINAIRE

1920 McEachran, D. "Osler and the Montreal Veterinary College" in *Sir William Osler, Memorial Number* (Montreal: Canadian Medical Association Journal), 35–38.

1955 "Symposium [on] Veterinary Education," *Veterinary Record* LXVII, 423–31, 435, 441–50.

1959 Penrose-FitzGerald, C. P. "The New Medical-Surgical Building at the Ontario Veterinary College," *Can. Jour. Comp. Med.* XXIII, 180–85.

1960 Henderson, J. A. "The Prospect before Us," *Canadian Veterinarian Journal* I, 3–10.

Jones, T. L. "Random Notes on Veterinary Education," *Canadian Veterinarian Journal* I, 41–44.

Murphy, D. A. "Osler, Now a Veterinarian," *Can. Jour. Comp. Med.* XXIV, 276–81.

1961 Saint-Georges, J. "75th Anniversary of the School for Veterinary Medicine of the Province of Quebec," *Can. Jour. Comp. Med.* XXV, 239–42.
1962 Gattinger, F. E. *A Century of Challenge: A History of the Ontario Veterinary College.* Toronto: U. of T. Press. Pp. 223.
Gattinger, F. E. "The Ontario Veterinary College at Confederation," *Canadian Veterinarian Journal* III, 97–100.
Gattinger, F. E. "Veterinary Instruction at Queen's and O.A.C.," *Canadian Veterinarian Journal* III, 174–77.
Jones, T. L. "Academic Environment," *Can. Jour. Comp. Med.* XXVI, 23–24.
Jones, T. L. "The Ontario Veterinary College is One Hundred Years Old," *Canadian Veterinarian Journal* III, 194–99.
McDonald, J. "The Veterinary Profession and Higher Education," *Can. Jour. Comp. Med.* XXVI, 147–49.

VOCATIONAL GUIDANCE : ORIENTATION PROFESSIONNELLE

1934 Smith, J. W. "Cinematography in Vocational Guidance," *Sch. Prog.* IV, no. 4, 13–14.
1951 Donald, R. V. "The Development of Guidance in the Secondary Schools of the Dominion of Canada." Unpublished M.Ed. thesis, Univ. of Manitoba.
1955 Axford, B. M. "The University Preparation, Orientation and Adjustment Programme." Thesis in Guidance, Toronto: Dept. of Education, Guidance Services Branch.
1956 Newstead, H. A. "Let's Take a New Look at Our Jobs," *Sch. Prog.* XXV, no. 4, 30–31, 48.
1958 Gagnon, F. « 'Motivation' des élèves qui fréquentent le collège », *Ens. Sec.* XXXVIII, 69–78.
Maranda, A. « L'Orientation professionnelle au Collège de Lévis », *Ens. Sec.* XXXVIII, 18–22.
Smith, R. N. "The Use of Vocational Interest Inventories in Secondary Schools," *Jour. Ed.* no. 2 (March), 83–90.
1959 Allen, P. « Les Carrières des affaires réclament l'élite des jeunes Canadiens français d'aujourd'hui », *Act. Nat.* XLVIII, 263–71.
Bertrand, R. « Une Expérience heureuse », *Instr. Publ.* III, 581–85, 588, 686–88, 722.
1960 Parmenter, M. D. *You and the University: A Text-Workbook of Information, Suggestions and Activities to Help You Make the Most of Present Opportunities and to Assist You in Planning Your Future.* Toronto: Univ. of Toronto, Ontario College of Education, Guidance Centre. Pp. 112. Revised annually.
1961 Desrosiers, F.-X. « Le Conseiller d'orientation à l'Externat Saint-Jean-Eudes », *Ens. Sec.* XL, no 5, 49–53.
1964 Auger, L. « Vers une conception dynamique de l'orientation », *Coll. et Fam.* XXI, no 1, 12–16.

G. GRADUATE STUDIES AND RESEARCH : ETUDES POST-GRADUEES ET RECHERCHE

1903 Cooke, C. K., ed. "Official Report of the Allied Colonial Universities Conference Held at Burlington House on July 9, 1903 . . . ," *Empire Review* [U.K.] VI, 65–128.

1909 Greig, R. B. *Agricultural Education and Research in Canada.* Aberdeen. Pp. 26.

1914 Royal Canadian Institute. *Cooperation between Science and Industry in Canada: The Royal Canadian Institute as an Intermediary for its Promotion: Establishment of a Bureau of Scientific and Industrial Research.* Toronto. Pp. 31.

1915 Arnoldi, F. *Presidential Address at Opening Meeting of Session, 1915.* Bulletin No. 1 of Bureau of Scientific and Industrial Research of School of Specific Industries of the Royal Canadian Institute. Toronto. Pp. 15.

1925 Banting, F. "Medical Research," *Annals of Clinical Medicine* [U.S.] III, 565–72.

1949 Imperial Order Daughters of the Empire. *Record of the Post-Graduate Scholarship Holders for the First Twenty Years of the First War Memorial 1920–1940.* Ottawa: The Order. Pp. 53.

1952 Williams, C. H. M. and A. W. S. Wood. "The Present Status of Dental Research in Canada," *Jour. Can. Dent. Assoc.* XII, 712–15.

1954 Haworth, E. "Research in the Canadian Universities," *Design Eng.* V, no. 7, 58–65.

1956 Ellis, R. G. "A Review of Dental Education Suggests a Fertile Field for Research," *Australian Dental Journal* I, 8–11.

Hamelin, L.-E. « Documents relatifs à la fondation d'un centre de recherches dans l'Ungava par l'Université Laval », *Act. Nat.* XLV, 592–612.

1957 Deane, S. G. "A Survey of the Financial Assistance Available for Graduate Study in the Field of Education at Canadian Universities." Unpublished M.A. thesis, Univ. of Alberta.

1958 Brehaut, W. "A Quarter Century of Educational Research in Canada: An Analysis of Dissertations (English) in Education Accepted by Canadian Universities 1930–55." Unpublished doct. dissertation, Univ. of Toronto. (*See* 1960, Brehaut.)

Sheffield, E. F. "How Many? How Much?—A Note on the Role of Statistics in Education," *Jour. Ed.* no. 2, 77–81.

1959 Beaulieu, P. "What Happens to Applicants for National Research Council Scholarships in Science and Engineering," *Eng. Jour.* XLII, 71–80.

Brehaut, W. "Canadian Education Theses—Bane or Boon?" *Can. Ed.* XIV, 49–52.

Canadian Education Association. *Proceedings of the Invitational Conference on Educational Research, Saskatoon, September, 1959* includes: Katz, J. "Curriculum Research in Canada," 45–65;

MacKinnon, A. R. "Research into Learning Processes," 66–68; Stein, H. L. "Some Theoretical Considerations of Measurement in Educational Research," 91–94; "Regional Report on Educational Research," 103–93. Toronto: The Association.

Currie, B. W. "Some Problems of Physics Teaching and Research in the Universities," *Physics in Canada* XV, no. 3, 8–16.

Dobson, W. A. C. H., G. M. Wickens, and N. Keyfitz. "Near and Far Eastern Studies; the Obligation of Canadian Universities: A Symposium," *N.C.C.U.C. Proc.*, 54–76.

Flock, D. L. "Petroleum Research at University of Alberta," *Oil in Canada* XII, 36–40.

Nock, F. J. "Foreign Languages as Graduate Study Requirement," *Mod. Lang. Jour.* XLIII, 129–34.

Reeves, A. W. "A Graduate Program in School Administration," *Can. Ed.* XIV, 26–35.

Taylor, H., F. T. Rosser, A. W. Trueman, and K. Goldschlag. "Scholarships and Fellowships: A Symposium," *N.C.C.U.C. Proc.*, 24–52.

Wade, M. "The Place of Canadian Studies in American Universities," *Queen's Q.* LXVI, 377–84.

Walsh, H. H. "The Challenge of Canadian Church History to its Historians," *Can. Jour. Theol.* V, 162–70.

1960 Brehaut, W. "A Quarter Century of Educational Research in Canada: An Analysis of Dissertations (English) in Education Accepted by Canadian Universities, 1930–55," *Ont. Jour. Ed. Research* II, 109–89.

Collins, C. P. "Educational Research in Canada" in *Education/3. A Collection of Essays on Canadian Education* (Toronto: Gage), 101–106.

Garigue, P. « La Recherche et le progrès économique des Canadiens français », *Act. Econ.* XXXV, 557–65.

Graham, G. A. "A Study of Programs for Advanced Degrees in Schools of Education in Canada." Unpublished doct. dissertation, Washington State Univ.

Hughes, F. N. "Graduate Study and the Canadian Research Conference," *Ont. Coll. Pharm. Bull.* IX, 2–6.

Kidd, J. R. "From Remedial to Continuing Education," *Food for Thought* XXI, 108–11.

MacKinnon, A. R. *et al.* "Insistent Tasks in Educational Research: A Symposium," *Can. Psychologist* Ia, 131–36.

Stock, E. H. and P. J. Beaulieu. "Science Postgraduates of Canadian Universities," *Canadian Public Administration* III, 326–30.

Taylor, K. W. "Economics Scholarship in Canada," *Can. Jour. Econ. Pol. Sci.* XXVI, 6–18.

Whitworth, F. E. "Is Research in Education Lagging?" *Ont. Jour. Ed. Research* III, 1–9.

Williamson, E. L. R. "Social Research or Suicide?" *Executive* II, no. 3, 36–41.

1961 Brierley, J. R. W. *Educational Research in Canada Today and Tomorrow*. Toronto: Gage. Pp. 145.

Canadian Education Association. *Second Canadian Conference on Educational Research, Macdonald College, Ste Anne de Bellevue, June 1961*. Toronto: The Association. Pp. 90.

Canadian Nuclear Association. *Survey of Nuclear Education and Research in Canadian Universities 1961*. Toronto: The Association. Pp. 28.

Canadian Teachers' Federation. *The Role of the Classroom Teacher in Educational Research*. Ottawa: The Federation. Pp. 75.

Collip, J. B. "The Place of Research in the Training of Physicians at Both Undergraduate and Postgraduate Levels," *Ont. Med. Rev.* XXVIII, 268–70.

Cook, W. H. *Support of Scientific Research in an Affluent Society*. Ottawa: National Research Council. Pp. 17.

Douglas, V. I. "Students' Attitudes towards Formal Requirements in Graduate Training," *Can. Psych.* IIa, 14–20.

Hand, R. J. "The Case for Graduate Education in Business," *Queen's Q.* XLVIII, 473–81.

Harman, E., ed. *The University as Publisher*. Toronto: U. of T. Press. Pp. 165.

Huston, M. J. "The Function of Graduate Studies in a Pharmacy College," *Can. Pharm. Jour.* XCVI, 22–24, 47.

Jackson, R. W. B. *Educational Research in Canada Today and Tomorrow*. Toronto: Gage. Pp. 145.

Macdonald, R. I. "Postgraduate Medical Education," *Ont. Med. Rev.* XXVIII, 274–78.

Marshall, M. R. "Graduate Medical Training: Its Organization and Administration," *Can. Med. Assoc. Jour.* LXXXIV, 695–97.

Ministère du Travail, Direction de l'Economique et des Recherches. *Le Canada et la migration des travailleurs intellectuels 1946–60*. Ottawa : Imprimeur de la Reine. Pp. 52.

"Odds on a Research Career in Canada," *Can. Chem. & Process Ind.* XLV, 97–99.

Rhodes, A. J. "Diplomas or Master's Degrees: Patterns of Postgraduate Education in Public Health," *Can. Jour. of Pub. Health* LII, 142–44.

Shand, F. J. M. "Administration of Government Sponsored Scientific Research." Unpublished M.A. thesis, Carleton Univ.

Spinks, J. W. T. "Trends in University Research in Science" in G. Stanley and G. Sylvestre, eds., *The Canadian Universities Today* (Toronto: U. of T. Press), 38–44.

Vanderkamp, J. R. "Study, Research and Travel Grants for University Professors," *C.A.U.T. Bull.* IX, 13–27.

1962 Adams, C. J. "The Institute of Islamic Studies," *Can. Geog. Jour.* LXV, 34–36.

Chapman, H. E. "Western Co-Operative College," *Continuous Learning* I, 288–92.

De Koninck, C., J. W. T. Spinks *et al.* "Graduate Studies and Research in the Humanities and the Sciences" in D. Dunton and D. Patterson, eds., *Canada's Universities in a New Age* (Ottawa: N.C.C.U.C.), 33–57.

Dumont, F. et Y. Martin. *Sélection de la Recherche sur le Canada français.* Québec : Presses Univ. Laval. Pp. 296.

Geoffrion, C. "Graduate Training as the Universities See It," *Physics in Canada* XVIII, no. 5, 5–12.

Lamb, W. K. "The National Library of Canada," *Can. Geog. Jour.* LXIV, 124–26.

Jackson, R. W. B. and W. Brehaut. "Educational Research in Countries other than the United States: Canada," *Review of Educational Research* [U.S.] XXXII, 234–46.

Jasmin, G. *et al.* « Les Départements de recherche à la faculté de médecine », *Montréal Méd.* XIV, no 2, 7–21.

Ostry, B. *Recherches sur les humanités et les sciences sociales au Canada.* Ottawa : Conseil Canadien de Recherche sur les Humanités et le Conseil Canadien de Recherche en Sciences Sociales. Pp. 66./*Research in the Humanities and in the Social Sciences in Canada.* Ottawa: Humanities Research Council of Canada and the Social Science Research Council of Canada. Pp. 58.

Risi, J. « L'Ecole des gradués », *Vieil Esch.* XIV, no 4, 4–8.

Ruel, P. H. « Le Rôle de la recherche en éducation », *Rev. Univ. Sherbrooke* III, 107–15, 173–82, 225–32.

Saucier, P. « Le Chercheur, Lazare de l'Université », *Maintenant,* 184–85.

Tremblay, A. "The Role of Research in Education," *Ont. Jour. Ed. Research* IV, 161–67.

Welsh, H. L. "Graduate Studies in Physics: Aims and Procedures," *Physics in Canada* XVIII, no. 5, 13–18.

Williams, E. E. *Resources of Canadian Libraries for Research in the Humanities and Social Sciences.* Ottawa: National Conference of Canadian Universities. Pp. 87./*Ressources des bibliothèques des universités canadiennes pour la recherche en humanités et en sciences sociales.* Ottawa: Conférence Nationale des Universités et Collèges Canadiens. Pp. 93.

1963   Brehaut, W. "Educational Research in Canada 1959–61," *Can. Ed. Research Digest* III, 128–31.

Cohen, R. "Afro-Asian Studies in Canada," *Bulletin des Etudes Africaines au Canada* I, no 1, 5–29.

Garneau, J. "Project for a French Cultural Community Scholarship and Fellowship Plan," *N.C.C.U.C. Proc.,* 51–54.

Harris, W. E. "The Graduate Chemistry Program in Canadian Universities," *Chem. Can.* XV, no. 1, 42–44.

Josie, G. H. "Research Methods in Public Health: An Annotated Bibliography with Special Reference to Canadian Problems and Experience," *Can. Jour. Pub. Health* LIV, 33–42.

MacDonald, W. R. "The Training of College Teachers: A Survey in the Atlantic Provinces," *Can. Ed. and Research Digest* III, 221–29.

Mitchener, R. D. "Why Not a University Centre for the Study of Higher Education," *C.A.U.T. Bull.* XII (December), 36–38.

Mooney, C. M. "Clinical Psychology Training in Canada," *Can. Psychologist* IVa, 74–86.

Robinson, G. de B. *et al.* "Research Policy Seminar" in *Proceedings of the Fifth Mathematical Conference* (Toronto: U. of T. Press), 75–87.

Thompson, W. P. *Graduate Education in the Sciences in Canadian Universities.* Toronto: U. of T. Press. Québec: Presses Univ. Laval. Pp. 112.

1964   Booth, A. D. "Engineering Research in the University of Saskatchewan," *Saskatchewan Engineer* XVIII, 9–11.

Grainger, R. M. "Dental Research at the University of Toronto," *Journal of Ontario Dental Association* XII, 23–24.

Hamlin, D. L. B. *International Studies in Canadian Universities.* Ottawa: Canadian Universities Foundation. Pp. 120.
    Bound with:
Lalande, G. *L'Etude de relations internationales et de certaines civilisations étrangères au Canada.* Ottawa : Fondation des Universités Canadiennes. Pp. 100.

Hoyt, R. "Financial Assistance Available in Canada for Students in Psychology," *Can. Psychologist* Va, 53–63.

Priestley, F. E. L. *The Humanities in Canada: A Report Prepared for the Humanities Research Council of Canada.* Toronto: U. of T. Press. Pp. 246.

Simon, B. V. *Library Support of Medical Education and Research in Canada. Report of a Survey of the Medical College Libraries of Canada, together with Suggestions for Improving and Extending Medical Library Sources at Local, Regional and National Levels.* Ottawa: Assoc. of Canadian Medical Colleges. Pp. 133.

H. ADULT EDUCATION : EDUCATION DES ADULTES

1935   MacLellan, M. "The Catholic Church and Adult Education." Unpublished doct. dissertation, Catholic Univ. of America.

1936   Falconer, R. A. "A Canadian Point of View," *Journal of Adult Education* [U.K.] VIII, 18–21.

1937   Maine, S. F. "The Universities and Adult Education," *Adult Learning* I, no. 3, 3–8.

1938   Wallace, R. C. "The Universities and Adult Education," *Adult Learning* III, no. 2, 4–7.

1939   Timmons, H. P. "An Analysis of the Religio-Cultural Aspects of the Nova Scotia Adult Education Movement." Unpublished M.A. thesis, Catholic Univ. of America.

1940 Bruchési, J. "Adult Education and Libraries in Quebec," *Ont. Lib. Rev.* XXIV (February), 12–17.

Feir, D. L. "A Survey of Adult Education in Canada." Unpublished M.A. thesis, Univ. of Alberta.

Kelly, M. G. "The Cooperative Movement and its Promotion by Catholic Leaders." Unpublished M.A. thesis, Boston Univ.

1941 Bates, A. C. "A Study of the Adult Education Movement in Nova Scotia." Unpublished M.A. thesis, Villanova College.

British Columbia Public Library Commission. *A Preliminary Study of Adult Education in British Columbia.* Victoria: King's Printer. Pp. 77.

Sheffield, E. F. "College for Employed Adults: A Survey of the Facilities in Canada for the Formal College Education of Employed Adults and a Study of the Characteristics and Achievements of the Faculty of Arts, Science, and Commerce of Sir George Williams College." Unpublished M.A. thesis, McGill Univ.

1944 O'Neill, F. M. "A Plan for the Development of an Adult Education Program for Rural Newfoundland." Unpublished doct. dissertation, Columbia Univ.

1945 Ottewell, A. E. "CKUA is on the Air," *New Trail* III, 57–60.

1946 "The Canadian Association for Adult Education," *Can. Ed.* I, 98–102.

1947 Glasgow, F. J. "The Role of Education and Rural Conferences in the Development of St. Francis Xavier University." Unpublished M.A. thesis, St. Francis Xavier Univ.

Manitoba, Royal Commission on Adult Education. *Report. . . .* Winnipeg: King's Printer. Pp. 170.

Wiggin, G. A. "Agricultural Adult Education Programs in Saskatchewan." Unpublished doct. dissertation, Univ. of Maryland.

1949 Henson, G. "Adult Education in Nova Scotia," *Can. Ed.* IV, 39–58.

Peers, F. "University Extension in Canada," *Food for Thought* IX, no. 5, 21–25.

Westmater, R. "A Study of the Work in Canada and Newfoundland of Canadian Legion Educational Services." Unpublished doct. dissertation, Univ. of Toronto.

1951 Sheffield, E. F. "Shaping University Extension Policy," *Food for Thought* XI, no. 6, 31–33.

Smith, D. *A Survey Report on Labour Education in Canada . . . 1949–50.* Toronto: Canadian Association for Adult Education. Pp. 40.

Wilhelm, J. O. "100 Years of Adult Education: The Royal Canadian Institute," *Food for Thought* XI, no. 5, 13–16.

1952 Friesen, J. K. *et al.* "Recent Trends in Adult Education," *Food for Thought* XII, no. 1, 24–33.

Ross, M. G. *Education in Canadian Institutions: A Study of Adult Education in Sanitoria, D.V.A. Hospitals, and Provincial Reformatories in Canada.* Toronto: Canadian Association for Adult Education. Pp. 43.

La Société Canadienne d'Enseignement Post-scolaire. *L'Education des adultes au Canada.* Montréal : La Société. Pp. 52.

1953 Curran, H. W. "Extra-mural Instruction by Correspondence Since 1889," *Proceedings of the Fourth International Conference on Correspondence Education,* 121–23.

Morin, R. and H. H. Potter. *Camp Laquemac: A Bilingual Adult Education Centre.* Toronto: The Canadian Association for Adult Education. Pp. 47.

1954 Canadian Jewish Congress. *Conference on Adult Education.* Abstract of Proceedings and Key Addresses. Toronto: Canadian Jewish Congress. Pp. 48.

Coady, M. M. *The Antigonish Way.* Antigonish: St. Francis Xavier Univ., Extension Department. Pp. 84.

1956 Sheffield, E. F. "Financing Adult Education in Canada," *Food for Thought* XVI, 423–29.

Thomas More Institute for Adult Education. *An Idea of Adult Liberal Education; Report After Ten Years.* Montreal: The Institute. Pp. 51.

1957 Gunn, C. R. "Adult Education in Pictou County, Nova Scotia." Unpublished M.A. thesis, Univ. of Toronto.

National University Labour Conference, Ottawa, 1956. *Labour–University Cooperation on Education; A Report on the National Conference on Labour Education; December 15–17, 1956.* Ottawa: Canadian Labour Congress. Pp. 60.

1958 Bissell, C. T. "Education for a Leisured Economy," *Canadian Journal of Accountancy* VII, 23–27.

Emard, C. H. "A Portrait of Adult Education in a Central Alberta Town." Unpublished M.A. thesis, Univ. of Alberta.

Wales, B. E. "The Development of Adult Education in British Columbia." Unpublished doct. dissertation, Oregon State College.

Wendt, G. "Science and Adult Education," *Food for Thought* XIX, 106–117.

1959 Adamson, E. "Ammunition coming up!" *Food for Thought* XX, 18–22.

University of British Columbia, Department of Extension. *A Submission to the Royal Commission on Education, British Columbia.* Vancouver. Pp. 57.

Canadian Association for Adult Education. *Voluntary Action.* Toronto: The Association. Pp. 99.

Canadian Association for Adult Education. *Western Regional Conference of the Canadian Association for Adult Education.* Toronto: The Association. Pp. 34.

Kidd, J. R. *Continuous Learning: An Address Given at a Banquet Held on Oct. 25th, 1958 to Mark the Opening of Saskatchewan House.* Regina: Saskatchewan House, Centre for Continuing Education. Pp. 16.

O'Connor, R. E. "Adult Liberal Studies," *Food for Thought* XX, 29–34.

Thomas, A. "The Making of a Professional," *Food for Thought* XX, 4–12.

Thomas, A. "The Public Library and Adult Education in British Columbia," *B.C. Lib. Assoc. Bull.* XXIII, 3–9.

1960 Earle, F. "Adult Education for Youth," *Food for Thought* XXI, 78–83.

Kapos, A. *Toronto Speaks: A Survey of the Educational Adjustment and Leisure Time Activities of Adult Residents in the West and Central Areas of the City of Toronto.* Toronto: U. of T. Press. Pp. 36.

Lobsinger, P. "A Psychological Approach to Adult Students Taking Extension Courses." Unpublished M.A. thesis, Univ. of Alberta.

Loosley, E. *Residential Adult Education: A Canadian View.* Toronto: Canadian Association for Adult Education. Pp. 44.

Renaud, A., ed. *Adult Education in Canada.* Toronto: U. of T. Press. Pp. 81./*Education des adultes au Canada.* Québec : Presses Univ. Laval. Pp. 81.

Robinson, E. W. "The History of the Frontier College." Unpublished M.A. thesis, McGill Univ.

Smith, C. H. "Federal Contributions to Education for Adults and to Certain Agencies of Cultural Diffusion: An Analytical Survey of Developments in Canada from 1920–1960." Unpublished M.A. thesis, Univ. of British Columbia.

Stearns, A. "Adult Education for World Citizenship," *Food for Thought* XX, 220–22.

Wohlfarth, H. "A Continuing Education," *Food for Thought* XXI, 11–16, 59–66.

Wohlfarth, H. "Towards a Philosophy of University Extension," *Food for Thought* XX, 323–26.

1961 Canadian Association for Adult Education. *The Literature of Adult Education.* Toronto: The Association. Pp. 75.

Canadian Association for Adult Education. *Report of the Conference on Government and Adult Education.* Toronto: The Association. Pp. 30.

Ironside, D. "Libraries and Adult Education," *Food for Thought* XXI, 341–45.

Jasmin, C. « L'Intellectuel contre le peuple », *Liberté* III, 698–710.

Joubert, M. « Un Problème urgent : la récupération scolaire », *Food for Thought* XXI, A, 18–27.

Kidd, J. R. *Continuing Education.* Conference Study No. 6. Ottawa: Canadian Conference on Education. Pp. 104.

Kidd, J. R. "The Creative Crusade," *Food for Thought* XXI, Supplement A, 37–46.

Kidd, J. R. *Eighteen to Eighty—Continuing Education in Metropolitan Toronto.* Toronto: Toronto Board of Education. Pp. 153.

Laidlaw, A. F. *The Campus and the Community: The Global Impact of the Antigonish Movement.* Montreal: Harvest House. Pp. 171.

Lalonde, M. « Le Bonheur, ou la vocation de vivre », *Liberté* III, 756–63.

« Manifeste sur la préparation des jeunes travailleurs et des jeunes travailleuses à la vie familiale », *Prêtre* XI, 412–19.

National Conference on Adult Education, Ottawa, 1961. *Report: Perspectives for the Next Ten Years; October 30–November 1, 1961.* Toronto: Canadian Association for Adult Education. Pp. 110.

Potter, G. "The Changing University," *Food for Thought* XXI, 16–21.

Selman, G. R. "The Extension Programme of the University of British Columbia," *B.C. Lib. Q.* XXIV, 11–16.

Vernon, F. "History of Adult Education in the Province of Ontario, 1800–1940." Unpublished Ed.D. thesis, Univ. of Toronto.

1962 Chapman, H. E. "Western Co-Operative College," *Continuous Learning* I, 288–92.

Dion, L. « Education des adultes : choix des buts », *Cité Libre* XIII, no 43, 6–13.

Institut Canadien d'Education des Adultes. *Mémoire à la Commission Royale d'Enquête sur l'Enseignement.* Montréal : L'Institut. Pp. 90.

Jones, G. "A Test of Validity of Place Residence as an Indicator of Socio-Economic Characteristics in University Non-Credit Evening Classes." Unpublished M.A. thesis, Univ. of British Columbia.

Kidd, J. R. *Financing Continuing Education.* New York: The Scarecrow Press. Pp. 209.

Kidd, J. R., P. H. Sheats *et al. A Symposium on the Continuing Education in the Professions.* Vancouver: Univ. of British Columbia. Pp. 62.

Légaré, II. F. "Continuing Education for Women," *Can. Home Econ. Jour.* XII, 85–90.

Rose, A. "Education for Community Living," *Continuous Learning* I, 149–61.

Thomas More Institute for Adult Education. *Appropriate Settings for Scholarship for Adults: A Documented Survey of an Experience in Liberal Arts and Science.* Brief submitted to the Royal Commission of Inquiry on Education, Province of Quebec. Montreal: The Institute. Pp. 64.

Thomas More Institute for Adult Education. *Planning for Responsible Growth and Stability of Purpose Within a Community of Adult Citizens.* Brief submitted to the Royal Commission of Inquiry on Education, Province of Quebec. Montreal: The Institute. Pp. 13.

Tough, A. M. "The Development of Adult Education at the University of Toronto before 1920." Unpublished M.A. thesis, Univ. of Toronto.

1963 Bonnier, J. « Un Projet audacieux : l'Institut Desjardins », *Education des Adultes,* Cah. no 13, 52–57.

Canada, Bureau Fédéral de la Statistique. *Participants à une éducation*

134   ADULT EDUCATION

supplémentaire au Canada. Ottawa: Imprimeur de la Reine. Pp. 51./Dominion Bureau of Statistics. *Participants in Further Education in Canada.* Ottawa: Queen's Printer. Pp. 51.

Corbett, E. A. "Atkinson College," *Continuous Learning* II, 22–25.

Kidd, J. R., ed. *Learning and Society: Readings in Canadian Adult Education.* Toronto: Canadian Association for Adult Education. Pp. 414.

Saskatchewan Association for Adult Education. *Residential Centres for Continuing Education in Saskatchewan.* Saskatoon: The Association. Pp. 13.

Selman, G. R. "A History of the Extension and Adult Education Services of the University of British Columbia." Unpublished M.A. thesis, Univ. of British Columbia.

Senter, J. *Adult Education.* Toronto: Globe & Mail. Pp. 22.

1964 "Adult Education in British Columbia," *Jour. Ed.* no. 10. Special issue which includes the following: Wales, B. E. "The Development of Adult Education," 5–16; Selman, G. R. "University Extension 1915–1963," 17–25; Cowan, J. "Public Financing of Adult Education 1950/51–1961/62," 75–83; Goard, D. H. "The Effect of Federal Aid to Technical and Vocational Education on the Total Educational Services," 84–98.

Hamilton, W. "Continuing Education," *Can. Nurse* LX, no. 1, 29–33.

MacKenzie, N. A. M. "Adult Education Extension Work and the New Universities," *Continuous Learning* III, 9–17.

5

THE PROFESSOR
LE PROFESSEUR

1954 Aikenhead, J. D.   "To Teach, or not to Teach." Unpublished Ph.D. thesis, Univ. of Oregon.
1958 Gingras, P.-E.   « Vers un statut professionnel », *Act. Nat.* XLVIII, 31–44.
1959 Armstrong, H. S.   *Academic Administration in Higher Education: A Report on Personnel Policies and Procedures Current in Some Universities and Colleges in Canada and the U.S.* Ottawa: Canadian Universities Foundation. Pp. 98.
Beach, D. B.   "The Use of Tests in English-speaking Institutions of Higher Learning," *Can. Psychologist* VIII, 87–93.
Lougheed, W. C.   "Return to Lagado: Teaching in the Universities," *Queen's Q.* LXVI, 240–48.
Plante, G.   « Proposition d'un concept administratif de la compétence pédagogique », *Coll. et Fam.* XVI, 67–72.
Underhill, F. H.   "Academic Freedom in Canada," *C.A.U.T. Bull.* VIII, 6–16.
Underhill, F. H.   "The University and Politics," *Queen's Q.* LXVI, 217–26.
1960 Committee on University Government.   "The Reform of University Government: A Statement by the Committee on University Government Presented to the Executive Council of the C.A.U.T.," *C.A.U.T. Bull.* IX, 10–35.
Décarie, V.   « Les Professeurs auront-ils la parole ? » *Cité Libre* XI, 13–15.
Read, L. M.   "The Crowe Case: Its History and Implications," *School & Society* [U.S.], 285–89.
"Staffing Canadian Summer Schools," *C.A.U.T. Bull.* IX, 35–41.
Thériault, A.   *La Soif et le mirage.* [A French Canadian teaching in an American College.] Montréal : Cercle du Livre de France. Pp. 222.
1961 Basmajian, J. V.   "Double Standards and the University Professor," *Queen's Q.* LXVIII, 249–55.
"Comparisons of University Salaries in Canada and the United States," *C.A.U.T. Bull.* X, no. 1, 13–25.
King, F. P.   "Retirement Plans in Canadian Universities," *C.A.U.T. Bull.* X, no. 1, 5–13.

Lucow, W. W. "Integrating Testing and Teaching," *Improving College and University Teaching* [U.S.] IX, 21–22.

McEachran, A. E. "Revamping my Teaching," *Improving College and University Teaching* [U.S.] IX, 23–25.

Matthews, T. H. "The Secret Profession," *Improving College and University Teaching* [U.S.] IX, 13.

Salter, F. M. "Inspection," *Improving College and University Teaching* [U.S.] IX, 14–15.

1962   "Canadian University Salaries—A C.A.U.T. Committee Report," *C.A.U.T. Bull.* no. 3, 7–13.

Crawford, D. G. and E. I. Signori. "An Application of the Critical Incident Technique to University-teaching," *Can. Psychologist* IIIa, 126–38.

Kinghorn, A. M. "The University Teacher in Canada," *Universities Review* [U.K.] XXXIV, 59–65.

MacDonald, R. "The Opinions of College and University Teachers in the Atlantic Regions of Canada Regarding the Preparation of College and University Teachers." Unpublished doct. dissertation, Cornell Univ.

McGrath, E. « Maîtres et professeurs », *Coll. et Fam.* XIX, nos 2–3, 47–55.

Ravier, A. « Les Vraies Richesses du maître », *Coll. et Fam.* XIX, nos 2–3, 90–99.

1963   Labrie, R. « La Formation du professeur du cours classique », *Ens. Sec.* XLII, no 4, 3–8.

MacDonald, W. R. "The Training of College Teachers: A Survey in the Atlantic Provinces," *Can. Ed. Research Digest* III, 221–29.

McIntyre, J. A. "The Academic and the Administrator: A Comparative Analysis," *C.A.U.T. Bull.* XII, no. 2, 23–35.

1964   Hart, J. "A Science Chairman's Lament," *C.A.U.T. Bull.* XII, no. 3, 42–48.

"Memorandum Concerning R.C.M.P. Activities on University Campuses," *C.A.U.T. Bull.* XII, no. 4, 36–40.

Turner, G. H. "Academic Freedom and Tenure: Notes on Investigational Procedures," *C.A.U.T. Bull.* no. 3, 48–54.

Weynerowski, W. "Preliminary Report on Current [1963–64] Pension and Sabbatical Arrangements at Canadian Universities and Colleges," *C.A.U.T. Bull.* XII, no. 4, 16–24.

6

THE STUDENT
L'ETUDIANT

1939   Dunn, E. J. "Prediction of Freshman Success in the University of British Columbia." Unpublished M.A. thesis, Univ. of Washington.

1949   Chevrier, J.-M. « Prédiction de succès à la première année du cours technique ». Unpublished L.Paéd. thesis, Univ. of Montréal.

Hayes, H. O. "A Comparative Study of Three Hundred Student Veterans in the Faculty of Arts at the University of British Columbia." Unpublished M.A. thesis, Univ. of British Columbia.

Nelson, L. D. "The Prediction of Achievement in First Year Engineering." Unpublished M.Ed. thesis, Univ. of Alberta.

Safran, C. "A Study of the Relationships between Veterans' Scores in Pre-Matriculation School and University." Unpublished M.Ed. thesis, Univ. of Alberta.

1950   Martin, J. I. "Predicting Success of Education Students in Academic Courses and in Teaching." Unpublished M.Ed. thesis, Univ. of Alberta.

1952   Line, W. *et al. The Veteran at Varsity: An Enquiry Concerning the Impact of the Veteran Student on Policy and Practices in the University of Toronto, 1945–51*. Toronto: Univ. of Toronto Bookstore. Pp. 49.

1953   Baskerville, D. R. "A Survey of Student Personnel Services in English-Speaking Canadian Colleges and Universities with Particular Reference to the Role of the Dean of Women." Unpublished M.A. thesis, Syracuse Univ.

1954   Arvelo, H. P. "A Study of Students' Opinions Regarding Teaching Practices." Unpublished M.Ed. thesis, Univ. of Toronto.

Fleming, W. G. "Factors Affecting the Predictive Accuracy of Ontario Upper School Results." Unpublished doct. thesis, Univ. of Toronto.

1955   Hay, C. M. "A Method for Evaluating or Measuring the Attitudes of (a) Responsibility and (b) Co-operation." Unpublished M.Ed. thesis, Univ. of Alberta.

Vaillancourt, R. F. "Local College Prediction with the Otis and the Otis-Ottawa." Unpublished M.A. thesis, Univ. of Ottawa.

1957   Atkinson Study on Utilization of Student Resources. *Report* (1957–63), 10 vols. to date. Toronto: Univ. of Toronto, Ontario College of Education, Dept. of Educational Research.

1. Fleming, W. G. "Background and Personality Factors Associated with Educational and Occupational Plans and Careers of Ontario Grade 13 Students. 1957. Pp. 158.
2. Fleming, W. G. "Ontario Grade 13 Students: Who Are They and What Happens to Them? 1957. Pp. 59.
3. Fleming, W. G. "Aptitude and Achievement Scores Related to Immediate Education and Occupational Choices of Ontario Grade 13 Students." 1958. Pp. 380.
4. Fleming, W. G. "Ontario Grade 13 Students: Their Aptitude, Achievement, and Immediate Destination." 1958. Pp. 56.
5. Fleming, W. G. "Personal and Academic Factors as Predictors of First Year Success in Ontario Universities." 1959. Pp. 137.
6. Brehaut, W. "A First-Year Follow-Up Study of Atkinson Students who Enrolled in Hospital Schools of Nursing." 1960. Pp. 58.
7. Fleming, W. G. "A Follow-Up Study of Atkinson Students in Certain Non-Degree Courses of Further Education Beyond Secondary School." 1960. Pp. 35.
8. Pipher, J. A. "Barriers to University." 1962. Pp. 53.
9. Fleming, W. G. "The Use of Predictive Factors for the Improvement of University Admission Requirements." 1962. Pp. 76.
10. Fleming, W. G. and G. R. Eastwood. "From Grade 13 to Employment—A Follow-Up Study of Students who Entered Employment Immediately After Leaving School." 1963. Pp. 66.

Supplementary Reports:
1. Savage, H. W. "An Evaluation of the Cooperative English Test of Effectiveness of Expression for Use in Ontario." 1958. Pp. 39.
2. Fleming, W. G. "The Kuder Preference Record—Vocational as a Predictor of Post-High School Educational and Occupational Choices." 1959. Pp. 49.
3. Savage, H. W. "An Evaluation of the Brown-Holtzman Survey of Study Habits and Attitudes for Use in Ontario." 1961. Pp. 34.
4. Flowers, J. F. "An Evaluation of the Kuder Preference Record—Personal for Use in Ontario." 1961. Pp. 31.

Verney, R. E., ed. *The Student Life: The Philosophy of Sir William Osler.* Edinburgh & London: E. & S. Livingstone. Pp. 214.

1958 Crompton, O. "The Prediction of University Freshmen Performance on the Basis of High School Achievement in British Columbia." Unpublished M.A. thesis, Univ. of British Columbia.

1959 Anderson, R. O. "Leisure Time Interests and Activities of First Year Women at the University of Alberta." Unpublished M.Ed. thesis, Univ. of Alberta.

Bushnell, J. R. R. *Provincial Student Aid Programmes for Higher*

*Education; a Paper Presented to the University Counselling &
Placement Association, Saskatoon, June 12, 1959.* Ottawa: Canadian Universities Foundation. Pp. 31.

Canada, Bureau of Statistics, Education Division, Research Section.
University Student Expenditure and Income in Canada 1956–57.
Ottawa: Queen's Printer. Pp. 91.

Fleming, W. G. *Research into the Utilization of Academic Talent—
Contributions of the Atkinson and Carnegie Studies.* Educational
Research Series No. 31. Toronto: Department of Educational Re-
search, Ontario College of Education, Univ. of Toronto. Pp. 26.

Kieran, J. W. and W. W. Muir. "What University Degrees Mean in
Applicants for Office Jobs," *Office Equipment and Methods* V,
36–39.

Rideout, E. B. "A New Dimension in the Measurement of Educational Need and Ability to Pay," *Ont. Jour. Ed. Research* I,
no. 2, 161–67.

Smith, D. D. "Traits and College Achievement," *Can. Jour. Psych.*
XIII, 93–100.

Taylor, H., F. T. Rosser, A. W. Trueman, and K. Goldschlag.
"Scholarships and Fellowships: A Symposium," *N.C.C.U.C. Proc.*,
24–52.

Wipper, K. A. W. "Fitness of First Year Students at the University
of Toronto between November and March, 1956–57." Unpublished M.A. thesis, Univ. of Toronto.

Zurowsky, J. "Predicting Freshman Success in Seven Science and
Two Business Administration Courses at the University of
Alberta." Unpublished M.Ed. thesis, Univ. of Alberta.

1960 « Les Conditions de la gratuité scolaire », *Relations* XX, 198–200.

Dufresne, G. « Il faut payer les étudiants », *Cité Libre* XI, 8–9.

Fournier, P. A. "Government Aid to Students in Quebec," *Can.
Ed.* XV, 29–36.

Gagnon, G. « L'Action étudiante », *Cité Libre* XI, 17–19.

Pipher, J. A. "An Appraisal of the Use of the Dominion Group
Test of Learning Capacity (Advanced) in the Atkinson Study of
Utilization of Student Resources," *Ont. Jour. Ed. Research* III,
no. 1, 17–25.

Seaman, B. E. "A Study of Academic Under-Achievement among
Education Students at the University of Alberta." Unpublished
M.Ed. thesis, Univ. of Alberta.

Whitworth, F. E. "The Cost of a Year at University" *in Education*/3.
A Collection of Essays on Canadian Education (Toronto: Gage),
89–93.

1961 Anderson, R. O. "Leisure Time Interests and Activities of First-
Year Women," *Alberta Journal of Educational Research* VII,
65–73.

Beattie, L. S. *The Development of Student Potential.* Conference
Study No. 3. Ottawa: Canadian Conference on Education. Pp. 63.

Clarke, D. B. *et al.* "Problems of Overseas Students in Canada,"
N.C.C.U.C. Proc., 23–53.

Hoyt, R. "Financial Assistance Available in Canada for Students in Psychology," *Can. Psych.* IIa, 6–14.

Joly, G. W., R. N. Smith, and M. Wisenthal. "Problem Students," *Improving College and University Teaching* [U.S.] IX, 26–31.

Macdonald, N. W. "Some Factors Affecting the Frequency and Status of University Students' 'Dating Behaviour'." Unpublished M.A. thesis, Univ. of British Columbia.

MacFarlane, J. D. "A Follow-Up Study to Determine the Effect of Enrichment Programs in a High School upon Achievement at University." Unpublished M.Ed. thesis, Univ. of Manitoba.

Smith, D. C. "Success and Failure in the First Year: An Investigation of Factors Distinguishing Successful from Failing Freshmen Students in the Institute of Education, McGill University, 1958–59." Unpublished M.A. thesis, McGill Univ.

Vanderkamp, J. R. *Provincial Programmes of Aid to University Students 1957–58 to 1960–61.* Ottawa: Canadian Universities Foundation. Pp. 27.

World University Service of Canada. *Problems of Overseas Students in Canada.* Toronto: The Service. Pp. 34.

1962   Brazeau, J. et al. *Les Résultats d'une enquête auprès des étudiants dans les universités de langue française du Québec ; rapport soumis à l'A.G.E.L., l'A.G.E.U.M. et l'A.G.E.U.S.* Montréal : Département de Sociologie, Univ. de Montréal. Pp. 198.

Eddison, R. F. "Opportunities for University Education," *Dalhousie Rev.* XLI, 466–72.

Jones, G. B. "An Experimental Application of the Principle of Incongruity Tolerance to the Counselling Setting." Unpublished M.Ed. thesis, Univ. of Alberta.

Roseborough, H. and J. Kurt. *A Report on a Survey of Students at McGill University, Sir George Williams University, and Bishop's University.* Montreal: McGill Univ. Students Society. Pp. 57.

Ross, M. G., D. L. Thomson *et al.* "Scholarships, Bursaries and Fellowships" in D. Dunton and D. Patterson, eds., *Canada's Universities in a New Age* (Ottawa: N.C.C.U.C.), 57–110.

1963   Easton, P. W. *Secondary School Survivors: A Follow-Up Study of Students Included in the 1955–57 Survey.* Educational Research Series No. 4. Toronto: Dept. of Educational Research, Ontario College of Education, Univ. of Toronto. Pp. 11.

Fédération des Collèges Classiques. *La Foi des étudiants.* Document no 20. Montréal : La Fédération. Pp. 123.

Gibson, F. W. "The University and the Student in a Changing Society," *Queen's Q.* LXX, 273–79.

National Federation of Canadian University Students' Committee, Loyola College. *Student Summer Employment in Canada.* Montreal: The Federation Committee at Loyola College. Pp. 33.

1964   Fieldhouse, H. N. "The University Student: Selection and Admission" in *Ninth Congress of the Universities of the Commonwealth, Report of Proceedings* (London: Clark), 120–27.

7

UNIVERSITY FINANCE
FINANCES UNIVERSITAIRES

1921 Royal Commission on University Finances. *Report.* . . . Toronto: King's Printer. 2 vols.
1937 Ikin, A. E. "Educational Endowments in the Dominion of Canada" in E. Percy, ed., *The Year Book of Education* (London: Evans Brothers Limited), 294–307.
1946 Baird, N. B. "Educational Finance and Administration for Ontario." Unpublished doct. dissertation, Univ. of Toronto.
1950 MacKenzie, N. A. M. and D. C. Rowat. "The Federal Government and Higher Education in Canada," *Can. Jour. Econ. Pol. Sci.* XVI, 353–70.
1951 Legault, G. « Pour une aide provinciale aux universités », *Thémis* I, 79–85.
1953 Canada, Teachers' Federation. *Educational Finance in Canada.* Ottawa: The Federation. Pp. 80. Revised 1954, 1958.
1954 MacKenzie, N. A. M. "Government and Universities" in *Seventh Congress of the Universities of the Commonwealth* (Cambridge: Cambridge Univ. Press), 22–26.
1956 Bissell, C. T. "Problems in University Planning for the Next Ten Years," *N.C.C.U. Proc.*, 82–87.
Brunet, M. « L'Aide fédérale aux universités : quand le gouvernement acceptera-t-il de se soumettre à la constitution ? » *Act. Nat.* XLVI, 191–215.
Sheffield, E. F. "Financing Adult Education in Canada," *Food for Thought* XVI, 423–29.
1957 Bissell, C. T., ed. *Canada's Crisis in Higher Education.* Toronto: U. of T. Press. Pp. 272.
Fédération des Collèges Classiques. *Frais de scolarité et de pension dans les collèges classiques.* Document no 4. Montréal: La Fédération. Pp. 49.
Industrial Foundation on Education. *Reports* (1957–62), 14 vols.:
1. "The Case for Corporate Giving to Higher Education." 1957. Pp. 63.
2. "The Case for Increasing Student Aid." 1958. Pp. 87.
3. "The Case for Increasing Student Motivation." 1958. Pp. 59.
4. "Programmes of Industry and Commerce for Financial Assistance to Higher Education." 1958. Pp. 54.

5. "The Case for Corporate Giving to Higher Education (1958 Supplement)." 1958. Pp. 57.
6. "The Case for Corporate Giving to Higher Education (1959 Supplement)." 1959. Pp. 49.
7. "The Case for Corporate Giving to Higher Education (1960 Supplement). 1960. Pp. 53.
8. "Public Fund-Raising by Canadian Universities and Colleges." 1960. Pp. 16.
9. "The Case for Increasing Student Motivation (1960 Supplement)." 1960. Pp. 35.
10. "Scholarships and Bursaries Provided by Business and Industry." 1961. Pp. 72.
11. "The Case for Increasing Student Aid (1961 Supplement)." 1961. Pp. 42.
12. "The Case for Corporate Giving to Higher Education (1961 Supplement)." 1961. Pp. 63.
13. "Company Matching—Gifts Programmes." 1962. Pp. 23.
14. "The Case for Corporate Giving to Higher Education (1962 Supplement)." 1962. Pp. 54.

Moffat, H. P. *Educational Finance in Canada*. Toronto: Gage. Pp. 95.

Trudeau, P.-E. « Les Octrois fédéraux aux universités », *Cité Libre* XVI, 9–31.

1958 Canadian Teachers' Federation. *Educational Finance in Canada, 1946–1956*. Research Bulletin No. 1, February 1958. Pp. 58.

Woodside, W. *The University Question*. Toronto: Ryerson. Pp. 199.

1959 Bushnell, J. R. R. *Provincial Student Aid Programmes for Higher Education: A Paper Presented to the University Counselling & Placement Association, Saskatoon, June 12, 1959*. Ottawa: Canadian University Foundation. Pp. 31.

Gauthier, A. « A propos des octrois fédéraux », *Act. Univ.* XXV, no 4, 7–8, 26–27.

McLean, J. F. "Unions on the University Campus," *Canadian Personnel and Industrial Relations Journal* VI, 39–45.

Parenteau, R. « Le Financement des commissions scolaires », *Act. Econ.* XXXIV, 660–69.

1960 Beauchemin, G. « Contribution de l'Eglise à l'enseignement classique », *Bull. Féd. Coll.* VI, no 2, 1–3.

Canada, Bureau Fédéral de la Statistique. *Traitements des professeurs d'université 1937–1960*. Ottawa: L'Imprimeur de la Reine. Pp. 35./Canada, Dominion Bureau of Statistics. *University Teacher's Salaries, 1937–1960*. Ottawa: Queen's Printer. Pp. 35.

Fédération des Collèges Classiques. *Droits annuels et courses d'études dans les collèges classiques*. Document no 10. Montréal : La Fédération. Pp. 44.

Fédération des Collèges Classiques. *Problèmes d'administration financière*. Document no 14. Montréal : La Fédération. Pp. 86.

Fournier, P. A. "Government Aid to Students in Quebec," *Can. Ed.* XV, no. 3, 29–36.

Moffat, H. P. "Educational Finance in Canada," *Canadian Research Digest* I, no. 8, 155–69.

Rideout, E. B. "A New Dimension in the Measurement of Educational Need and Ability to Pay," *Ont. Jour. Ed. Research* I, 161–67.

Sheffield, E. F. "Canadian Government Aid to Universities," *Vestes, The Australian Universities Review* III, no. 2, 20–25.

Sheffield, E. F. *Financial Needs of Canadian Universities and Colleges, 1960.* Ottawa: Canadian Universities Foundation. Pp. 15./*Besoins financiers des universités et des collèges au Canada, 1960.* Ottawa: Fondation des Universités Canadiennes. Pp. 15.

Smith, C. "Federal Contributions to Education for Adults and Certain Agencies of Cultural Diffusion: An Analytical Survey of Developments in Canada from 1920 to 1960." Unpublished M.A. thesis, Univ. of British Columbia.

Tremblay, A. « Les Subventions fédérales aux universités », *Cité Libre* XI, 3–12.

1961   Angers, F.-A. « Octrois aux universités et position constitutionnelle du Québec », *Act. Nat.* L, 222–32, 330–42.

Brown, G. A. "The Financing and Administration of Some Aspects of Education Shared by Dominion and Provinces." Unpublished M.A. thesis, Carleton Univ.

"Canada" in *Economic Factors Affecting Access to the Universities* (Geneva: World University Service), 4–10.

Canadian Federation of Mayors and Municipalities. *The Costs of Education: Data Assembled for the 1961 Annual Conference of the Canadian Federation of Mayors and Municipalities, Held at Halifax, Nova Scotia, May 30th to June 3rd, 1961.* Montreal: The Federation. Pp. 37.

Canadian Teachers' Federation. *The Cost of Education—Challenge of the Sixties.* Ottawa: The Federation. Pp. 40.

Deutsch, J. J. "The University and Its Finances" in G. Stanley and G. Sylvestre, eds., *Canadian Universities Today* (Toronto: U. of T. Press), 80–86.

Fédération des Collèges Classiques. *Uniformisation de la comptabilité.* Document no 16. Montréal : La Fédération. Pp. 97.

The Financing of Higher Education in New Brunswick. Sackville: Mount Allison Univ. Pp. 22.

Gingras, P.-E. « Gratuité scolaire et enseignement libre », *Act. Nat.* L, 539–45.

McCordic, W. J. *Financing Education in Canada.* Conference Study No. 5. Ottawa: Canadian Conference on Education. Pp. 61.

Moran, H. O. "Canada's Educational Aid Programs," *Can. Ed. Research Digest* I, no. 4, 5–12.

Parenteau, R. « Finances provinciales », *Act. Econ.* XXXVII, 155–68.

Parizeau, J. « Finances fédérales », *Act. Econ.* XXXVII, 169–80.

Sheffield, E. F. *Sources of University Support.* Ottawa: Canadian Universities Foundation. Pp. 23./*Provenance de l'appui financier aux universités.* Ottawa : Fondation des Universités Canadiennes. Pp. 15.

Soucy, E.　« Cette Aide serait-elle un piège ? » *Act. Nat.* LI, no 1, 60–64.

Vanderkamp, J. R.　*Provincial Programmes of Aid to University Students, 1957–58 to 1960–61.* Ottawa: Canadian Universities Foundation. Pp. 27./*Programmes provinciaux d'aide aux étudiants d'université, 1957–58 à 1960–61.* Ottawa : Fondation des Universités Canadiennes. Pp. 27.

World University Service of Canada. *Problems of Overseas Students in Canada.* Toronto: The Service. Pp. 34.

1962　Ares, R.　« La Conférence canadienne sur l'éducation. l'aide fédérale et le 'Montreal Star' », *Act. Nat.* LI, 660–65.

Kidd, J. R.　*Financing Continuing Education.* New York: The Scarecrow Press. Pp. 209.

Le Sieur, A.　« Le Rôle du militaire dans l'aide financière fédérale accordée aux universités canadiennes ». Thèse de doctorat, Univ. d'Ottawa.

MacKenzie, N. A. M.　"Universities, Colleges, and Government Grants," *Dalhousie Rev.* XLII, 5–17.

Sheffield, E. F. and C. M. ApSimon.　*University Costs and Sources of Support/Dépenses des universités et provenance de l'appui financier.* Ottawa: Canadian Universities Foundation. Pp. 35.

1963　Brunet, M.　*Le Financement de l'enseignement au Québec.* Montréal : L'Académie Canadienne-française. Pp. 31.

Canadian Universities Foundation. *Brief to the Prime Minister of Canada Presented . . . May, 1963.* Ottawa: The Foundation. Pp. 20.

Smiley, D. N.　*Conditional Grants and Canadian Federalism.* Toronto: Canadian Tax Foundation. Pp. 72.

1964　Canadian Association of University Teachers. "Brief to the Minister of Finance on the Financing of Universities," *C.A.U.T. Bull.* XII, 25–35.

Deutsch, J. J.　"The Role of the Layman in Respect of Finance in University Government" in *Ninth Congress of the Universities of the Commonwealth, Report of Proceedings* (London: Clark), 91–95.

Québec, Ministère de la Jeunesse. *Les Besoins financiers de l'éducation au Québec, 1964–1967 : problèmes et options.* Etude du Bureau de la Planification publiée par le service de l'information du Ministère de la Jeunesse. Québec : Imprimeur de la Reine. Pp. 38.

Wylie, T. J.　*Financing Higher Education in Canada No. 5, Government Support of Universities and Colleges/Le Financement de l'enseignement supérieur au Canada no 5, appui financier accordé aux universités et collèges par les gouvernements.* Ottawa: Canadian Universities Foundation. Pp. 45.

8

UNIVERSITY GOVERNMENT
GOUVERNEMENT DES UNIVERSITES

1951 Laurendeau, A. « Autonomie universitaire et autonomie provinciale », *Act. Nat.* XXXVIII, 161–64.
1953 Salter, F. M. "The University in a Democratic Age," *N.C.C.U. Proc.* 45–53.
1954 MacKenzie, N. A. M. "Government and Universities" in *Seventh Congress of the Universities of the Commonwealth, Report of Proceedings* (Cambridge: Cambridge Univ. Press), 22–26.
1956 Rowat, D. C. "The Government of Canadian Universities," *Culture* XVII, 268–83, 364–78.
1957 Rowat, D. C. "Faculty Participation in Canadian University Government," *American Association of University Professors Bulletin* XLIII, 461–76.
Stewart, C. H. "The Government of Canadian Universities," *C.A.U.T. Bull.* V, no. 2, 8–10.
1959 Armstrong, H. S. *Academic Administration in Higher Education: A Report on Personal Policies and Procedures Current in Some Universities and Colleges in Canada and the U.S.* Ottawa: Canadian Universities Foundation. Pp. 98.
1959 Fowke, V. C. "Who Should Determine University Policy," *C.A.U.T. Bull.* VII, 4–13.
Smith, J. P. "Let Professors Control the Universities," *Saturday Night* (February 28, 1959), 18–19, 40.
Underhill, F. H. "Academic Freedom in Canada," *C.A.U.T. Bull.* VIII, no. 2, 6–16.
"University Government in Canada as Illustrated by the Case of United College, Winnipeg," *Universities Review* [U.K.] XXXI, 43–48.
1960 Canadian Association of University Teachers. "The Reform of University Government," A Statement by the Committee on University Government Presented to the Executive Council of the Canadian Association of University Teachers, *C.A.U.T. Bull.* IX, 10–35.
Décarie, V. « Les Professeurs auront-ils la parole ? » *Cité Libre* XI, no 29, 13–14.
Smith, J. P. "University Government," *C.A.U.T. Bull.* VIII, 4–15.
Smith, J. P. "University Government in Canada and the Case of Professor Crowe," *Science and Freedom* [U.K.] no. 15, 26–30.

Thompson, W. P. "University Government," *C.A.U.T. Bull.* IX, no. 2, 4–8.

1961   MacKenzie, N. A. M. "Faculty Participation in University Government," *C.A.U.T. Bull.* IX, no. 4, 8–14.

Morton, W. L. "University Government: The Alienation of the Administration," *C.A.U.T. Bull.* IX, 5–13.

1962   Morton, W. L. "The Evolution of University Government in Canada," *Can. For.* XLI, 243–47.

Rowat, D. C. "The Uniqueness of the University Administration," *C.A.U.T. Bull.* no. 4, 22–27.

1962   Story, G. M. (Chairman). *University Government: A Report of the Memorial University of Newfoundland Teachers' Association.* St. John's: Memorial Univ. Pp. 54.

1964   Belshaw, C. S. *Anatomy of a University.* Vancouver: Univ. of British Columbia. Pp. 67.

Freedman, S. "University Government," *C.A.U.T. Bull.* XIII, no. 1, 14–26.

Lower, A. R. M. "Administrators and Scholars," *Queen's Q.* LXXI, 203–13.

MacKenzie, N. A. M. "Can Faculty Members Take Control," *Saturday Night* LXXIX (September 1964), 14–15.

Sissons, C. B. "The University and Democracy" in *Nil Alienum: The Memoirs of C. B. Sissons* (Toronto: U. of T. Press), 143–66.

Whalley, G., ed. *A Place of Liberty.* Toronto: Clarke, Irwin. Pp. 224.

9

TECHNICAL INSTITUTES, COMMUNITY COLLEGES, ETC.
AUTRES INSTITUTIONS D'ENSEIGNEMENT SUPERIEUR

1919 Buteau, J.-A. *Notre enseignement technique industriel*. Québec. Pp. 124.

1925 MacLean, J. A. and W. C. Murray. "The Junior College in the United States and Canada," *N.C.C.U.C. Proc.*, 27–33.

1927 Sandiford, P. "Junior High Schools and Junior Colleges," *Queen's Q.* XXXIV, 367–83.

1933 McLeish, I. "Technical and Industrial Education in Quebec," *Sch. Prog.* I, no. 8, 17–20, 24, 26–27.

"Technical Education" in E. Percy, ed., *The Year Book of Education* (London: Evans Brothers Limited), 527–31.

1934 Fox, W. S. "Report on the Junior College Situation in Canada in 1934," *N.C.C.U.C. Proc.*, 65–71.

McQueen, J. "The Development of the Technical and Vocational Schools of Ontario." Unpublished M.A. thesis, Columbia Univ.

Thompson, W. P. "The Junior College within the University," *N.C.C.U.C. Proc.*, 72–74.

1939 Sexton, F. H. "Technical Education in Canada" in H. V. Usill, ed., *The Year Book of Education 1939* (London: Evans Brothers Limited), 604–34.

1941 Johns, R. J. "Origin and Development of Technical Education in Canada." Unpublished M.Ed. thesis, Colorado State College of Agriculture and Mechanic Arts.

1949 "The Ryerson Institute of Technology," *Sch. Prog.* XVI, no. 3, 30–33.

1958 Woodside, W. "The Role of the Junior College" and "More Technical Institutes" in *The University Question* (Toronto: Ryerson), 116–29.

1959 Letendre, G. « Un Beau Rêve qui devrait devenir une heureuse réalité », *Act. Nat.* XLVIII, 180–87.

Royal Commission on Education in Alberta. *Report*. . . . Edmonton: Queen's Printer. Pp. 451.

1960 Boston, R. E. "The Training of Engineering Technicians," *Jour. Ed.* no. 4, 79–84.

Canada, Department of Labour, Interdepartmental Skilled Manpower

Training Research Committee. *Acquisition of Skills.* Report No. 4. Ottawa: Dept. of Labour. Pp. 68.

Mitchener, R. D. "Junior Colleges in Canada," *Junior College Journal* [U.S.] XXX, 400–12.

1961 Canada, Senate. *Final Report of the Committee of the Senate on Manpower and Employment.* No. 25. Ottawa: Queen's Printer. Pp. 76.

Comité d'Etude sur l'Enseignement Agricole et Agronomique. *Rapport...* Québec : Imprimeur de la Reine. Pp. 267.

Deschamps, R. « Ecole Forestière de Duchesnay », *For. et Cons.* XXVII, no 7, 10.

Goodings, B. H. "The Engineering Technician—His Present and His Future," *Design Eng.* VII, no. 1, 38–40.

"No Faculty Can Train Engineer and Technician," *Can. Consulting Eng.* III, no. 6, 38–41.

Pigott, A. V. *A Brief on Manpower and Employment.* Toronto: Canadian Association for Adult Education. Pp. 42.

Ross, A. M. "Why We Need More Junior Colleges," *Saturday Night* LXXVI (September 16, 1961), 22–25.

1962 Association des Diététistes du Québec. *Mémoire sur l'enseignement ménager, présenté à la Commission Royale d'Enquête sur l'Enseignement.* Montréal: L'Association. Pp. 61.

Canada, Ministère du Travail, Direction de la Formation Technique et Professionnelle. *Education technique et professionnelle au Canada.* Ottawa: Imprimeur de la Reine. Pp. 30.

Canadian Department of Labour, Information Branch. *Technical and Vocational Education in Canada.* Ottawa: Queen's Printer. Pp. 16.

Cohen, P. *Another Look at Occupational Trends and Their Implications for Education, Training and Guidance.* Ottawa: Economics and Research Branch, Dept. of Labour. Pp. 14.

Comité d'Etude sur l'Enseignement Technique et Professionnel. *Rapport...* Québec : Imprimeur de la Reine. 2 vols.

Craighead, D. H. "The Institute of Technology in English Canada," *N.C.C.U.C. Proc.*, 65–69.

Cousins, W. J. "The Junior College," *N.C.C.U.C. Proc.*, 52–55.

Dolan, R. C. « L'Institut de Technologie dans la Province de Québec », *N.C.C.U.C. Proc.*, 58–64.

Goard, D. H. "Two Comments on Terminal Programs," *Continuous Learning* I, 90–93.

Hall, O. and B. McFarlane. *Transitions from School to Work.* Report No. 10, Research Program on the Training of Skilled Manpower. Ottawa: Queen's Printer. Pp. 89.

Macdonald, J. B. *Higher Education in British Columbia and a Plan for the Future.* Vancouver: Univ. of British Columbia. Pp. 119.

Sch. Prog. Issue devoted to Technical/Vocational Education. XXXI, May.

Simon, F. "History of the Alberta Provincial Institute of Technology and Art." Unpublished M.A. thesis, Univ. of Alberta.

Sinclair, S. "Technical and Vocational Training: Are We on the Right Road?" *Can. Bus.* XXXV, no. 4, 42–44, 103–104, 107–10; no. 5, 66–70, 73–77.

Whitworth, F. E., ed. *Skills for Tomorrow.* Ottawa: Canadian Conference on Education. Pp. 73./*Vers le climat technique de l'avenir.* Ottawa : Conférence Canadienne sur l'Education. Pp. 73.

1963   Beattie, L. S., *et al. A Study to Determine the Need for Technical Education in North York Township.* Toronto: Board of Education for the Township of North York. Pp. 70.

Canada, Department of Labour. Research Program on the Training of Skilled Manpower. *Occupational Trends in Canada 1931 to 1961.* Report No. 11.

Canada, Ministère du Travail, Bureau de la main-d'œuvre féminine. *Formation professionelle et technique pour les jeunes filles aux niveaux de l'école secondaire, de l'école post-secondaire et de l'école de métiers au Canada.* Ottawa : Imprimeur de la Reine. Pp. 111.

Committee of Presidents of Provincially Assisted Universities and Colleges of Ontario. *Post-Secondary Education in Ontario, 1962–1970; Report of the Presidents of the Universities of Ontario to the Advisory Committee on University Affairs, May 1962.* Toronto: U. of T. Press. Pp. 44.

Committee of Presidents of Provincially Assisted Universities and Colleges of Ontario. *The Structure of Post-Secondary Education in Ontario. Supplementary Report No. 1, June 1963.* Toronto: U. of T. Press. Pp. 30.

Dayon, M. « Réformer les instituts familiaux », *Maintenant,* 13–15.

Jasmin, J.-J. « Où en est rendu l'Institut de Technologie Agricole de St.-Hyacinthe ? » *Agr.* XX, 100–102.

Jasmin, J.-J. « L'Ingérance du gouvernement fédéral dans le domaine de l'enseignement technique et professionnel », *Agr.* XX, 139–41.

Ontario, Legislative Assembly, Select Committee on Manpower Training. *Report, February, 1963.* Toronto: Queen's Printer. Pp. 136.

Sch. Prog. Issue devoted to a consideration of junior community colleges. XXXII, July.

Sch. Prog. Issue devoted to Technical/Vocational Education. XXXII, May.

1964   Hamilton, F. A. (Chairman). *Report of the Grade 13 Study Committee, 1964: Submitted to the Honourable William G. Davis, Minister of Education, June 26, 1964.* Toronto: Ontario Dept. of Education. Pp. 35.

Royal Commission on Health Services. *Report.* . . . Ottawa: Queen's Printer. 2 vols.

Sch. Prog. Issue devoted to Technical/Vocational Education. XXXIII, May.

10

FICTION
ROMANS ET LITTERATURES DRAMATIQUES

1853 Chauveau, P.-J.-O. *Charles Guèrin*. Montréal : G. H. Cherrier. Pp.
359. Le problème de l'encombrement des professions libérales —
sacerdoce, droit, médecine — vers le milieu du XIXe siècle au
Canada français.

1879 Withrow, W. H. *The King's Messenger; or, Lawrence Temple's
Probation, a Story of Canadian Life*. Toronto: Methodist Book and
Publishing House. Pp. 232. An important section of this novel
about a Methodist clergyman is devoted to his years at Burghroyal
College, where "learning was not divorced from religion, nor
science made the handmaid of scepticism."

1897 Pettit, M. *Beth Woodburn*. Toronto: Briggs. Pp. 158. The heroine,
an aspiring novelist from Norfolk County on the Lake Erie shore,
attends the University of Toronto briefly.

1900 Carman, A. R. *The Preparation of Ryerson Embury, a Purpose*.
Toronto: Publisher's Syndicate. Pp. 248. The hero loses his faith
while at a Methodist College and is converted to socialism on
reading Henry George's *Progress and Poverty*. An interesting picture of college life in the 1880's.

Choquette, E. *Carabinades*. Montréal : Deom Frères. Pp. 226. Souvenirs romancés d'un ancien « carabin » à l'Université Laval, sous
forme de contes.

1903 Dick, V.-E. *Le Roi des étudiants*. Saint-Henri : Decarie, Hébert et
Cie. Pp. 262. Les aventures invraisemblables de quatre étudiants
en médecine. Roman publié d'abord en feuilleton en 1876.

1904 Connor, R. *The Prospector: A Tale of the Crow's Nest Pass*.
Toronto: Westminster. Pp. 401. Chapter II contains the famous
account of a football game between Toronto and McGill.

1906 Connor, R. *The Doctor: A Tale of the Rockies*. New York: Grosset
& Dunlop. Pp. 399. The student careers of two brothers who
become respectively doctor and clergyman are described (inci-
dentally) in this melodrama. Barney's graduation from Trinity
Medical School is described.

Machar, A. M. *Roland Graeme; Knight: A Novel of Our Time*.
Toronto: Briggs. Pp. 285. This novel by the daughter of John
Machar, Principal of Queen's 1846–54, is similar in theme to
Carman's *The Preparation of Ryerson Embury* (see above).

O'Higgins, H. J. *Don-A-Dreams: A Story of Love and Youth*. New

York: Century. Pp. 412. Part II of this four-part novel is set at University College, University of Toronto in the 1890's. It gives a fairly detailed account of student life, particularly in the residence.

1907 Barr, R. *The Measure of the Rule.* London: Constable. Pp. 308. Primarily concerned with the Normal School at Toronto (which the author attended 1873–74), but includes a vivid picture of University College and of its Principal, John McCaul, during the hero's "university career of half-a-day."

1917 Seton, E. T. *The Preacher of Cedar Mountain.* New York: Doubleday. Pp. 426. The hero ("illiterate, penniless and already twenty three") spends an unhappy year at a small theological college in Ontario in 1877.

1921 Genest, F. D. *The Letters of Si Whiffletree—Freshman.* Montreal: The Author. Pp. 69. Why Stephen Leacock bothered to contribute a preface to this collection of (intentionally) illiterate letters, originally published in the *McGill Daily*, remains a mystery.

MacKinnon, L. V. *Miriam of Queen's.* Toronto: McClelland and Stewart. Pp. 310. Love and lectures at Queen's University, Kingston, in the early years of this century.

1926 Davidson, F. J. A. *Du vieux vin dans des bouteilles neuves.* Paris : Editions Baudinière. Pp. 342. Contient le récit de sa carrière d'étudiant à une université à peine déguisée que l'on croit être l'Université de Toronto ; une sorte de roman à clé.

1947 McCourt, E. A. *Music at the Close.* Toronto: Ryerson. Pp. 228. Chapters V and VI find the hero, aged 25, a freshman at the University of Saskatchewan taking Latin, French, History, Economics, Philosophy, and English. His problems with English receive detailed attention. The time is the late 1920's.

1948 Callaghan, M. *The Varsity Story.* Toronto: Macmillan Company of Canada. Pp. 172. The University of Toronto *circa* 1930 sentimentally viewed by the Warden of Hart House.

1949 Davies, R. *Fortune My Foe.* Toronto: Clarke, Irwin. Pp. 99. A drama depicting the conflict between the idealism of a young professor who wants to leave for the greater opportunities in an American university and the cynicism of an older professor who has long been resigned to staying. The scene is Kingston, Ontario.

1950 Lockquell, C. *Les Élus que vous êtes.* Montréal : Editions Variétés. Pp. 197. Une jeune frère enseignant entre en fonctions dans un collège dirigé par sa communauté.

1951 Boyle, G. *The Poor Man's Prayer.* New York: Harper. Pp. 207. A biographical novel about Alphonse Desjardins, founder of Caisses Populaires and the study clubs of Quebec.

Bullard, M. *Wedlock's the Devil.* London: Hamish Hamilton. Pp. 271. One of the central characters is a professor of Anthropology at the University of New Glasgow (Toronto).

Davies, R. *Tempest-Tost.* Toronto: Clarke, Irwin. Pp. 376. Amateur players in a university city, possibly Kingston, attempt a performance of *The Tempest*. The company includes Professor Vambrace "that bony and saturnine hatchet-man" of the Salterton Little

152 FICTION

Theatre. Hero is Hector Mackilwraith "an indisputable B.A." of Waverly University, possibly Queen's.

1952   Irwin, G. *Least of All Saints*. Toronto: McClelland & Stewart. Pp. 302. The University of Toronto and more specifically the Faculty of Divinity of Victoria College feature prominently in this novel which concerns a veteran of World War I who belatedly enters the ministry. The time is the 1920's.

1954   Davies, R. *Leaven of Malice*. Toronto: Clarke, Irwin. Pp. 312. The novel is, like *Tempest-Tost*, set in the university city of Salterton and again features Professor Vambrace, head of the Department of Classics. The central figure is Solly Bridgetower, a junior instructor in English who is "out of love with his work." The new course in American-Canadian Literature (AmCan) is hilariously described, as are the ideas of a professor of educational psychology.

Lewis, W. *Self-Condemned*. London: Methuen. Pp. 407. Assumption College, now part of the University of Windsor, and to a much lesser extent, the University of Toronto, provide part of the background of this semi-autobiographical novel.

1955   Birney, E. *Down the Long Table*. Toronto: McClelland and Stewart. Pp. 298. The involvement of the central hero with the communist party in this novel of the 1930's begins when he is a graduate student at the University of Toronto.

1959   Bodsworth, F. *The Strange One*. New York: Dodd, Mead. Pp. 400. The central figure is a young biologist whose undergraduate and graduate school days are spent at the University of Toronto. At the end he is a lecturer in the Department of Zoology. Whether an Indian wife (Kanina Beaverskin) would be a handicap to his advancement in the Department is one of the problems with which he wrestles.

1959   Bruce, C. *The Township of Time: A Chronicle*. Toronto: Macmillan. Pp. 234. One of the self-contained but related tales in this chronicle of the descendants of a group of United Empire Loyalists who disembarked at Halifax in 1786 involves a graduate student at the University of Toronto—"Duke Street, 1896." A second—"The Wind in the Juniper, 1945"—presents the final thoughts of an atomic physicist fatally injured in a radiation accident, among them recollections of his undergraduate years at Cardinal College in the Maritimes.

MacLennan, H. *The Watch That Ends the Night*. Toronto: Macmillan. Pp. 373. Partially set at McGill.

1961   Bessette, G. *Les Pédagogues*. Montréal : Cercle du Livre de France. Pp. 309. Un professeur de « l'Institut Pédagogique de Montréal » se révolte contre les pressions, politiques et autres, de sa vie professionnelle.

1963   Carbonneau, R. *Le Destin de Frère Thomas*. Montréal : Editions de l'Homme. Pp. 157. La vie d'un frère enseignant, mort à vingt-six ans.

McCourt, E. A. *Fasting Friar*. Toronto: McClelland and Stewart. Pp. 222. A novel about academic freedom set in a provincial university in one of the prairie provinces.

Index

Lightning Source UK Ltd.
Milton Keynes UK
UKHW010001210722
406167UK00001B/227